THE LETTERS OF

William James

AND

Théodore Flournoy

William James (seated) and Théodore Flournoy in the garden of
Edouard Claparède, Geneva, May 18, 1905.

THE LETTERS OF

William James

AND

Théodore Flournoy

EDITED BY

ROBERT C. LE CLAIR

THE UNIVERSITY OF WISCONSIN PRESS

MADISON, MILWAUKEE, AND LONDON 1966

Published by the University of Wisconsin Press
Madison, Milwaukee and London
U.S.A.: Box 1379, Madison, Wisconsin 53701
U.K.: 26–28 Hallam Street, London, W.1

Printed in the United States of America
by Kingsport Press, Inc., Kingsport, Tennessee
Library of Congress Catalog Card Number 66–13803

Foreword

Lovers of William James will be grateful for the correspondence here between James and his friend, the Geneva psychologist, Théodore Flournoy. James, as the lyric and intensely personal writer of letters, is already known through the collection of his letters by his son, Henry James, and the skillfully edited treasury of letters in R. B. Perry's *The Thought and Character of William James*. Other Jamesian letters continue to appear. There is something much more, however, in the present collection than the mere addition to the total available mass.

Flournoy was a psychologist of exceptional range and exceptional sensitivity, who served as a superb sounding board for James's ever revolving and ever scintillating mind, but in return gave much from his own European scholarship, erudition, and universal high seriousness. The conversations here are a beautiful reflection of the thought of two profound students of human nature over the turn of the century; it is a remarkable epitome of thought about human beings as the modern world was facing, without knowing it, the end of the great expansionist and optimistic period and preparing for the unremitting crisis that began with World War I. It is a world of vast charm, delicacy, radiance; a world still poignantly re-

flected in the pressed flowers, the Baedekers, the postcards of
serene withdrawn valleys of the Alps, the British midlands,
or the New Hampshire mountain country. A world of very
deep and genuine intellectual and esthetic delight breathes
steadily in these pages, asking the guide only to point to it,
not to describe it. It is a world of books, pictures, statues,
music, from which philosophy and psychology emerge in a
natural and gracious manner. There was another psychology
then, too—the emerging "hard" psychology of the laboratories—
but neither James nor Flournoy thought in these terms, as
this book will make clear, and what there is of clinical psychology is of the intensely personal rather than the medical
and scientific types which have, of course, in more recent times
won their way.

To document more explicitly the extraordinary vitality of
the literary culture within which these men lived, I will quote
one passage about Tolstoy:

> Of course you have read Tolstoi's War & Peace and Anna
> Karenina. I never had that exquisite felicity before this summer, and
> now I feel as if I knew *perfection* in the representation of human
> life. Life indeed seems less real than his tale of it. Such infallible
> veracity! The impressions haunt me as nothing literary ever
> haunted me before.

And to document James's extraordinary sensitivity to the
whirlwind cultural changes that were going on in his own
country, I will quote the paragraph about Chicago:

> I wish you were here with me to see Chicago and its institutions.
> It is a stupendous affair—the "storm-centre" of our Continent, and
> already outstripping New York in civilization, size and importance.
> It is practically less than 40 years old, and its original founders
> still live & take part in guiding its affairs. It is a place of vast
> ideas and titanic energy, and the largeness and ambitiousness of
> its beginnings must determine its character for all time. Money for
> public purposes is poured out like water, and although there is
> crime and corruption *ad nauseam*, there is greatness of the greatest
> sort. They have a University 5 years old, which will probably very

soon be the leading one of the country and is already doing first-rate work. All the prosperity has come about because of a geographical position which forced the navigation of the Great Lakes and the railroads connecting East West and South to converge at the place.

And, while still referring to the events at the turn of the century, there is this about the Spanish War:

But the *great* passion undeniably now is the passion for *adventure*. We are in so little danger from Spain, that our interest in the war can only be called that in a peculiarly exciting kind of *sport....* Civilization, properly so called, might well be termed the organization of all those functions that resist the mere excitement of sport.

The limpid, generous, and delicate words of Flournoy are less easily quotable, partly because we Americans are less familiar with his style, partly because he appears half-consciously to be playing the part of devoted interlocutor with James, as indeed most of James's correspondents did. Flournoy manages, however, to convey the beauty of his French through the lucid channel of the English translation, and to remind us continually of the solidity of Alps and of European culture against the brilliant, flowing words of James. It is a relation between equals that is sustained here, but one in which the wisdom of the old world is willing to allow itself to shine with a steady glow in contrast to the stellar brilliance of America's most brilliant philosophical intellect.

GARDNER MURPHY

Preface

Several years ago the late Dr. Henri Flournoy and his sister, the late Madame Georges Werner-Flournoy, of Geneva, kindly permitted me to see some unpublished letters of William James to their father, Dr. Théodore Flournoy, first professor of psychology at the University of Geneva. A few items indicated that the two men had carried on an extensive correspondence, the bulk of which is now deposited in the Houghton Library at Harvard—Flournoy's letters in French, James's in English. In translating Flournoy's letters, I had the invaluable help of Madame Werner-Flournoy, as well as that of Thomas C. Elliott of London. I am very much indebted to the late William James of Cambridge for reading the manuscript and to the James family for approving it for publication. Mrs. Bailey Aldrich of Cambridge also read the manuscript and made many helpful suggestions. Professor Henri Reverdin of Geneva, one of Flournoy's students and a member of the last class that James taught at Harvard, gave me helpful advice. I wish to thank the Staff of the Houghton Library for their help and many kindnesses.

Of the correspondence there are extant over seventy letters and postcards from James and fifty-four from Flournoy. Except as indicated by footnotes, all letters and postcards have been printed in full. Seventeen of the James letters were published wholly or in part in *The Letters of William James*, 2 volumes, edited by his son Henry James (1920), and in *The Thought and Character of William James*, 2 volumes, by Ralph Barton Perry (1935), and again in *The Selected Letters of William James*, edited by Elizabeth Hardwick (1961). Two of the Flournoy letters appear in part in Perry's two volumes. There are, however, over one hundred letters and cards which, as far as can be ascertained, have not previously been published.

As to the question of punctuation, I have followed, as closely as possible, that of James's original letters and typescripts and with Flournoy's have stayed as close to the original as the translation would allow. Both men wrote spontaneously, informally, and often in haste, all of which is part of the charm of the letters. Too formal an editing would detract from the free, warm flow of thought and feeling. Flournoy, it is true, was a more reserved person than James, yet in spirit and temperament they were very much alike. Both men were accomplished letter-writers with remarkable command of the resources, as well as the mechanics, of their respective tongues.

ROBERT C. LE CLAIR

Elsah, Illinois
December, 1965

Contents

Introduction

The correspondence of William James and Théodore Flournoy is the record of a growing affinity between kindred spirits. Even before they met in Paris at the International Congress of Physiological Psychology in 1889, Flournoy had read James's articles and sensed a mind and temperament close to his own. *"C'est mon homme!"* he murmured to himself. Two decades later, in one of the last letters he wrote, James confided to his Swiss colleague: "Through all these years I have wished I might live nearer to you and see more of you and exchange more ideas, for we seem two men particularly well *faits pour nous comprendre*. Particularly, now, as my own intellectual housekeeping has seemed on the point of working out some good results, would it have been good to work out the less unworthy parts of it in your company."

Covering two decades, 1890–1910, with every year being represented by one or more letters, the correspondence expresses directly the writer's presence, whether the subject is the latest professional meeting, the Spanish-American War, the Dreyfus Affair, or the miracles at Lourdes. Keen wit, warm humor, a rich sense of the human spirit permeate the pages, Flournoy's originally in French, James's in English, though each had a good command of the other's tongue. Neither man thought of himself as literary, and their exchange of thought was not intended for publication. Yet almost the entire correspondence has been preserved—over seventy items by James and fifty-four by Flournoy, in a style which many men of letters might well envy.

Among James's many correspondents, Flournoy was in a special class. Between them were striking points of resemblance. Both began by studying medicine and turned from physiology to psychology. Both wearied rapidly of laboratory research, and both became increasingly interested in philosophy. At Flournoy's death James H. Leuba pointed out that "the ideas of the Swiss psychologist were on many problems so near to those of James that in *La philosophie de William James* (1911), it is at times difficult to tell when Flournoy expounds the views of the great American and when his own." Yet, parallel professional interests alone cannot account for the depth and extent of the friendship. Far more significant are the intangible forces of the human spirit which mutually attracted them, especially that "inward palpitating human quality, gracious and tender, precise, fierce, scornful, humorous by turns," as James wrote of his father, to whom he was indebted for much of his personal charm and intellectual brilliance.

While of a quieter nature, Flournoy shared with James a warm spontaneity of thought and feeling, a cordial attitude toward people, and an unimpeachable integrity that was impatient with sham and humbug of every sort. What he especially admired in his American friend was the fine sense of fair play, of always giving a man the benefit of the doubt. As James's eldest son said of him later: "He made the other man feel that he had no desire to pigeon-hole him and dismiss him from further consideration, but that he rejoiced in him as a fellow creature, unique like himself and forever fascinating."

Behind both men lay rich heritages of family and fortune,

education and culture, which prepared each of them for the rare personal intercourse they enjoyed. So well known has become the James family story and William's part in it that no rehearsal is necessary here. But who was Théodore Flournoy and what were the special qualities which brought him the enduring affection and profound admiration of William James?

Originating in Champagne, France, the Flournoy forebears arrived in Geneva in 1600, Protestant refugees from religious persecution. A family of pastors, historians, doctors, and men of letters, the Flournoys had attained considerable prominence by the mid-nineteenth century. Thédore's father, Alexandre, was a banker, a man of fine sensibilities; his mother, a beautiful woman, was Caroline Claparède of an equally distinguished French refugee family which had fled to Geneva after the revocation of the Edict of Nantes, in 1685. Théodore's uncle, René Edouard Claparède, the only man of science the families had produced, was a naturalist known for his work on infusoria and annelida. Admired for his open-mindedness, scientific curiosity, vigor, clarity, and independence of thought, he was a strong influence on his nephew, who was seventeen when Claparède died in 1871. Nearly two decades later Flournoy discovered in William James most of the qualities he had admired in his uncle, including marked intellectual capacity, a strong spiritual sense, and a fine ability in polemics.

During the first twelve years of his life Flournoy suffered from extreme timidity, which he struggled for years to overcome. He also had to contend with a youthful tendency to pay attention only to what interested him, doing in an perfunctory way whatever else was required. The records of his early years at Calvin's Collège are amusing on this point. The boy was apparently intelligent, *"mais distrait et mobile."* *"Pas toujours sage ... causeries et distractions fréquentes."* He showed little sign of becoming a distinguished scholar with prodigious powers of concentration. As an extracurricular activity, he developed his interest in science, first collecting shells with great care and perseverance, then carrying on a few elementary experiments in physics and chemistry. Using an abandoned orangery on his grandfather's property in Champel, he succeeded in making a Leyden jar and setting up an electric telegraph between his workshop and the house. His interests in science seemed natural and the boy felt that his career was determined, and to some extent it was.

After the Collège, Flournoy entered the University of Geneva in 1871, where William James had been a student in 1859–1860. Taking a degree first in letters, then in mathematics and sciences, he studied under Carl Vogt, Marginac, and Wartmann. Intellectually he was not happy, however, because of the incompatibility between what his professors taught and his own philosophy of life. He had already arrived at a clear distinction—to which he held the rest of his life— between the scientific method and his moral idealism. He had plenty of opportunity to hold to this distinction. Darwinism was being vigorously advanced by Huxley, Haeckel, Moleschoot, and Büchner, and prevailed on all sides. In resisting the widespread enthusiasm of the evolutionists and not being taken in by the ironic, droll sarcasm with which men like Vogt treated metaphysical matters, Flournoy showed singular independence of thought. What was admirable in a young man still in his teens was his ability to admire such biological research without scorning the philosophy behind it. This is an important trait which he had in common with James. Their subsequent investigations of spiritualism, Flournoy's support of the Church of Geneva (without active participation in services), and James's *Varieties of Religious Experience* are a few of the many evidences that both men were endowed with a deep spiritual sense which, however, was kept in abeyance and not confused with their scientific research.

In 1876, Flournoy's religious interests caused him to enroll in the School of Theology at Geneva, but one semester was enough. He withdrew, he said, because to him theology comprised *"trop de chinoiseries!"*—an opinion James had inherited from his father. The elder James had dropped out of the Princeton Theology School in 1837 after two years of futile effort to accept orthodox theology.

Flournoy next turned to the study of medicine, going for a year to Freiburg, Germany, then to Strasbourg, where he specialized in anatomy and received his M.D. in 1878. As was the case with James, after obtaining an M. D. Flournoy never practised medicine. Most of the following year Flournoy spent in Leipzig, studying under Wundt, who was then establishing the first European laboratory of experimental psychology. In 1880, after a few months in Paris, he returned to Geneva and, feeling that his formal education was complete, read extensively, integrating and enlarging his interests in preparation for teaching. He made a special study of Kant, who was for a time his intellectual and spiritual guide. In fact, the first course which Flournoy gave as a *privat-docent* at the University in Geneva in 1885 was on the philosophy of Kant. Three years later he inaugurated his course in physiological psychology. Two direct results were the publication of his *Métaphysique et psychologie,* 1890, and his appointment to the Chair of Experimental Psychology, created for him by the Faculté des Sciences in 1891. This promotion constituted official recognition of Flournoy's ability and also of psychology as a discipline separate from the field of philosophy in which it had previously been included.

At the same time, William James was achieving professional recognition with his now classic work, *Principles of Psychology,* 1890. He and Flournoy had met the previous August in Paris. In sending a copy to Flournoy, James cemented their acquaintance into a permanent friendship, and Flournoy's letter of appreciation for the volumes launched the correspondence which continued until James's death in 1910. As propitious as were the time and circumstances, it is doubtful how much their connections might have developed without James's love of travel, since Flournoy was reluctant to leave home for any reason. As in the friendship of Carlyle and Emerson, their personal contacts were dependent upon the expansive American spirit and willingness to travel abroad. While Flournoy occasionally gave addresses in Paris, he declined most invitations to lecture outside of Switzerland, including one from Harvard, being too *sauvage,* as he pleaded with James, though he was, like James, an excellent lecturer. Humorously, he replied to another friend, Aloys Naville, who invited him to go to Ceylon: *"Ce n'est pas aller de Genève à Ceylan qui m'affraie; c'est d'aller de Florissant à la gare de Cornavin!"* From his home to the railroad station was about as extensive a trip as he cared to make. Fortunately, James's peripatetic travels and education as a boy had instilled in him a delight in travel that never declined. On the nine trips abroad that he made in the last twenty years of his life James seldom failed to visit the Flournoys, bringing Mrs. James occasionally, as well as one or more of their five children. Madame Flournoy, nèe Mlle. Marie-Hélène Burnier of the Canton of Vaud, was a gracious hostess with whom Mrs. James had much in common. The six Flournoy children developed attachments with the Jameses that deepened the whole relationship. Thus, domestic and family news occurs often, as does the subject of ill health, from which both men suffered. It was an important bond of sympathy between them.

Predominantly, the letters concern professional interests, news of publications and meetings, colleagues and commitments. Each reviewed the other's books, Flournoy undertaking the translations of James's or arranging for their translation and in every way possible proclaiming their excellence. James's rich, active life was filled with interesting people of whom he wrote Flournoy uninhibitedly, often giving candid vignettes that are as amusing as they are significant. The names comprise a veritable Blue Book of distinguished individuals, ranging from Münsterberg, Renouvier, Santayana, and Bergson to Admiral Dewey, John D. Rockefeller, and Giovanni Papini.

Yet, what the reader is finally left with is a vivid impression of two extraordinary human spirits coming often into tangency, charged with what James called "the electric current of sympathy that binds the world together." From Lake Geneva, Wisconsin, he wrote Flournoy in 1896: "I have thought of you a great deal without writing, for truly, My dear Flournoy, there is hardly a human being with whom I feel as much sympathy of aims and character, or feel as much 'at home,' as I do with you." While Flournoy's natural shyness never permitted him such effusive expressions of fraternal feelings, both sides of the correspondence are permeated with the spirit of rejoicing as fellow beings blessed with a rare capacity of communion in heart and mind.

THE LETTERS OF

William James

AND

Théodore Flournoy

I

Beginning of a Spontaneous Friendship

1890–1895

About a year after they had been introduced in Paris, William James sent Théodore Flournoy a copy of *Principles of Psychology*. In response to this scholarly courtesy, Flournoy wrote a letter which initiated their correspondence of twenty years. Neither man had any idea of the extensive exchange of letters which would follow, but from the tone of these opening pages one senses a promise of an enduring friendship. Although James was Flournoy's senior by twelve years, both were entering upon the first full maturity of their careers; both were happily married, and each had four children of about the same ages. James had been Professor of Philosophy at Harvard for five years and had just published his major work, *Principles*, which established his already high reputation and greatly extended his influence. In the same year, 1890, Flournoy published his first important work, *Métaphysique et psychologie*, followed three years later by *Des Phénomènes de synopsie*. In 1891 he was appointed Professor of Physiological Psychology by the Faculté des Sciences at Geneva. These were auspicious years for them both, an ideal time in which to have their friendship begin.

Greatly in need of a year off from teaching, James with his

wife and children sailed for Antwerp in May, 1892. After a tour of the Black Forest the family spent several happy weeks that summer at Vers-chez-les-Blanc in the mountains above Lausanne, where the Flournoys were staying. Here the friendship deepened quickly. It continued in a lively fashion by exchange of letters during the next several months while the Jameses lived in Florence, vacationed in Lucerne, and visited Henry James in London before sailing for home in August, 1893.

In the first five years of the correspondence, references are made to people of mutual interest. Charles Ritter was a fellow student of James's at the University of Geneva in 1859–60. They had brief reunions on several of James's visits to Switzerland and kept in touch mostly through Flournoy. Hugo Münsterberg, whose name appears often over the years, played an important role in certain aspects of James's career. A student of Wundt, he came to Harvard in the fall of 1892 to relieve James of the directorship of the laboratory work. He remained for three years; then, after a two-year absence in Europe, returned to Harvard permanently. Münsterberg was highly skeptical of spirit communication and had very little sympathy for the psychic research which increasingly interested James and Flournoy. James's early enthusiasm for Münsterberg went through certain fluctuations, as his comments to Flournoy indicate.

Not widely known, but of considerable importance to Flournoy, was Edouard Claparède, whom James came to admire in many ways. He was a nephew of the famous Swiss naturalist René Edouard Claparède and was also Flournoy's cousin. Together, in 1901, they founded the *Archives de psychologie*. In addition to his career at the University of Geneva, Claparède was one of the founders of the Institut Jean-Jacques Rousseau in 1912, still an outstanding school of education. As the letters reveal, he became more and more helpful to Flournoy by taking over the laboratory work and performing tedious duties at professional meetings and "congresses" which they attended together.

Important references occur in James's letters, mostly in the early years, to Charles Bernard Renouvier, the noted French philosopher, who was probably one of the strongest influences upon James's development, especially in the 1870's. Renouvier's two leading ideas, to which James inclined, were dislike of the unknowable and reliance on the validity of personal experience. Liberty he considered to be man's fundamental characteristic. For a discussion of Renouvier's work and his relationship with James, one should see R. B. Perry, *The Thought and Character of William James* (Boston, 1935), I, 654–710.

Prominent in early letters is the name Frederic W. H. Myers. Myers was an English psychologist, poet, and essayist, one of the founders in 1882 of the Society for Psychical Research, which James joined in 1884, remaining active for many years. The two were together in southern France for a holiday in 1900, and James was with him in Rome when Myers died the following year. His main work was *Human Personality and Its Survival of Bodily Death*, published posthumously in 1903. James called it "the first attempt to consider the phenomena of hallucination, hypnotism, automatism, double personality, and medium-ship, as connected parts of one whole subject."

By 1895, the tone of the letters had changed from the pleasant formality of the beginning to a warm intimacy. Writing from Colorado that year, James said: "I wish I could by telephone at this moment hear just where and how you all are, and what you are all doing. In the Mountains somewhere, of course, and I trust all well." Flournoy, in turn, says that he could not pass the Diablerets, a section in the Ormonts, "without recalling, with more intensity than usual, our excursion of 1892 to Pillon and to Col de la Croix!" The warmth, solicitude, even tenderness of the friendship had been firmly established.

The first letter was written by Théodore Flournoy to James in 1890.

9 Florissant, Geneva
October 15, 1890

Sir,

I have just received from Henry Holt and Co. of New York your two fine volumes. After glancing over the preface, I wish to thank you immediately for this delightful present and to assure you that I shall be one of those people, less rare than you think, who will read your fourteen hundred pages from one end to the other and who will devote much thought to them. I promise myself a great deal of profit and pleasure from this study. For, as I told you a year ago, when I had the privilege of meeting you at the Congress of Psychology, on a number of occasions your articles, either in *Mind* or in *La Critique philosophique,* have given me the deep pleasure of finding exact, well-put ideas which were merely drifting vaguely through my mind. Very often they suggested to me, in their richness and originality, views of which I hadn't dreamed, but the truth of which struck me and stayed with me. Consequently, if I am not in accord with you on all points (which would be unlikely), those on which I do agree are so numerous and so important that I am forced frequently to say, in speaking of you, "C'est mon homme!" That is why I took the liberty of mentioning you in the introduction to the little brochure [*Mètaphysique et psychologie*], of which I sent you a copy three months ago; and I certainly owe you even more than I realize.

If, through your articles, you have often been the companion of my thoughts and the guide to my reflections, that will be even more the case henceforth. In a fortnight, in fact, I shall begin my course in Psychology in the Faculté des Sciences—

which is to say that your work is going to become my favorite daily reading all winter and that my students will hear your name very often!

In several months, when I have had the time to study in this way your *Principles of Psychology*, I shall take the liberty of sending you my impressions and my difficulties or objections. Permit me in the meantime to extend to you my warmest congratulations on having carried through successfully a work of this scope, in the impartial and positive spirit which permeates your preface, and to express my profound gratitude for your kindness in sending it to me.

Please accept, dear sir, my cordial greetings and believe me your devoted and grateful,

Théodore Flournoy

JAMES TO FLOURNOY

95 Irving St.
Cambridge, Mass.
May 31, 1891

My dear Mr. Flournoy

I received the Journal de Genève a week ago, with your review of my psychology in it, and I need hardly say that it afforded me very acute pleasure. Unrestricted and unqualified praise is after all the real thing which authors crave, and the adjectives need not fear to make themselves too superlative! It is easier, however, to be a "noble et forte personalité" in a book, than in the bosom of one's family; and it is perhaps well that you wrote your review of the book before you had acquired a greater degree of intimacy with its author! But, joking and modesty apart, the review pleased me more than any other which I have yet seen, because, in spite of its being untechnical and avoiding every detail, I seemed to feel that you had better than anyone else caught the "point of view" of my lengthy pages. I am the more sure of this since I have read your "Metaphysique et psychologie." When it arrived last Autumn I laid it aside for a propitious moment; and finally as my year got fuller and fuller of drudgery and reading for my lectures, it took its place in a pile of books destined to be read in the summer vacation. The last lecture took place 3 days ago; the blessed vacation has almost begun—we have but two weeks more for examinations—and I have just finished your little book. It has really delighted me, no less by the extraordinary vitality of the style than by the admirable good sense of the matter. This is to be really "scientific" without being a bavarian into the bargain, as so many of our "scientists" are! You have a great future as a writer; and I hope as a thinker, although as yet you have shown so little of your hand. It behoves all of us who on the whole agree in aims and methods to close up our ranks and give each other a helping hand, and perhaps our "School" will prevail!

Thanking you once more most heartily for your so cordial and all too flattering words, I am yours faithfully

Wm James

Pray keep on writing! I have been reading myself to sleep of late by means of Voltaire, and I assure you that your style does not suffer by close comparison.

JAMES TO FLOURNOY

Hôtel Föhrenbach
Freiburg i. B.
June 13, '92

Dear Mr. Flournoy,

You will be surprised at seeing the above address to a letter signed with my name; but here I am, having come to Europe with my entire family [1] to spend fifteen months at least. I

1. William and Alice Gibbens James had five children: Henry (Harry), 1879–1947; William (Billy), 1882–1961; Hermann, 1884–1885; Margaret Mary (Peggy, Peg), 1887–1950; Alexander Robertson (Tweedie), 1890–1946.

write to you as to one of my very few Swiss acquaintances, to ask for a little practical advice, which I hope it will cost you but little trouble to give.

I have four children, the oldest being thirteen years old, and much travelling is for them out of the question. What I desire is to find some quiet and rural spot in Switzerland where we can settle down quietly *en pension* for two months or even more. It must be cheap, not too hot for us, or too cold for the baby; of not too high an altitude for me (as I sleep badly on mountain heights); the neighborhood must be beautiful; and a good house, not too primitive, is indispensable! You see how modest are my requirements! Can you, out of your doubtless copious knowledge of your incomparable country, give me any indications as to the region towards which I had better turn, when in a week I shall start forth as *éclaireur* to discover the promised land, and telegraph to my wife to follow. It occurs to me that you may know of some one special pension, off the beaten track of tourists, which would be just the thing I wish.

I sincerely trust that you will pardon the liberty which I take in thus appealing to you. If philosophers will not help each other, who shall help them? I am writing simultaneously to my old friend Charles Ritter (whom I suppose to be still in Geneva) to see what *he* will say. If you write to me *here* (as above) your letter will get me, since I stay at least a week longer.

Münsterberg, whom I am glad to say we have captured for Harvard University, gives me good news of you—Professorship, Laboratory, etc. I heartily congratulate you on it all, and look forward eagerly to the pleasure of meeting you again this summer, either in Geneva or elsewhere. Naturally, I expect, myself, to do some walking and travelling in Switzerland. I may have to write to you later to ask if you can recommend me a young man who could be a tutor to my boys for the summer. Shall you be at the London "Congress"? At present my own intention is not to go. I have had bad cerebral fa-

tigue for a year past, and although it will doubtless be interesting to be there, I think it will do me more good to stay
away. Moreover the journey is too *kostspielig.*

Believe me, with cordial regards,

Yours sincerely
Wm James

Monday evening
[June, 1892]

Dear Sir,

After several vain telephone calls, I got a response from
Professor *David,* at Beaumont near Lausanne, who will shortly
have a room free in which he will be able to accommodate
your two sons for July, August, and September, if that is
agreeable to you. In case you have not yet found a pension
for your sons, I urge you strongly to go see this one. Monsieur
David is one of my best friends, a very original man, a little
brusque in demeanor, but good at heart and of a high intellectual and moral character. He married a cousin of my wife,
so that we know them very well, and I can recommend them
to you in every respect.—I do not know, however, if he still
keeps up his Latin enough to teach it to your sons, but he
could easily find a Latin teacher in Lausanne to give them
lessons. He teaches history at the high school for girls and
mathematics at the Gaillard College in Lausanne. He has three
young daughters, the eldest of whom is about seven, and three
or four young men boarding with him of whom he takes as
much care as of his own children. He occupies a villa (Beaumont), 20 minutes above Lausanne, superbly situated, with
excellent air, splendid view, fine walks of all kinds in the
neighborhood; it would be difficult for you to find a better
place for your sons during the summer months.

In the event that, after having seen M. David and his house, you would prefer another *pension,* here are three addresses which I can give you and which are completely recommended: Monsieur *Biélèr,* director of the Agricultural Institute, Rue Agassiz, *Lausanne;* Monsieur Paul *Oltramare,* master at the College of Geneva, Quai Pierre-Fatio, *Geneva;* Monsieur *Thévenaz,* also a master at the College of Geneva, Rue de l'Hôtel de Ville, *Geneva.*

These three gentlemen take a few boarders and go with them during vacation to the country or the mountains, but I don't know where. Moreover, I do not know if they still have rooms available now.

Of the three, I should recommend especially M. Oltramare, one of my good friends, excellent in Latin (and even in Sanskrit, but your sons are not yet up to the Vedas!) You could see him tomorrow morning at his home (Quai Pierre-Fatio— but I don't know the number—but anyone can tell you) or more probably at the College.

Looking forward to the pleasure of seeing you again tomorrow, please believe me, dear Sir, your very devoted,

Th. Flournoy

P.S.   M. David, Beaumont near Lausanne, has a telephone, if you wish to make an appointment with him.

JAMES TO FLOURNOY

Lucerne, July 4, 1892

Dear Colleague,

I presented your card duly at M. David's, and was charmed both by him, his wife and his place. But I found later something that promises to be both cooler, cheaper, and fuller of picturesque character, and which will allow us to live very near our boys, so I have written to M. David to consider me out of the game. There are two pastors, one at Ormonts (Vers l'Église), the other at Gryon (sur Bex) who will take our boys into their family and teach them, and at Gryon we can have a Chalet with *large* rooms—a great thing! I take the family there in a day or two, and for the present Gryon will be my address.

M. David pleased me so much personally that I feel very sorry he isn't at Gryon as a duplicate pastor, but the world is wrongly put together.

I shall long remember your kindness to me at Geneva, & trust I may in some way be able to repay it in future. With my best regards to Madame Flournoy, to whom my wife wishes also to be remembered, I am always faithfully yours

Wm James

JAMES TO FLOURNOY

Grand Hôtel de Riche-Mont
Lausanne, July 17, 1892

My dear Flournoy—

I hope you will let me follow our anglo-saxon custom and drop titles of ceremony between such colleagues and *gleich-gesinnten* Menschen as we now are, you of course doing the same.—I have travelled and seen almost as much as Ulysses since I left you on Saturday night exposed to the fury of the tempest, and I only hope you got safely home. Without going into details I may say that I know of several places in either of which my boys would be well off. Tomorrow I go (I might have gone today, with a little more energy)—to Gryon to talk it all over with my wife, and decide on the best combination. Meanwhile, I cannot *now engage* the rooms at Madame Cru-chon's and must run the risk of losing them, though I think they might well be the best thing we could do in August. Will you kindly say this to Madame Cruchon? My wife writes that she is getting fonder and fonder of the mountains, in spite of the rain, and does not wish to abandon that region. I will let you know in a couple of days just what we shall have done. I meant to have told you last time for the sake of M. Claparède that there is now at Lucerne (Pension Stutz) a charming young American lady, an admirable musician, who has a most elaborate system of chromatic symbols accompanying sounds, letters of the alphabet, and names, also a number diagram, of all of which she can probably give an intelligible account. To a remark which I made, she said "my mind must be like a sort of little Switzerland, for picturesqueness, compared with yours." She has had these things as long as she can remember.

Will you please present my best respects and regards to Madame Flournoy, and believe me always truly yours

Wm James

For a week my address will be Gryon—if I go they will forward letters.

JAMES TO FLOURNOY

Pensione Villa Maggiore [Pallanza]

Sept. 19, 1892

My dear Flournoy,

Your most agreeable letter [2]—one of those which one preserves to read in one's old age—came yesterday. I had only been waiting, to write to you, until our plans should be more definitely known. We are waiting now for a word from our friend the American doctor at Florence to know whether it is safe to take the baby there immediately. If so we shall go. If not, I think we shall go to Alassio for two or three weeks. (A. is a watering place on the Mediterranean near Genoa).— We were driven from Château d'Oex by the cold and wet after a week, but had a fine day on the Simplon, and have been at this place for eight days. The house is fine but very dirty and ill-kept, and the weather fine, but hot as hades. The lake is beautiful enough, but the town repulsive. I am

2. This letter from Flournoy has apparently been lost.

glad to have got into such prosaic, practical, and common-place relations with a place which for most people is as ex-clusively romantic as the Lago Maggiore. A delightful Swiss pension in the Country at Canobbio near the head of the lake was full so we couldn't get into it, and this place is so bad as to table etc. that we can't stay much longer.

The material perfections of Switzerland seem quite ideal now that one has turned his back on them forever!—but I sincerely hope not forever.

I am *much* obliged to you for the paper by Secrétan,[3] and (unless you deny me the permission) I propose to keep it, and let you get a new one, which you can do more easily than I. It is much too oracular & brief, but its *pregnancy* is a good example of what an intellect gains by growing old: One says vast things simply. I read it stretched on the grass of Monte Motterone, the Righi of this region, just across the Lake, with all the kingdoms of the Earth stretched before me, and I realized how exactly a philosophic Weltansicht resembles that from the top of a mountain. You are driven, as you ascend, into a choice of fewer and fewer paths, and at last you end in two or three simple attitudes from each of which we see a great part of the Universe amazingly simplified and summar-ized, but nowhere the entire view at once. I entirely agree that Renouvier's system fails to satisfy, but it seems to me the classical and consistent expression of *one* of the great attitudes, that of insisting on logically intelligible formulas. If one goes beyond, one must abandon the hope of *formulas* altogether, which is what all pious sentimentalists do; and with them M. Secrétan, since he fails to give any articulate substitute for the "Criticism" he finds so unsatisfactory. Most philosophers give formulas, and inadmissible ones, as when Secrétan makes a *mémoire sans oubli* = duratio tota simul = eternity!

3. Charles Secrétan (1815–1895), a French-Swiss, was professor of philosophy at the University of Lausanne. He considered Christian dogmas as being purely ethical and wanted them trans-lated into terms that did not contradict the critical scientific spirit.

I have been reading with much interest the articles on the will by Fouillée [4] in the Revue Phil. for June and August. There are admirable descriptive pages, though the final philosophy fails to impress me much. I am in good condition now, and must try to do a little methodical work every day in Florence, in spite of the temptations to flânerie of this sort of life.

I did hope to have spent a few days in Geneva before crossing the Mountains! But perhaps for the holidays you and Madame Flournoy will cross them, too and see us at Florence. The Vers chez les Blanc-days are something that neither she nor I will forget! You and I are strangely contrasted as regards our professorial responsibilities, you are becoming entangled in laboratory research and demonstration just as I am getting emancipated. As regards *demonstrations,* I think you will not find much difficulty in concocting a program of classical observations on the senses etc. for students to verify;— it worked much more easily at Harvard than I supposed it would when we applied it to the whole class, and it improved the spirit of work very much. As regards *research,* I advise you not to take that duty too conscientiously, if you find that ideas and projects do not abound. As long as a man is working at anything, he must give up other things at which he might be working, and the best thing he can work at is usually the thing he does most spontaneously. You philosophize, according to your own account, more spontaneously than you work in the laboratory. So do I, and I always felt that the occupation of philosophizing was with me a valid excuse for neglecting laboratory work, since there is not time for both. Your work as a philosopher will be more *irreplaceable* than what results you might get in the laboratory out of the same number of

4. Alfred Jules Emile Fouillée (1838–1912). The articles referred to are "Existence et développement de la volonté," and "Le Developpement de la volonté." Fouillée was interested in reconciling metaphysical idealism with naturalistic and mechanical standpoints of science by means of his *idées-forces.*

hours. Some day I feel sure that you will find yourself impelled to publish some of your reflections. Until then, take notes and read, and feel that your true destiny is on the way to its accomplishment! It seems to me that a great thing would be to add a new course to your instruction. Au revoir, my dear friend! My wife sends "a great deal of love" to yours, and says she will write to her as soon as we get settled. I also send my most cordial greetings to Madame Flournoy. Remember me also affectionately to those charming young *demoiselles* who will, I am afraid, incontinently proceed to forget me.

Always affectionately yours
Wm James

FLOURNOY TO JAMES

Florissant, Geneva
Dec. 30, 1892

My dear James,

Here is the end of the year, with its whirlwind of activities, a joyful week for the children,[5] a terrible one for the parents! In the midst of this confusion, I must not let the occasion slip by without sending our very best wishes to you and yours. I hope that the New Year passed in Europe will leave you no bad memories; that the beautiful Tuscany sunshine will cheer you up and warm you in place of the icy fog which we have here; that you, Mrs. James, and your children are in good health and that you have good news from all your relations on the other side of the water. May nothing disturb the calm and tranquility which you have come to seek in our Old World, and may your sojourn in the country of Galileo and Fra Angelico inspire in you a philosophy of art

5. Théodore and Marie Burnier Flournoy had six children: Alice, 1881–1965; Blanche, 1882–1905; Marguerite, 1883–1963; Henri, 1886–1955; Hélène, 1891——; Ariane-Dorothée, 1896——.

and an *Erkenntnisslehre* which will counterbalance your Psychology.—

I have read the two articles which Marillier has devoted to you in the Revue philosophique; but, without being able to offer very precise objections, I have not been satisfied with them. His exposé is much less clear than the original and it does not convey, in my opinion, a general impression which tallies with that made by your book. It is true that his work is not yet complete;—moreover, I am probably not impartial with regard to Marillier, whose turn of mind and personality are not very congenial to me. But at least it gives me very great pleasure to see your book presented to the French public by an article of wider range than an ordinary summary report would give, and that leaves me hopeful that the plan to translate your textbook will finally be carried through. This would be the greatest service which could be rendered to French psychology. I use it often for my course and I appreciate very much its conciseness and clarity. There are, however, chapters like the one on *space*, which I prefer in your large work, because they lose more than they gain in being condensed and abridged. I read with great interest in The Philosophical Review your article Thought before Language, about which you spoke to me last summer and which is very thought-provoking.

I do not speak to you of my laboratory, which bores me more and more and in which I accomplish nothing worth while. I ought to give a great deal more time to it; perhaps then I should find interest in it, but I am too harassed on all sides during the winter, although I decline all social invitations and hardly ever go out. A literary and philosophical group of Eastern students have asked me to give them a talk on the philosophy of Kant. You can imagine how easy it is to explain "criticism" in one single hour to a group of Serbs, Bulgarians, and Romanians who can hardly understand French!

We are all well. Since yesterday the children have been skating with Mlle. Hühnersdorf [6] with whom we are perfectly satisfied, but whom the children torment occasionally beyond all limits! Please accept, my dear James, and Mrs. James as well, for yourselves and your children, our very best wishes, and believe me, always

Your respectfully affectionate
Théodore Flournoy

JAMES TO FLOURNOY (postcard)

16 P[iazz]ᵃ dell' Indipendenza,
Florence. October 19, 1892

I send you a reprint of my last years' assistant's articles on Pleasure & Pain. He believes in specific Nerves, & it seems to me that his reasons & theories have some merit. He has asked me to distribute some of the reprints. We are *settled,* at last, the boys have begun school, and a certain routine of life has commenced. Florence is *delicious,* and if the children don't freeze this winter, we shall be happy. I hope that you are all well and flourishing in your own house, and that the bad weather hasn't yet set in. Warmest regards *from both to both!*

W.J.

JAMES TO FLOURNOY

16 Pᵃ dell' Indipendenza
Florence, Jan. 3, 1893

My dear Flournoy,

Your letter of new-year's greeting was a most gratifying event yesterday. I had been thinking of you and of your family all the week, and "innervating" myself to write, but the muscular discharge fell short of accomplishment! I am sure you

6. Fräulein Hühnersdorf had been governess to the James children in Cambridge and was employed by the Flournoys, on the recommendation of the James family.

can forgive the weakness of an ultra-lazy man. Now that your letter supplies the stimulus, no effort is required—quite the reverse. Your hopes about the *beau soleil de la Toscane,* etc. sound rather ironical in the midst of the cloudy skies we have been having for a month. But we have had no cold below the freezing point, and very little as low as that, and no such bad weather in general as seems to have prevailed north of the alps. The only inconvenience of our life is the small size of the living room in which the boys and their parents both have to huddle when they are all at home together, in the latter part of the day. But now that we are embarked on January and steering straight for Spring and Freedom, my spirits rise. They have also risen since a dinner, at which we had four friends on Sunday night, has proved that the resources of the establishment, glass, spoons, cook, & *bonne,* are adequate to a dinner party of six. So that hereafter we may accept an invitation, without feeling that to return it will be an impossibility. The streets of Florence are everlastingly interesting, but the evolution of italian art is much too complicated for the successive steps in its evolution to be traced in any clear way. It seems as if a large number of men coordinately made most of the advances. I see here a couple of young men who are devoted to Italian painting in a streng-wissenschaftlich manner, their principal interest being the re-naming of all the pictures in the galleries. I have also another friend, who is an entomologist, blessed with a great memory for details and who has taken up Kunstgeschichte in an entomological manner. Alongside of their severity there seems little room for a merely loving relation to the pictures. But the good thing about a work of art is that it tells all sorts of things to different spectators, of none of which things, the artist ever knew a word.—

You speak of Marillier's articles, of which the third was brought by the postman an hour ago. I fear that during eternity I can never indemnify him for the trouble my unfortunate volumes have given him. His exposition seems to me excellently clear and faithful, and the whole thing is an immense compliment to me, but I don't believe in such very long compte-rendus. They are necessarily colorless and tame compared with the originals, and yet they are difficult reading. I should rather any day read a hundred pages of an original author than 30 pp. of a compte rendu. Then it grieves me to find that the Lord has hardened poor Marillier's heart against the reception of so many of my truths. In spite of the pains he has taken, I fear he will not be saved! He *is* conscientious, though, is he not?—I have just read, all but the last 100 pp., Wundt's System der Philosophie.⁷ That man can write more pages on any given theme than anyone who ever lived. Intelligent too, and clear; but it's all surface and plausibility, and the success with which he escapes saying anything really decisive or important is astounding in a man who has done such an awful *quantity* of hard thinking and study. I think that some machinery will have to be organized to *pay* men for not writing books, from whom there is reason to think that the world is threatened. Wundt ought certainly to be pensioned off now—we have labored enough over his pages. I should like to be present at your Kant-session with the Orientals. Of course you have read that wonderful thing of [Friedrich] Paulsen's "Was Kant uns sein Kann" in the earlier years of the Wertelisch? Don't take your laboratory too severely, or let it weigh on your soul. Your two little contributions were well worth the years you spent.

Best love from both of us and wishes for the New Year to both you, Madame Flournoy & the children, Peggy & Tweedy got the pretty Christmas cards & Peggy sends love and thanks. Please give our cordial greetings also to Fr. Hü[h]nersdorf.

[W. J.]

7. Wilhelm Max Wundt (1832–1920), the German philosopher and psychologist whose *Physiological Psychology* James had reviewed in 1875 in *The North American Review* and with whom Flournoy had studied in Leipzig in 1879–80.

JAMES TO FLOURNOY (postcard)

16 Pᵃ. Dell' Indipendenza

Florence, Jan. 30, 93

I send you herewith an essay of mine on Ethics [8] of wh[ich] you may remember my speaking to you last summer. It seems to me "chock-full of truth!—but rather too condensed, so pray don't read it till you have leisure and an unoccupied mind— next summer perhaps. In any case don't think it necessary to "react" on paper by addressing critical or appreciative remarks to me!—I congratulate you that the 30th of January of this hard winter is reached. We have had no bad cold in Florence, but I rejoice nevertheless at the prospect of some *warmth* soon. All goes well with us, rather too much interruption from casual acquaintances is all we have to complain of. Wife, chidren, and myself extremely well. Love to you & yours from all of us.

Wm James

JAMES TO FLOURNOY

Pension Gottlieben

Meggen, bei Luzern

May 5, 1893

My dear Flournoy,

Madame Flournoy's delightful letter to my wife came the day before yesterday, and gave her the greatest pleasure. She will soon write herself, but as I have had an envelope, directed to you, lying on my table for a week past, I "get ahead." She is probably going early next week to Munich to pay a visit of 3 to 5 days to our Harry, to see whom she has a maternal longing. If you are kind enough to write Billy, I am sure he will be highly pleased. But I advise you to wait for a fortnight longer. He will speak better then; and

8. The essay may have been "The Moral Philosopher and the Moral Life."

until he gets into entire equilibrium with his environment at la Chiésaz, he had better not be disturbed. His address there is chez M.A. Ceresole, pasteur, la Chiésaz, sur Vevey.—*This* place is a paradise, and we shall very likely spend the whole month of May here. I find I can read and walk and sleep, and I enjoy it very much. My brother [9] arrived yesterday from London, or rather from Paris.

Can you name me any simple book on the differential calculus which gives an insight into the philosophy of the subject. I was struck by your saying last summer that you tho't Renouvier's view was mistaken. [Kurt] Lasswitz in his Atomistik would seem to hold also what R. would call a mystical view. I have just been through a short treatise by one of my colleagues, but it is a thicket of particular formulas & calculations without one general idea, and I want ideas and not formulas. Can you also indicate to me any little manual explaining the political constitution of Switzerland? There must be something for school: but don't take *any trouble* about either of these things! There is a young German Gelehrter, Carl Hauptmann by name, here in the house, very modest and simple, author of a book, "die Metaphysik in der heutigen Physiologie-Beiträge zu einer Dynamik der Lebewesen." The book is a terribly abstract and unreal affair, insisting that life is pure mechanism but without a single concrete suggestion as to what the mechanism may be. But the man is a charming and human individual with a very pretty and innocent young wife.

Warmest regards!
W. J.

9. Henry James, the novelist, who was living permanently in London.

Geneva, Wednesday morning
May 10, 1893

My dear James,

Here is something to divert you during these rainy days.
I have only a vague recollection of the content of this literature. Your letter has supplied me with a good pretext to request the return of two of these works from a student who
had monopolized them for a long time. That is why I was
not able to reply immediately. It is Freyer that I remember
if not most clearly, at least most sympathetically. Cohen has
always seemed to me atrociously laborious to read. The French
are so clear that they make me feel doubtful. Since the
infinitesimal, the space element, cannot possibly be either
zero or anything measurable, even the smallest assignable
quantity, it seems to me more natural to make of it, as Freyer
does, a unique idea, *sui generis*—a notion of intensity opposed
to extension—despite the mystical character of the thing—rather
than to escape the difficulty with the evasive notion of "under
any assignable quantity."—But as it is eight years since I have
concerned myself with these abstruse questions, I should perhaps take a different view now if I had the time to ponder
it a few days, which is what I count on doing under your
direction when you publish your Epistemologie!—On rereading your letter, I notice to my confusion that I totally forgot
to inquire about a manual on the constitution of our republic.
You can guess that left to myself, never even knowing who
the President of our Confederation is, nor how many members
there are in our federal houses, I am unable to tell you of
a handbook on this subject; but in two or three days' time,
I shall certainly meet some lawyer who will be able to tell
me of one for you. As for these volumes, keep them as long
as you wish; I do not need them at present.

We are very sorry for the domestic difficulties you are
having with your Hélène; my wife will answer Madame James

shortly, to whom we wish to send all our best wishes, and a thousand thanks from my wife for her charming letter.

I have been very interested recently by a certain man named Kreps; who uses a form of mental suggestion on his daughter, at the circus. She guesses all the objects, numbers, etc. shown to her father, at a great distance from her, so perfectly and in circumstances so extraordinary that I got them to come yesterday morning to the Laboratory to examine them with my students. Quite certainly there isn't the least trace of mental suggestion but a process of mnemonics and of imperceptible, wonderfully skillful signs. My wife has had the great pleasure of making the acquaintance of Mlle. Rodgers; unfortunately, we were not home when these ladies called several days ago; we are waiting for the end of the wind and the rain to invite them to come for an afternoon at Florissant. The same for Billy. The return of good weather would be preferable, to have him come, and since you would prefer that this not be for several days, this is good.

My pamphlet on colored hearing drags on lazily to great length. I should like to have the manuscript finished in some ten days, but I dare not count on it. One of my students, two weeks ago, had a case analogous to the one reported by one of your students, which you told me about last summer. Upon awakening in the morning, already broad daylight, he had the *positive* image of his lamp, ⌂ , with his eyes open, just as he had seen it on turning it off the previous night. Unfortunately, he did not take notes at the time, telling me of it two days later, and not having seen the phenomenon since then (I had been speaking to him about it several days before). As he is subject to hypnotic hallucinations and to several other peculiarities, I hope that he will make new observations of this sort. I have recommended that he take notes immediately.

Your visit was a very pleasant surprise, three weeks ago, but it was too short! Won't you be coming back to our neighborhood to get Billy? I must stop to correct some proofs. Please accept, my dear James, our most affectionate greetings and believe me your most devoted,

Th. Flournoy

JAMES TO FLOURNOY (postcard, in French)

Meggen, bei Luzern

May 12, 1893

A thousand thanks, my dear Flournoy, for your more than kind parcel, which I am going to set myself the task of understanding a little. The volumes give me a terrifying idea of your erudition and profundity. Why am I deprived of a mathematical sense? All mathematical propositions seem to me not only unintelligible, but *false!* Renouvier always pleases me by his exposition; he makes me feel that I ought to go back to school again!

My wife is staying in Munich for a week.

W. James

JAMES TO FLOURNOY (postcard)

Meggen, May 18 [1893]

Returning from Zurich with Mrs. James who has been a week in Munich I find a note from our Billy saying he goes to you on Wednesday, and that you have invited him for a week. That seems to me too much for your family. It seems to me better that he should return to Vevey on Sunday, and I write him a word to that effect. You are very kind to him, and we both hope you won't have cause to repent your hospitality.—In great haste, with warm regards.

Wm James

JAMES TO FLOURNOY

34 De Vere Gardens [London]

June 26 [1893]

My dear Flournoy,

I received your card with the article by Baldwin many days ago, and send back with this your copy of the program of the Etudes modernes. We are staying in my brother's rooms, he being in the country, and enjoying to the utmost the glorious [sic] of London at this season, sombre, rich, immense, nothing on the continent can be compared to it. My wife takes to it as a fish to the water. The great thing is simply to ride through the streets on the tops of omnibuses over the softly rumbling wooden pavement. I wish you both were here so that I might take your respective "reactions"— not the *time* of them, but the quality.

No decision yet as to how we return.

The amount of literature indicated in the Enseignement moderne is enormous. It looks as if it must be an indigestion. It certainly will require skilful teaching, and I shall be extremely curious to know, after 10 years trial of the system, what the results are judged to be. Certainly if the program can be successfully taught to youths under 20, it is safe to say that their education will be more really "humanistic" than on the classic plan.

The evening spent with you is a delicious remembrance. When we get back to Switzerland we shall immediately communicate with you. With love from both, to both. Yours always

Wm James

JAMES TO FLOURNOY (postcard, in French)

Queenstown, Ireland

August 25 [1893]

Our ship stops here for an hour before confronting the waves of the Atlantic, and I have taken this moment to send you our last farewells. All is favorable to the utmost degree; our twenty-eight large pieces of luggage and our innumerable small parcels have been put on board without damage or confusion; our cabins and places at table are of the best, and (the principal thing!) the sea is as calm as I have ever seen it. Farewell, "sabbatical year," adieu Canton de Vaud,[10] goodbye youth! And may God bless you all, young and old, my dear Flournoy.

Wm. James
Alice H. James

FLOURNOY TO JAMES

Geneva, December 18, 1893

Dear James,

Since you left our old continent—which becomes more dangerous every day because of anarchist dynamite explosions and bombs (someone even threatened to blow up our peaceful Hôtel de Ville)—we have had news of you three times. First, your kind card from Queenstown, telling us of your happy departure, and we were very touched by this last farewell, so cordial and affectionate, which you took the time to send us at the moment of sailing. The signature of Mrs. James beside your own makes this card doubly dear to us and we are carefully preserving it!—Sometime afterward, a note from H[erbert] Nichols informed me, in a postscript, of your happy arrival at Cambridge; I hope that the crossing was made without any seasickness at all for any of you, and without damage to your twenty-eight large pieces of luggage and the army of small packages. What a curious impression, *sui generis*, it must make on one's return home after fifteen months' absence on the other side of the ocean; your children, particularly, must have found that everything had become singu-

10. Vaud is the section of Switzerland in which the James and Flournoy families had vacationed together in the summer of 1892.

larly small, and the ceilings very low, during their travels, which must have produced a notable growth in their stature. —Several weeks ago, my worthy colleague, Monsieur [Louis] Wuarin told me, at last, that he had had the privilege of being a guest in your home. I thank you for receiving him so pleasantly. He had the good fortune to attend one of your classes, and what he told me makes me regret once more not being fifteen years younger. Upon reading the *Principles of Psychology* three years ago, I thought that were it not for my age and family I would set sail at once for Harvard for some semesters of study!—So you have resumed your courses, and now all the germinal ideas—which I need hardly say you did not gather in Europe, but rather received "by the back stairs" [11] during your year of holiday and rest—now these seeds are about to germinate and to produce such rich harvests. I am impatient for and will be delighted to see the results in your next articles or books.—Monsieur Wuarin brought back to me Münsterberg's brochure which he published about the Harvard laboratories. I won't say that the description of all these numerous instruments or the magnificence of that organization made my mouth water, because decidedly I do not feel as if I am up to all that; and I feel a shiver of awe before that arsenal of instruments, which gives me a strong sense of my incapacity, and I bless the destiny which has wisely adjusted my position to my faculties. I do not complain any more about having an inadequate laboratory, without suitable quarters, without resources—and without serious students—now that I know that my present laboratory is all I need, and that I should certainly lose my head if I had the responsibility of more space, more instruments, and more students. This universe is certainly orderly and cared-for!

This year I have only three hard-working students (two of

11. In English in the original.

them women!) in the laboratory; I have them do an elementary laboratory course, helping myself from Sanford, from
Nichols' notes, and adding to these experiments that can be
carried out with material at my disposal and which I glean
from my reading. My theoretical course brings together, as
a rule, about 35 regular auditors. The fact that scarcely one-
tenth frequent the laboratory (which costs nothing) proves
to me that experimental psychology is not yet in demand
here; the students prefer to be given the results and the
conclusions of other people's research, rather than to begin,
themselves, to observe and verify.—I try to penetrate into the
spiritualistic world of our city, but it is rather difficult. At
the present time they do not have very outstanding mediums;
I should be very content, indeed, if I were only able to
observe closely those who experience the phenomena about
which I hear, but they surround themselves with solitude and
darkness. I am now deep in Myers's articles in the *Proceedings of the Society for Psychical Research;* I have been asked
to give two talks in a series of public lectures, after the New
Year, and I shall do them on Verifiable Hallucinations, Visions
in the Crystal Ball, etc.

I have nothing particularly interesting to tell you about my
family. Fraülein Hühnersdorf is always a great help to us,—
and we hope that you will be satisfied with the helpers whom
you took with you upon leaving Switzerland! Our little
Riquet [12] entered school this autumn; he works hard, likes his
teachers very much, and is always among the first in behavior—but, alas, it is otherwise for the sciences, and as for
arithmetic, geography, grammar, or other things, he remains
prudently at the bottom of his class! I console myself by
thinking that his very rapid physical growth holds back his
intellectual development for the moment—all the same, your
compatriot, W. Townsend Porter of St. Louis, has shown in

12. Henri Flournoy

a brochure which I happened to read that there is some correlation between mental precocity and bodily weight.

I must stop for the present. My wife and children intend to reply directly to Mrs. James and your family, but I fear that their letters which still remain in the realm of good intentions will reach you too late, after the New Year. Please give my respectful good wishes to Mrs. James and kind regards to your children, and believe me always, my dear James, your grateful and affectionate

Théodore Flournoy

I was forgetting to give you all our best wishes for happiness and health in the New Year.

JAMES TO FLOURNOY (dictated)

[95 Irving Street] Cambridge
Dec. 31, 1893

My dear Flournoys,

We must address you in the plural as we are ourselves plural. She is holding the pen and I am dictating the words because a sharp of attack of tonsillitis keeps me from writing myself and I don't want 1893 to pass by without your receiving a word of greeting from us. We had a most magnificent voyage home and found everything in our house charmingly clean and cheerful. But I found it terribly hard to get at any teaching again. One loses so quickly an artificial discipline like that of a professor's life that in my 15 months I had quite reverted to the "feral" state. I seemed to have forgotten all my psychology and the subject of psychology *Ueberhaupt* had shrunk to nothing in my consciousness. I had two months of profoundest melancholy from which I gradually emerged and am now all right again. But I now know that 15 months is too long for a vacation for a man whose work, at all times, is done with effort. In another way too, we are both melancholy after our vacation. So much Italy and so much Switzer-

land make one's native land seem *strange* to one. A non-con-
ducting film has grown up between us. We both look back
to Switzerland as the terrestrial paradise and I must say, my
dear Flournoy, that your position in the world as a citizen of
that fortunate republic, with your pleasant house in Geneva,
and your not-too-burdensome professorship, with those salubrious mountains open to you for your summer vacation, with
your central position for travelling etc. etc. make you a most
enviable man. The impression Switzerland leaves on us is that
of extraordinarily healthy civilization. The neurotic *fin-de-
siècle* element which is killing the larger countries, including
our own, has got but comparatively little hold on you as
yet. All human lives have their dissatisfactions but the alge-
braic sum of these and the healthy satisfactions seem to me
on the whole to be a maximum just where you are placed.

We had last week a meeting of most of the psychologists
of the country in New York. On the whole a very profitable
two days. When you see all the little homunculi from whom
the work comes, its majesty of the latter shrinks, but at the
same time it *solidifies* in one's imagination. Münsterberg is a
great success here. In so far as I can see he hasn't a personal
fault. He is very enthusiastic about America too and con-
siders that ideality is a distinguishing trait of the American
character—rather a pleasant contrast to the usual German accusation that we have no soul for anything but dollars.

We are starting a new Psychological Journal of which you
will receive a specimen and possibly become a subscriber.
Everyone seems to be publishing a Psychology in these days.
Ebbinghaus, Külpe, Müller, Ladd, Stout, and who knows who
besides. It seems as if some precipitation of truth ought to
result from all this industry and I hope it will. Those who
wait before emitting their own thunder till all this irrigating
shower has passed by, and fertilized the ground will be in
the best position to write something good. Madame Flournoy
will be pleased to hear that our two Swiss women are perfect

treasures—the best women we have ever had in the house. And they, like Münsterberg, take an optimistic view of America. How we should like to look in on you by some sort of telepathy this morning. I think the sight of *ces demoiselles* would instantly cure my tonsillitis.

Let Madame Flournoy take this letter from both of us, and believe in the sincere affection with which we wish you each and all (not forgetting the Good Fräulein) a happy New Year.

Yours ever faithfully,
Wm James

FLOURNOY TO JAMES

Geneva, March 18, 1894

My dear James

Here I am two long months late in thanking you for several things: your excellent photograph, which adorns my chimney-piece and reminds me of precious, happy times; your kind letter written jointly with Mrs. James; the first number of The Psychological Review, the interesting contents of which made me decide at once to take out a subscription; finally, the much too kind and long account which so generously devoted to "Synopsie" [13] in the January issue of The Philosophical Review. That is a long list to add to all the other causes for gratitude and to increase my indebtedness to you!—You were ailing when you wrote to us and enduring a painful angina; I hope that this illness did not last long, that the rest of the winter passed without trouble to you and yours, and that your next postal card (which will come very soon, I hope) will give us excellent news of you all.—It is Easter vacation here, but this is only a semblance of holiday for us because we have been victims of masons, plasterers, and varnishers,

13. The reference is to Flournoy's most recent work, *Des Phénomènes de synopsie,* Geneva and Paris, 1893.

for the past eight days and will be for three or four months to come. We are changing the arrangement of our house and installing a hot-water heating system; I am moving my study to the second floor, as we are enlarging the dining room. All this amuses the children very much, but tires the parents, and Fräulein Hühnersdorf is a very great help in all this disorder and confusion which results from the upset condition. Yesterday, I finished my winter course, which was complicated this year by several public lectures from which I was not able to escape; two among others on "occult psychology." I had a considerable audience, given the attraction which the subject has for the not always very healthy curiosity of the public toward such mysterious subjects. I need hardly tell you that by ending without coming to any conclusions, on a prudent question mark, I displeased almost everybody; the medical people, kurzsinnig and einseitig, hold me in small esteem because I did not bluntly and a priori reject telepathy and spiritism—and the spiritualists are angry with me for not having hoisted their flag. The fact is that my position is not settled; far from it. The few mediums and subjects of telepathic hallucinations etc. whom I have been able to reach in the last three months in Geneva have not furnished me with decisive phenomena; and it is upon some passages of your "Principles of Psychology" and in the *Proceedings of the Society for Psychical Research* (especially the article by Myers on subliminal consciousness) that I have drawn for the greatest part of my two lectures and my nonconclusive conclusions; so that I have nothing new to report to you in that respect.

Several days ago at a soirée, I met an elderly woman physician, Dr. Harriet Clisby, who had studied in America, had been entertained in the home of your parents, and remembered you and your brother Henry James very well; but perhaps this recollection is not reciprocal because you were only 5 or 6 years old when she knew you. This lady is at present giving a series of three lectures, in English, on "Physiology of Character." I heard the first one, but unfortunately my ear is so unaccustomed to your fine language that only a few fragmentary snatches of Mlle. Clisby's ideas were conveyed to me.

I learned with grief of the premature death of Dr. Myers, and I have not been able to judge at all from the very brief card with which F. W. H. Myers replied to my letter how and to what extent he has been affected by this loss.—Remember us, please, to Mrs. James and your children, tell us soon by a word on a card that you are in good health; and believe me, my dear James, your very devoted and grateful

Théodore Flournoy

JAMES TO FLOURNOY

Chocorua [New Hampshire]

August 1894

My dear Flournoy,

I have thought of you often in this summer season, as the contrast between the last two summers and this one has brought you up in memory as an "associate" of the bygone periods. I wonder whether you are again at Salvan, or have passed to some new mountain height unknown to us. Wherever it be, I hope it is as good a place as the Vers-chez-les-Blanc and Pension Cruchon which you introduced to us, and which now stand apart in my imagination as places of almost unique tranquility, salubrity, and happiness. Here in this warmer and lower region, expressive as it is artistically, I find myself thirsting for that incomparable strong and sweet air, and recollecting how it felt when one began to get it above the Croisettes, after walking or driving in the Postwagon at the end of a hot day at Lausanne or on the Lake. Everything disappears in the maelstrom of time, and I much doubt whether I ever see the Pension Cruchon again!—But I must not get into the Obermann vein, which I find of late is rather growing upon me, but tell you of our destinies, which are much what they always were. I got through the University year somewhat haltingly, having the influenza at Christmas time, and being so fatigued at the end of March that in desperation, and at the advice of a medical friend who had had good success with it in his practice, I tried Brown-Sequard's famous injections. The result after eight of them was an abscess which kept me in bed 5 weeks. But between Royce [14] and Münsterberg my instruction got given and the year closed happily. I got off to the North Carolina Mountains early in June, and since then have been for the most part here with the family, who are all well, save little Tweedy who today has a rather severe bronchial attack. Our little lakeside and Mountain slope look pretty, even after Switzerland, only the air has not that magnificent quality. Having spent so much money abroad, we are living on an economical basis, without horse, man, cow, or pig. But *es geht,* and although I lose freedom, by having to do a good deal of work which naturally would be taken by the man, and by the necessity of going on foot when otherwise I should drive, it is probably good for my constitution. My intellect is somewhat stagnant. I enjoyed last year reading a good deal of stuff which might connect itself with lectures on "Cosmology," but no reactions of my own have yet set in, and as for psychology, it has passed away from me altogether since the publication of my book. Münsterberg now lectures very fluently & on the whole very effectively in English and creates enthusiasm amongst the students. He is still in Cambridge conducting a "summer school" in psychology. The University gets such professors as are willing, to give these summer schools for the benefit of teachers who come from all parts of the country to work up particular

14. Josiah Royce (1855–1916), James's colleague and friend at Harvard, professor of philosophy there from 1885 until his death. For his relationship with James, see Henry James, ed., *The Letters of William James* (Boston, 1920), I, 200, 201.

subjects. Each subject is lectured on every-day for six weeks. There are 500 students in all, this year, of whom Münsterberg has 40, half men, half women. It is very useful work, and it shows his energy that he should be able to take it. On the whole he is one of the most *faultless* men whom I have ever known, in point of character.—By the way, if a young *Wadsworth*, formerly of Harvard, has made your acquaintance in Geneva, be a little cautious with him. He is very intelligent, acute and witty, but with a distinct tendency to mental aberration. He left Cambridge with a delusion about Münsterberg having insulted him, and was going to Geneva to study with Schiff, so that it is very likely you may have met him.—

I have just read a book "Appearance and Reality" by F. H. Bradley, [15] pub'd a year ago, which is destined to bring the whole of english philosophical discussion up to a higher plane, dialectically, than it has ever known before. I mistrust it, both premises and conclusion; but it is one of those vigorous and original things that have to be assimilated slowly. Your Colleague [Jean-Jacques] Gourd would probably enjoy it, although it is so different from his own book in the thesis it defends, because it is pure metaphysics from beginning to end. It undoubtedly will be epoch-making in our literature.—But enough! This is only to let you all know that we love you. Those dear demoiselles! How I should like to see and hear them. Our Harry is now bigger than I am, and the brief period of about six months in which I could get rid of clothes that I didn't like by transferring them to him, is now gone forever, alas. Pray send a line before the summer is

15. Francis Herbert Bradley (1846–1924), Professor of Philosophy at Oxford University, restated, after Hegel, the case for idealism, particularly in the book here mentioned. The main thesis, toward which both James and Flournoy were unsympathetic, was that the totality of reality is beyond finite mind and that therefore our adjustments can never be free of error. Spirit he called "The Absolute" and, as James said, tended toward pure metaphysics.

over to let us know how it has fared with you all. Accept
the affectionate regards of both of us for both yourself and
Madame Flournoy, and believe [me] always and faithfully
yours,

Wm James

Our regards also to Fraülein Hühnersdorf, who I hope is with
you still.

FLOURNOY TO JAMES

Geneva, October 2, 1894

My dear James

I received your good letter six weeks ago at the same time
that I returned from Salvan, where we spent our vacation,
as we did last year. My intention was to reply immediately,
and then, as usual, I had to wait indefinitely before doing so.
If *graphophobia* is not yet officially a form of neurasthenia,
it is nevertheless real and causes me torment, whether it is
a question of revising a lesson or of writing very freely to a
friend who holds a special place deep in my heart and to
whom I have the greatest desire to reply without delay. The
mere fact of taking up my pen and sitting down before a
blank piece of paper paralyzes me completely. It is only after
several useless attempts, separated by days and even weeks
in which it is impossible even to make a new attempt, that
I give birth, with great effort, to a few lines. This incapacity
to write is a great trial to me; it is really becoming an illness.
The idea of resorting to the Brown Sequard injections occurred to me last winter; but the failure of this treatment
for a friend of mine, who has pretty nearly the same trouble,
made me put off the treatment; and your letter does not
encourage me to try it! I hope that you are entirely free
from your illness of last winter and that your active life in
the country during vacation has had splendid effects.—I have
not been lacking in physical activity this year, though it fa-

tigued me rather more than it refreshened me. Last March
we began remodeling our house, which you know; we crowded
into one part while the other was given over to workmen,
then we moved into the former part and thus moved back
and forth several times, because all this has been enormously
complicated by the installation of a hot-water heating system,
with the heater in the basement. Our house, constructed long
ago in the old method, lent itself badly to remodeling, and
it has not been easy. It's been 7 months since the work began,
and although we are nearly through, we still have workmen
here, and the heating system is not yet completely finished.
My library is now on the second floor and opens onto a large
balcony over the veranda; our old dining room has become
a small room (=Wohnstube) where the children will be able
to play more freely than before with Fraülein Hühnersdorf
(who has spent three months of vacation with her family,
this summer, and will return to us in several days). Finally,
we added a much more spacious dining room, formed by
joining my old study with an adjoining room. If our heating
system goes well, we will be much more comfortable than
ever before, and several rooms on the second floor are now
enlarged and have become more habitable, whereas previously
they weren't at all so, being impossible to heat sufficiently
during winter.

If I have spoken at length of these material things, it is
because they have been, by force of circumstance, our principal preoccupation for a year. I have been singularly involved
in all this and neglected philosophy and psychology. I have
been carpenter, locksmith, painter, mover, and I have done
my University duties only with aversion and in the most mediocre manner. Never have I felt to such an extent the profound
inanity, the abnormality, if I may say so, of cerebral speculations, and the blessings of manual labor; and I do not understand people who, able to become blacksmiths or carpenters,
believe they choose the better part in devoting themselves

to study. For a year, I have ignored The Philosophical Review, Mind, Philosophical Studies, and tutti quanti—however, I have read with interest a work on Bunyan by your friend Royce; and I was extremely pleased to read the note in The Psychological Review, in which you roundly dispose of Wundt, as he deserves!

Other than these two or three articles, I haven't read anything, have not kept abreast, and I see with terror the winter term approaching. I had hoped that these few months of occupation with material things would rest my philosophical nerve centers. Alas! it is not at all so. I have merely become rusty and have a hard time getting back to work. I returned from the mountains several weeks ahead of my regiment (some of the children are still in Lausanne at the home of my wife's parents; my wife will bring them home tomorrow—the others will not be here for a month) in order to try to work on an article that Binet [16] has asked from me on our laboratory work, for a volume he is preparing, but I simply do not know how I shall get through the situation.

The "demoiselles" are pleased with your remembrance, as is also my wife. Alice has grown like a weed and has the air of a young lady of 15 or 16, even though she is only 13½. Blanche remains small and thin as a matchstick, but quick and light as a chamois; the mountains are better for her than the plains. Marguerite is a butterball; Henri has started school and conducts himself prudently, with a respectable average that leaves much room for improvement. The little youngest one is spoiled by everyone, and I have fears about the effect of this on her character.

16. Alfred Binet (1857–1911), the French experimental psychologist, had just become in 1894 director of the psychological laboratory at the Sorbonne. The following year, with Ribot and others, he began the publication of *L'Annee psychologique.* He is best known for his work on intelligence tests, done in the following decade.

My wife started a letter several weeks ago addressed to Mrs. James. But when will she find the time and the strength to finish it? She is very tired because of these repairs and she goes frequently to Lausanne to see the children. We hope you are all well. Remember us to your children and accept for Mrs. James and yourself our kindest regards. Believe me, my good friend, your most devoted

Théodore Flournoy

P.S. Please convey my compliments to Münsterberg. I am extremely pleased for him and for you, about his success.

Thank you for warning me about Wadsworth—I haven't yet seen him and will do nothing to make his acquaintance.

JAMES TO FLOURNOY

Glenwood Springs, Colorado

Aug. 13, 1895

My dear Flournoy,

Ever since last January an envelope, addressed to you has been lying before my eyes on my library table. I mention this to assure you that you have not been absent from my thoughts; but I will waste no time or paper in making excuses. As the sage Emerson says, when you visit a man do not degrade the occasion with apologies for not having visited him before. Visit him now! Make him feel that the highest truth has come to see him in you its lowliest organ. I don't know about the highest truth transpiring through this letter, but I feel as if there were plenty of affection and personal gossip to express themselves. To begin with, your photograph and Mrs. Flournoy's were splendid. What we need now is the photographs of those fair *demoiselles!* I may say that one reason of my long silence has been the hope that when I wrote I should have my wife's photograph to send you. But alas! it has not been taken yet. She is well, very well, and is now in our little New Hampshire country-place with the children, living very quietly and happily. We have had a rather large *train de maison* hitherto, and this summer we are shrunken to our bare essentials—a very pleasant change.

I, you see, am farther away from home than I have ever been before on this side of the Atlantic, namely in the state of Colorado, and just now in the heart of the Rocky Mountains. I have been giving a course of six lectures on psychology "for teachers" at a so-called "summer-school" in Colorado Springs. I had to remain for 3 nights and 3 days in the train to get there, and it has made me understand the vastness of my dear native land better than I ever did before. Colorado Springs is a pulmonary resort at the foot of Pike's Peak, 14,000 odd feet high, and is a really exquisite place both for climate and for beauty. On the West the magnificent mountains, the rocks being mostly of pinkish colour, and beautifully sculptured by the weather, and on the East the illimitable prairie stretching delicately tinted and very gently undulating surface to the sun, and interrupted at long intervals by low "bluffs" or cliffs. The altitude is 6,000 feet, and the climate perfect all the year round. The most *fin de siècle* civilization coexists here with the most primeval nature. Around every railroad station one sees mere caverns in the clay banks with three pieces of wood to make a doorway, and in these certain human beings live, and yet the hotel in which I now am (4 years old) is really handsomer and more comfortable than the best Swiss hotel that I have ever seen. In admirable good taste too. Its raison d'être is certain hot springs, very wonderful fountains playing, and a great warm swimming tank 400 feet long on the grounds. The trouble with all this new civilization is that it is based not on saving, but borrowing; and whenever hard times come, as they did come 3 years ago, everyone goes bankrupt. But the vision of the future, the dreams of the possible, keep everyone enthusiastic, and so the work goes on. Such conditions have never existed before on so enormous a scale. But I must not write you a treatise on national economy!—I got through the year very well in regard to health, and gave in the course of it what I had never done before, a number of lectures to teachers in Boston and New York. I also repeated my course in Cosmology in the New Woman's College which has lately been established in connexion with our University. The consequence is that I laid by more than a 1000 dollars, an absolutely new and proportionately pleasant experience for me. To make up for it, I haven't had an idea or written anything to speak of except the "presidential address" [17] which I sent you, and which really contained nothing new.

Münsterberg is a perfectly triumphant success, and left us with the liveliest hope on the part of everyone that he will return after two years. He is more made up of ideal qualities than anyone I know, his only defect being a sort of naiveté and optimism that come from the almost pathologically free and harmonious working of all his faculties together. Nothing gives him any difficulty. He makes the most effective orations in English, (though his accent remains poor), and, what is unusual in a man of so many new ideas, he is a perfect monster of method and order, and does everything punctually according to a fixed program. His departure throws the entire burden of Psychology on me next year. There are two good assistants in the laboratory, however, trained by him, so with the aid of Heaven, I shall doubtless pull through, though I have no more capacity for experimental psychology than for being captain of a steamer. My boy Harry has pleased us very much by passing all the examinations for the Univeristy at the early age of 16. Billy will, we hope, do the same. Peggy has improved very much, and I beg you tell Fräulein Hühnersdorf that *her* "Tweedy" is *great* man of the

17. Given in December, 1894, in Princeton at a meeting of the American Psychological Association, this talk, "On the Knowing of Things Together," was included in part in *The Meaning of Truth*, p. 43, under the title "The Tigers in India."

family. He is really fine. I regret to say, however, that his french is growing very bad. He says "Donne moi ca! C'est *mon!*" etc. This is in consequence of the loss of our 2 Swiss *bonnes* whom we bro't over. Though we treated them like children of the house, they became infected with the American disease of living for the possible rather than the actual and left us 3 months ago to better their situation. One of them has been very unhappy over it but we do not take her back, as she was rather inefficient.

And now is not that enough gossip about ourselves? I wish I could by telephone at this moment hear just where and how you all are, and what you are all doing. In the Mountains somewhere, of course, and I trust all well, but it is perhaps 15 or 20 years too soon for transatlantic telephone. My surroundings here, so much like those of Switzerland, bring you before me in a lively manner. I enclose a picture of one of the streets at Colorado Springs for Madame Flournoy, and another one of a "cowboy" for that one of the *demoiselles* who is most *romanesque*. Alice, Blanche—but I have actually gone and been and forgotten the name of the magnificent third one, whose resplendent face I so well remember notwithstanding. *Dulcissima mundi nomina,* all of them; and I do hope that they are being educated in a thoroughly emancipated way, just like true American girls, with no laws except those imposed by their own sense of fitness. I am sure it produces the best results!—How did the teaching go last year? I mean your teaching. Have you started any new lines? And how is [Daniel Auguste] Chantre? and how Ritter? And how Monsieur Gourd? Please give my best regards all round, especially to Ritter. Have you a copy left of your Métaphysique et psychologie? In some inscrutable way my copy has disappeared, and the book is reported *épuisé.*

With warmest possible regards to both of you, and to all 5 of the descendants believe me ever faithfully yours

W. James

Geneva, September 4, 1895

My dear James,

Your affectionate letter was so well timed and gave me such pleasure that for once I am going to make an exception to my dilatory and lazy habits and reply without delay, for fear that if I postpone one or several semesters will pass before I would find the opportunity and time to thank you! In my thought, I have followed you with envy to the heart of the Rocky Mountains, reading your lively descriptions of the splendid and unusual surroundings in which you are spending the summer. This contrast and unusual mingling of wild nature with refined civilization ought singularly to stimulate the mind and strengthen the body; I hope that you will bring back from your vacation all the vigor and enthusiasm you need for giving your course in psychology.

The pleasant picture of Münsterberg which you gave me pleases me greatly,—but at the same time makes me understand how much you lose by his departure and the void he is going to leave in your laboratory. I saw in the University schedule that he is going to resume his courses at Freiburg [Breisgau, Germany]. If only I could send my students off to him (if I have any this winter) and close my laboratory, which is at present the biggest thorn in my life!—We spent the months of July and August at Le Sépey near Aigle, in a delightful châlet where we were by ourselves, without the boredom of pension food and the promiscuities of a hotel. The first half of our sojourn was lovely; magnificent weather, beautiful walks all about the Ormont region; you can imagine that I did not pass by the Diablerets without recalling, with more intensity than usual, our excursion of 1892 to Pillon and Col de la Croix—But after four perfect weeks, I got— I do not know how—congestion of the lungs which kept me in bed all the second half of our stay. It was the first time in my life that I found myself seriously ill. My wife was very upset. Fortunately, we were only a half-hour's distance from her brother, who is a medical doctor at the sanatorium of Leysin; it was precisely to be near him during the summer that we had chosen Le Sépey, but we never thought we would have need of his services! For three weeks, he came every day to auscultate me, percuss me, drug me, treat me with cupping, with mustard plaster, etc.; and thanks to his good care I escaped, at least till now, from pleurisy and pneumonia. I don't know what we would have done without him—for there is at Le Sépey neither doctor nor pharmacy. As soon as my strength permitted, we returned to Geneva where we were recalled by the children's lessons and schooling and where I am more comfortably situated than in a mountain chalet to recover. My right lung has not yet returned completely to normal, and I am condemned to a quantity of treatments and tiresome precautions. But at last, thank God, I am considered out of danger. My poor wife was even more tired than I was by this illness. As for me, the complexities and weaknesses of my nature are such that I do not know if I ought to hope to be soon free from a stubborn cough and pains in my side, which exhaust me very much, or if I may on the contrary decently hope that the cough and pains will continue so long as to prevent me from resuming laboratory work this winter! Decidedly, that Laboratory is becoming a fixed, morbid idea, a real phobia with me. Mrs. James will have learned, by a letter that my wife wrote her from Le Sépey a few days before I fell ill, that we no longer have Fräulein Hühnersdorf. It was certainly not in order to replace her with someone else that we let her go, for we will never find anyone so pleasant and precious from all points of view. But, given the character of my wife and me, we have finally perceived that a governess is a useless mechanism and even an inconvenience in our household. Owing to my natural laziness, I had come to the point where I hardly concerned myself with the children and even saw them very

seldom, leaving them always in Fräulein's care; and since basically, now that they are at their lessons most of the day, we
have all the time to spend with them, my wife and I, during
the few hours when they are free, we've decided that the
time has come to give up the help of a governess in order
to be obliged to spend time with them ourselves. Fräulein
wanted to stay for another year in a French place, if possible
Paris, in order to finish learning the language she already
knows so well. Unfortunately, our efforts to find her a place
all this spring have not succeeded; there are so many German
girls available who work at no cost or for ridiculous salaries
to learn French that it is very difficult to find a position with
remuneration such as Fräulein has the right to ask. At the
moment she is still in Germany; she has made several visits
to the homes of various members of her large family; she
has often written to us as well as to the children, who were
naturally very attached to her; we do not know yet what
her plans are for the autumn and winter; she was hesitating
between looking for a place in Germany, even, or in Paris,
or finally returning to America. She is a person of warmth
and intelligence, for whom we would wish fate to be most
favorable in proportion to her virtues, to say the least! We
shall not forget that it is because of you that we have had
the privilege of having had her; I can say that during these
three years she has not ceased to do honor to your recommendation. We have always been perfectly content with her
—and I hope that for her part she will not have carried away
a bad memory of her stay under our roof.

I congratulate you on the brilliant success of your son
Harry, in whose footsteps Billy will not fail to follow. Whom
do they take after! "The apple never falls far from the tree."
I do not have such good news to report about our children,
who remain at an honest average—*aurea mediocritas*—which,
at the same time, keeps them from retaking examinations and
from the pride of recompense. They seem to have some taste
for music, which is a nice example of atavism because my

father was an enthusiastic musician, although I absolutely am not, and my wife hardly more so. Marguerite and Alice play the piano; Blanche began the violin several months ago, and Henri just started the 'cello this week. I assure you that I must have great paternal devotion to accept the prospect of an unlimited number of years of exercises and cacophonies. Fortunately my study is separated from the rest of the house by a thick wall almost impenetrable to harmony.

I did not know that [George Trumbull] Ladd had thought it worth his while to refute me and I thank you for the information. I immediately ordered the *Philosophy of Mind* from my bookseller, and it will not be long before I have it. I shall try to find a copy of "Metaphysique et psychologie" to send to you. From time to time, I can put my hand on one, at the home of friends or at a second-hand book dealer's.

I was forgetting to tell you what has interested me most during the last six months; it is a certain medium (nonprofessional, unpaid) of a spiritualist group into which they agreed to accept me in spite of my neutral position. I have attended about twenty of the seances, of which a third were here at my home; psychologically, it is very interesting, because this woman is a veritable museum of all possible phenomena and has a repertoire of illimitable variety: she makes the table talk,—she hears voices,—she has visions, hallucinations, tactile and olfactory,—automatic writing—sometimes complete somnambulism, catalepsy, trances etc. All the *automatism, sensory and motor*, of Myers,—all the classical hysterical phenomena—present themselves in turn, in any order and in the most unexpected fashion, varying from one time to another. The *contents* of these phenomena are always of former events, going back a few or many years, being perfectly correct, generally having to do with the ancestors of the persons present. The good faith of the medium is indisputable, and the strangeness of her revelation well calculated to convince the spiritualists of this group. However, in the 5 or 6 cases which concerned deceased members of my family, I finally had proof that these persons all had had, some fifty years ago, personal contacts with the parents of the medium; and the most natural supposition is that these revelations, invariably exact and dealing with odd facts, are reminiscences of accounts which the medium had heard from the mouth of her parents in her childhood. By induction, I suppose that in cases concerning people other than myself, and on which I cannot undertake any research, it is the same. I have still as yet seen nothing, in these seances, which seems to me to prove the intervention of disincarnated spirits; a certain number of episodes appear to me to indicate that there is an unconscious mental suggestion on the part of the spectators, but, I cannot yet state this with certainty. The great majority of the phenomena were evidently the automatic reproduction of forgotten memories—or memories registered unconsciously. There is actually in the nature of this medium a second personality who perceives and recalls incidents which escape ordinary awareness; for example, the medium lost a gold brooch one day, put a notice in the papers without results, and ten days later the table dictated that this brooch would be found in a certain street, at a certain spot, where actually the medium had passed on the day she lost the brooch. This is included in the facts published by Myers, and I have the definite impression that the extraordinary revelations obtained in the seances, for the most part, if not all (and certainly all those concerning me, as yet) are phenomena of "Cryptomnesia."—What is irritating in this kind of observation is the difficulty of making it precise, the medium and the members of the group having a holy terror of everything which resembles an "experiment," such as, for instance, verifying whether or not the hand which moves the table is consciously directed. This is why I doubt whether I can write a paper, worthy of publication, on this case which certainly is full of interesting psychological and physiological phenomena.

My wife greatly appreciates the view which you sent her and the "cowboy" was awarded to Blanche, not as the most romantic,—in this respect it is difficult to decide between Alice and her (and moreover they are perhaps too little romantic for your taste) but as the most capable of appreciating this wild horseman. Actually her ideal and her dream have always been to become one day a "circus rider," which constitutes for her the nec plus ultra of happiness. She is beginning to understand that these gymnastic aspirations are not of the most elevated order, but she will not renounce them without regret! This is too long a letter, my dear James. Won't you come next summer, for the Congress of Psychologists at Munich, and also for our National Swiss Exposition at Geneva? All good wishes from us all to you all, and especially my regards to Mrs. James. Thank you again for your letter. Believe me always your most affectionate

Théodore Flournoy

The "demoiselles" were very appreciative of your kind thoughts, and we will certainly send you their photographs when we have some.

JAMES TO FLOURNOY (postcard)

Cambr. Nov. 8, '95

I thank you heartily for your post card and the copy of your immortal essay, just received. I thank you still more for your noble letter of Sept. 4 to which I was on the point of sending a long and *immediate* answer. Something prevented that, and here I am, two months later, with a postcard! I am already bowed down with too much work and no *letter* can be written for some time to come. I was truly grieved to hear of your illness, and hope that there will be no relapse, but a solid recovery. I sympathize with you in re laboratorie. I am suffering similarly in M—berg's absence. A true nightmare.

W. J.

II

Bonds between Diverging Careers

1896–1900

Although James spent a good portion of the next five years in Europe, he was not often in Geneva, and the correspondence continued with even greater vigor. Ill health became a major topic, particularly with James, whose heart condition was serious. In an endless search for help, he visited many specialists and took treatments at several spas, but with little encouragement. The marked personal courage with which he carried on his activities under these conditions was a great inspiration to Flournoy, who was often in poor health and far less active and optimistic. One notes in these years the growing imbalance of the two careers. Professional opportunities developed in many ways for James, taking him to Wisconsin, California, London, and Edinburgh. Flournoy remained in Geneva, with an occasional trip to Lausanne and Paris for lectures or meetings. Both saw that the relationship was an uneven one, yet the friendship flourished, James writing more frequently and always with warmth of feeling and stimulating ideas on a variety of things. Their candid comments on colleagues, current affairs, family joys and tribulations flow across the pages of the letters with refreshing ease and charm, often with real tenderness and solicitude.

Finding himself staying at Lake Geneva, Wisconsin, in August, 1896, James writes with wry humor of the connecting links between that body of water and Lake Léman. He was lecturing at different summer schools and other special audiences on material which he gathered into his next two books, *The Will to Believe and Other Essays in Popular Philosophy,* 1897, and *Talks to Teachers and Students on Some of Life's Ideals,* 1899. In 1896–1897 he delivered the Lowell Institute Lectures. Most important of all, perhaps, was his invitation to give the "Gifford Lectures on Natural Religion," at the University of Edinburgh. This took him abroad in July, 1899, for what proved to be a much longer sojourn than he intended, for ill health kept him from giving the first series of lectures until May, 1901. After a few months at home, he returned to Edinburgh for the second series in 1902, publishing the lectures that June as *The Varieties of Religious Experience.* Far less productive, Flournoy published but one book at this time, *Des Indes à la planète Mars,* in 1900, the work which brought him his widest recognition.

James's being in Europe from 1899 to 1901 afforded many opportunities to meet colleagues in whom he and Flournoy were interested. Among those frequently mentioned were Charles Robert Richet, editor of the *Revue scientifique,* whom Flournoy called "the most truly and completely *human*" of his French connections, and Marie Felix Pierre Janet, editor of the *Journal de psychologie normale et pathologique.* There was also François Pillon, whom James had met in 1880 through Renouvier, Pillon being Renouvier's closest collaborator and disciple. James dedicated his *Principles of Psychology* to Pillon and spoke of him as "the best of men." The Belgian philosopher Joseph Rémy Leopold Delboeuf, known for his work on logic and hypnotism, James considered "much the best teacher I've seen." In complimenting Flournoy on the quality of his French, James wrote "You and Delboeuf are the only worthy successors of Voltaire!"

After the Gifford Lectures, James moved away from psy-

chology toward philosophy, but he never completely gave up
his interest in the psychological aspects of spiritism and the
occult. Flournoy's concern with psychical research remained
his principal activity, and both men at the turn of the century
were at the peak of mutual interest and individual investigations. James had discovered Mrs. Piper, the Boston medium,
in 1885 and wrote many reports on her trance-states for both
the English and the American Society for Psychical Research,
the last one being his definitive article, "Mrs. Piper's Hodgson-
Control," published in 1909, the year before his death. Richard
Hodgson, born in Australia and educated at Cambridge, was
one of the most active workers in the Society for Psychical
Research. In 1887, he became secretary-treasurer of the American branch and resided in Boston, where he made extensive
investigations of Mrs. Piper's activities as a medium, working
in close contact with James. After Hodgson's death in December, 1905, James was asked to correlate and report on
the long series of sitttings with Mrs. Piper in which Hodgson
was presumed to be Mrs. Piper's control. Of his final report
on Mrs. Piper, James stated that after many tests he was
unable "to resist the conviction that knowledge appeared in
her trances which she had never gained by the ordinary
waking use of her eyes, ears, and wits. . . . What the source
of this knowledge may be I know not, and have not a glimmer
of an explanatory suggestion to make; but from the fact of
such knowledge I can see no escape." (*The Will to Believe*,
p. 319). (For a full account see *William James on Psychical
Research*, by Gardner Murphy and Robert O. Ballou.)

Of the European mediums, the most celebrated was the
Italian, Eusapia Palladino, who could produce remarkable
physical manifestations during her trances, creating widespread interest among scientists for over a decade. James,
however, became completely disillusioned with her when she
was brought to New York, and Flournoy, although at times
deeply impressed by her performance, remained skeptical

also. The Swiss medium, "Hélène Smith," was Flournoy's outstanding subject with whom he worked for six years, making extensive investigations of her séances. In 1900 he published the results of his research in *Des Indes à la planète Mars*.

Concerning contemporary affairs at the end of the century, Flournoy and James exchanged significant comments on the Dreyfus case—the sort of thing which aroused their indignation and violated their sense of justice. Alfred Dreyfus, a French Army officer, was convicted in 1894 of purloining secret papers from the German Embassy in Paris and was sent to Devil's Island off the coast of Guiana in 1895. In 1896, a certain Colonel Picquart accidentally came upon evidence which indicated that the real criminal was a Major Esterhazy. The case created enormous interest, heightened by violent anti-Semitic press campaigns. In 1898, Emile Zola published in *L'Aurore* his famous letter "J'accuse," for which he was tried and condemned to one year in prison. He appealed the decision, went to England for a time, and returned to France in 1900 when a general amnesty was declared for all those involved in the Dreyfus Affair. The case dragged on until 1906 when the sentence condemning Dreyfus was finally quashed by the Court of Appeal. In 1930, five years before Dreyfus died, extracts from the papers of Colonel Schwartzkoppen, a German military attaché in Paris at the time of the affair, confirmed Esterhazy's guilt and Dreyfus's innocence. James and Flournoy would have been greatly pleased with the ultimate resolution of the case.

Of greater interest, perhaps, was the Spanish-American War, in explanation of which James comments with keen insight on "the way history is made," the naïve humanitarianism of the American people, and the *psychologie des foules!* that was sparked by the blowing up of the "Maine" and Admiral Dewey's victories. Flournoy's carefully worded replies, conveying the European point of view on America's imperialistic policy and action, are characteristic of the profound respect each man had for the other's views while holding solidly to his own. The unimpeachable integrity repeatedly evidenced throughout the correspondence was the cement of this extraordinary friendship.

Lake Geneva, Wisconsin
Aug. 30, 1896

My dear Flournoy,

You see the electric current of sympathy that binds the world together—I turn towards you, and the place I write from repeats the name of your lake Leman. I was informed yesterday, however, that the lake here was named after Lake Geneva *in the State of New York,* and *that* Lake only has Leman for its Godmother. Still you see how dependent, whether immediately or remotely, America is on Europe! I was at Niagara some 3 weeks ago, and bought a photograph as souvenir, and addressed it to you after getting back to Cambridge. Possibly Madame Flournoy will deign to accept it. I have thought of you a great deal without writing, for truly, My dear Fournoy, there is hardly a human being with whom I feel as much sympathy of aims and character, or feel as much "at home" as I do with you. It is as if we were of the same stock, and I often mentally turn and make a remark to you, which the pressure of life's occupations prevents from ever finding its way to paper. I am hoping that you may have figured, or at any rate *been,* at the Munich "Congress" —that apparently stupendous affair. If they keep growing at this rate, the next Paris one will be altogether too heavy. I have heard no details of the meeting as yet. But whether you have been at Munich or not, I trust that you have been having a salubrious and happy vacation so far, and that Mrs. Flournoy and the young people are all well. I will venture to suppose that your illness of last year has left no bad effects whatever behind. I myself have had a rather busy and instructive, though possibly not very hygenic summer, making money (in moderate amounts) by lecturing on Psychology to teachers at different "summer schools" in this land. There is a great fermentation in "paedogogy" at present in the U.S., and my wares come in for their share of patronage. But although I learn a good deal and become a better American for having all the travel & social experience, it has ended by being too tiresome, & when I give the lectures at Chicago which I begin tomorrow I shall have them stenographed and very likely published in a very small volume, and so remove from myself the temptation ever to give them again. Last year was a year of hard work, and before the end of the term came, I was in a state of bad neurasthenic fatigue, but I got through outwardly all right. I have definitively given up the laboratory, for which I am more and more unfit, and shall probably devote what little ability I may hereafter have to purely "speculative" work. My inability to read troubles me a good deal; I am in arrears of several years with psychological literature, which, to tell the truth, does grow now at a pace too rapid for anyone to follow. I was engaged to review Stout's new book [1] (which I fancy is very good) for Mind, and after keeping it 2 months had to back-out, from sheer inability to read it, and to ask permission to hand it over to my Colleague Royce. Have you seen the colossal Renouvier's 2 vast vols. on the philosophy of history?—that will be another thing worth reading, no doubt, yet very difficult to read. I give a course in Kant for the first time in my life (!) next year, and at present and for many months to come shall have to put most of my reading to the Service of that overgrown subject. I wish you were here with me to see Chicago

1. George Frederick Stout (1860–1944). The book referred to is *Analytic Psychology*, 1896.

and its institutions. It is a stupendous affair—the "storm-centre" of our Continent, and already outstripping New York in civilization, size, and importance. It is practically less than 40 years old, and its original founders still live & take part in guiding its affairs. It is a place of vast ideas and titantic energy, and the largeness and ambitiousness of its beginnings must determine its character for all time. Money for public purposes is poured out like water, and although there is crime and corruption *ad nauseam*, there is greatness of the greatest sort. They have a University 5 years old, which will probably very soon be the leading one of the country and is already doing first-rate work. All the prosperity has come about because of a geographical position which forced the navigation of the Great Lakes and the Railroads connecting East West and South to converge at the place.—Of course you have read Tolstoi's War & Peace and Anna Karenina. I never had that exquisite felicity before this summer, and now I feel as if I knew *perfection* in the representation of human life. Life indeed seems less real than his tale of it. Such infallible veracity! The impressions haunt me as nothing literary ever haunted me before.

I imagine you lounging on some steep mountain side, with those demoiselles all grown too tall and beautiful and proud to think otherwise than with disdain of their elderly *commensal* who spoke such difficult french when he took walks with them at Vers-chez-les-Blanc. But I hope that they are happy as they were then. Cannot we all pass some summer near each other again, and can't it next time be in Tyrol rather than in Switzerland, for the purpose of increasing in all of us that "knowledge of the world," which is so desirable? I think it would be a splendid plan. At any rate, wherever you are, take my most affectionate regards for yourself and Madame Flournoy & all of yours, & believe me ever sincerely your friend

Wm James

FLOURNOY TO JAMES

Geneva, October 2, 1896

My dear James,

Many weeks ago I should have thanked you for the magnificent photograph of Niagara Falls, which you so kindly sent us. My wife was extremely pleased by this gracious attention from you, and immediately pinned the picture on the wall of her little sitting room, this view of a spectacle more grandiose than all those we have in our country. At the same time, we see in this kind remembrance an exact symbol of that whirling, boiling life in the New World, where even vacations are used to carry the treasures of science from city to city, where the spreading of truth never stops, and the rush of life and of research knows neither truce nor rest. This inspires me, at one and the same time, with envy and terror. Beside your inexhaustible and fruitful activity, the monotonous and drowsy course of my days and years gives me the effect of a puddle of stagnant waters compared with the cataracts of Niagara.

I hope that your course in Psychology at Chicago gave you the greatest satisfaction, and it pleases me to think that by this time you are taking the vacation which you so well deserve, before resuming your teaching at Harvard. Your letter was extremely interesting to us, and I thank you very much indeed. All year I had cherished the hope that I would see you in Munich and would bring you back to Switzerland, and I assure you that it was a profound disappointment to be deprived of that pleasure. You, on the other hand, did not lose a great deal; it did not seem to me that the Congress offered an interest proportionate to the abundance of its program; it is true that, as a consequence of the confusion produced by an agenda of 5 sections, I heard many things which did not interest me and missed others which I should have liked to hear. This system, of multiple simultaneous sections, should be good for individuals having the gift of ubiquity and several consciousnesses at their command, but it is worthless to ordinary mortals. At the end of August, we had here at Geneva the Congress of Criminal Anthropology, which was not divided into sections but so arranged that each of us could be present at every sitting, and so lose no detail of the endless battles (more amusing for the spectator than profitable to the scientist) between the adherents of the Lombroso theory and their opponents, determinists and spiritualists, etc.—But, to return to the Congress at Munich, it was a confused jumble which left me no clear ideas or comprehensive views, and I am waiting for the publication of the summary in order to guide myself through the maze. The only advantage I gained was in making a few acquaintances or meeting again certain people: Richet, Janet, Ochorowicz, etc. I had news of you from Münsterberg—and from Baldwin,[2] whom I had the pleasure of meeting. Mr. and Mrs. Baldwin spent several days in Geneva, but my wife's health, and the language difficulties, did not permit us to see them as much as we should have wished. Baldwin seemed to me to be one of those happy persons who write and publish with extraordinary facility, and who find means of working even while traveling. This ease of production bewilders me and makes me covetous, because with advancing years I have increasing trouble in drafting and composing my work.—

I was telling you of my wife's health; it is really only too good, for she spent the summer preparing for a little one who was born last Thursday, September 29th, in the form of a fifth little girl, Ariane-Dorothée, weighing 4 kilos 550 grams after 24 hours. The mother and child are doing marvelously well. From the aesthetic point of view, unity has

2. James Mark Baldwin (1861–1934), American philosopher and psychologist, taught at Princeton and Johns Hopkins, was prominent among experimental psychologists, became editor of the *Psychological Review* in 1909, and published several texts and studies of importance.

been carried a little too far against variety; five girls for one boy! Still, as we cannot complain so far about the elder four, we are thankful for the new arrival. And above all, it is a great relief that the event is now over and well done! My wife's condition caused us to remain in Geneva all summer. This loss of holiday (except for a week in Munich), combined with the apprehension which this sixth pregnancy gave me, and a certain amount of fatigue accumulated during last year had a depressing effect on my nervous system—I don't know whether to call the state of intellectual torpor, of exhaustion, of exaggerated emotional sensibility, that I have been in for several months *neurasthenia*—I only know that the condition is subjectively very painful and makes me very disagreeable to everyone around me. I see approaching, with distaste and repulsion, the moment to reopen the laboratory and take up my courses again, in four weeks; the laboratory particularly is a burden which I will not carry much longer. I congratulate you warmly and rejoice that you are definitely free from the laboratory, and I wish you as much pleasure as success in your new path, beginning with your course on Kant; would that I might follow it and dive once more, under your direction, into the old master's thickets; I dared, a dozen years ago, to tackle that rock (youth has no misgivings!) and two of my first courses as a "privat docent" were devoted to him. Today that epoch seems to me like the golden age of my studies!

You asked me if I have read Renouvier's Philosophy of History. Alas no; it has been a long time since I read anything. My brain refuses to work this year; and the indifference with which I see shelves of reviews and uncut volumes pile up seems to be a grave symptom of my mental state; I hope that less fatigue and some improvement will come with the new year.

Your proposition of a summer sojourn in the Tyrol is infinitely attractive to me. May the dream come true! It would be a very great joy for us all, as we have unforgettable memories of those all-too-short days in 1892 with you at Vers chez les Blancs. This is the second year that you have written me at the very moment you are far away from your home. It is very kind of you to take the precious time from your vacation to think of us, but we regret that you do not mention Mrs. James or your children; this no doubt means that they are all well, but nevertheless we all protest this obstinate silence and we would like very much to know something of your family. In any case, remember all of us to all of your family. Occasionally I meet your friend M. [Charles] Ritter and he has asked me to send you his greetings when I write. M. Chantre has had the sorrow of losing his younger son (consumption) this spring. He had already lost the first one a few years ago. I have not spoken of our National Swiss Exposition at Geneva this summer—nor of the Armenians—nor of the socialistic laws which our nation will reject, I hope, the day after tomorrow—nor of the Czar—nor of your presidential elections—even though these are our preoccupations of the moment. Believe me, my dear James, your most affectionate and devoted

Théodore Flournoy

Frl. Hühnersdorf is still at home. In the year since she left us she has not had a happy life and has lost her mother, her brother-in-law, and a nephew, and some of her brothers and sisters are ill.

JAMES TO FLOURNOY (dictated)

Cambridge, Mass.
Dec. 7, 1896

My dear Flournoy

Your altogether precious and delightful letter reached me duly, and you see I am making a not altogether too dilatory

reply. In the first place, we congratulate you upon the new-
comer,[3] and think if she only proves as satisfactory a damsel
as her charming elder sisters, you will never have any occasion to regret that she is not a boy. I hope that Madame
Flournoy is by this time thoroughly strong and well, and that
everything is perfect with the baby. I should like to have
been at Munich with you; I have heard a good many accounts of the jollity of the proceedings there, but on the
whole, I did a more wholesome thing to stay in my own
country, of which the dangers and dark sides are singularly
exaggerated in Europe. Your lamentations on your cerebral
state make me smile, knowing, as I do[,] under all your subjective feelings, how great your vigour is. Of course I sympathize with you about the laboratory, and advise you, since it
seems to me you are in a position to make conditions rather
than have them imposed on you, simply to drop it and teach
what you prefer. Whatever the latter may be, it will be as
good for the students as if they had something else from you
in its place, and I see no need in this world, when there is
someone provided somewhere to do everything, for anyone
of us to do what he does least willingly and well. *I* have got
rid of the laboratory forever, and should resign my place immediately if they reimposed its duties upon me. The results
that come from all this laboratory work seem to me to grow
more and more disappointing and trivial. What is most needed
is new ideas. For every man who has one of them one may
find a hundred who are willing to drudge patiently at some
unimportant experiment. The atmosphere of your mind is in
an extraordinary degree sane and balanced on philosophical
matters. That is where your forte lies, and where your University ought to see that its best interests lie in having you
employed. Don't consider this advice impertinent. Your tem-

3. Ariane-Dorothée, 1896, the youngest of the six Flournoy
children.

perament is such that I think you need to be strengthened from without, in asserting your right to carry out your true vocation.

Everything goes well with us here. The boys are developing finely; both of them taller than I am, and Peggy healthy and well. I have just been giving a course of public lectures of which I enclose you a ticket to amuse you.[4] The audience, a thousand in number, kept its numbers to the last. I was careful not to tread upon the domain of Psychical Research, although many of my hearers were eager that I should do so. I am teaching Kant for the first time in my life, and it gives me much satisfaction. I am also sending a collection of old essays through the press, of which I will send you a copy as soon as they appear.[5] I am sure of your sympathy in advance for much of their contents. But I am afraid that what you never will appreciate is their wonderful English style! Shakespeare is a little street boy in comparison!

Our political crisis is over but the hard times still endure. Lack of confidence is a disease from which convalescence is not quick. I doubt, notwithstanding certain appearances, whether the country was ever morally in as sound a state as it now is, after all this discussion. And the very silver men who have been treated as a party of dishonesty, are anything but that. They very likely are victims of the economic delusion, but their intentions are just as good as those of the other side.

Münsterberg, it appears, is a bone of contention at Zurich. I strongly want him to return here, and I fancy that his going to Zurich now would not definitively defeat that possibility. If he should go to Zurich and stay, however, why wouldn't

4. Eight lectures on "Abnormal Mental States" delivered at the Lowell Institute in Boston but never published. See Perry, *William James*, II, 169.

5. *The Will to Believe, and Other Essays in Popular Philosophy,* 1897.

that be a solution of some of your laboratory troubles? One psychological laboratory is surely enough for a country of the size of Switzerland. Students of that subject would go to him, whilst you could take those in other branches of philosophy.

If you meet my friend Ritter, please give him my love. I shall write to you again ere long *eigenhändig*. Meanwhile believe me, with lots of love to you all, especially to ces demoiselles, and felicitations to their mother,

Always yours,
Wm James

M. le Professeur. My wife wishes me to convey to Madame Flournoy her most loving regards, and hopes for the little one.

FLOURNOY TO JAMES

Geneva, March 25, 1897

My dear James,

Your letter of December 7th has spent the entire winter on my table, right under my eyes;—many times I have reread it with the intention of replying, and always my courage failed me—and yet what "courage" is needed to write such a friend as you! But it is the courage to act "überhaupt." I experienced a period of listlessness, dullness, apathy etc. in which I had great difficulty in just facing the most pressing daily demands, my courses, my family, etc. You will have learned by a letter from my wife to Mrs. James of the affliction, as terrible as unexpected, which fell upon us at the beginning of November. My brother-in-law, Dr. Burnier (whom you perhaps had the occasion to see at Vers chez les Blanc when we were there) was assassinated by one of his patients whom he had been obliged to send away from the establishment at Leysin because of his bad character and conduct. Burnier was one of the best examples that I have ever known of energy and of physical and moral activity; he was adored by his patients, and was a kind of cornerstone in my wife's family—and also in his own wife's family. His horrible and tragic end was a veritable disaster for the two families, and at the same time a terrible blow to his patients, several of whom did not recover from it and have died. I tell you that, beyond personal grief (Burnier was my best friend, an old school-comrade, the first promoter of our marriage—and, younger and stronger than I, the notion that he could go before me had never occurred to me), I had the poignant spectacle of the grievous emotions of the whole family, with the sad realization of my impotence to do anything at all to relieve this irremediable affliction. My wife, who cherished her brother, has been profoundly affected and psychologically shaken by this blow which struck her a short time after her confinement and while she was still nursing the baby. A day still does not pass when she does not weep, and sometimes several times, and what can I say or do before these tears and this sorrow which I share and from which even the presence of the children brings only superficial and passing distraction. Then, not to mention my wife's parents, already elderly, there is especially my sister-in-law and her two sons (of whom the elder is 12 years old) who inspire in us an unspeakable pity and for whom one knows not what to do! I go from time to time to Vevey, where my sister-in-law is staying, near her own family. And it is she, whose happiness has been irretrievably snatched in a second, who serves as the example to everyone by her admirable energy, her religious resignation, her heroic efforts to hide her tears from her children and to teach them to—live! And all the sadness and the tribulations of the month of November were renewed and revived a short time ago in the most cruel way by the trial of the murderer, a Bulgarian named Paroucheff, which lasted two days. One can hardly present, in view of what happened, the complicated and contradictory impressions to which this event has subjected the victim's family. The criminal's defense made a magnificent eulogy of my brother-in-law, but he very cleverly touched a sensitive chord in speaking of the assassin's mother, an old woman with white hair, who had hastened here from the heart of Bulgaria and whose presence in the audience was well designed to soften the heart of the judges. Then, the medico-legal report of the psychiatrists encouraged an extenuation of responsibility because of hereditary degeneracy and mental disequilibrium. So that the murderer, in spite of the jury's very severe verdict (which showed itself on this occasion much firmer than is usually the case in our country), has been sentenced by the court to only the minimum punishment of 15 years' confinement. After 10 years, according to practise, if he behaves well in prison, Paroucheff will be free and can inflict on some other doctor his unbalanced impulses. With us, as elsewhere, the conflict between the ancient juridical point of view of responsibility and the anthropological point of view of the psychiatry-experts, ends in practice in the result that the more dangerous the criminal is, the less morally responsible he seems, and the sooner, consequently, he will be released into society.

But that is enough on our personal circumstances. They will explain to you, however, my dear James, my long and guilty silence towards you by the atmosphere of depression and despondency in which I have lived for five months. Physically, we have been in good health, thank God, the children having had a good winter. Little Ariane is not very aware of her mother's upset emotions and is the joy of her elders. I hope that you and Madame James, your children, and yourself are in good health.

You were kind enough to send me your discourse on Agassiz,[6] which I read with renewed admiration for this great man—but even more for *your* manner of thought and presenta-

6. Louis Agassiz (1807–1873), the Swiss-born American naturalist and Harvard professor with whom James went on the Thayer Expedition to Brazil in 1865–66. The discourse Flournoy mentions was later published in *Memoirs and Studies* (1911), pp. 3–6.

tion! I followed your advice and neglected the laboratory a great deal this winter—it is so easy and pleasant to follow advice which falls in line with one's own natural indolence!—but, alas! I have not counterbalanced this freedom on the one side by an increase of effort on the other, and the absorbing and depressing circumstances of which I have given you an account have prevented all serious work; I could hardly endure the ordinary routine of my courses.—I gave your regards to M. Ritter, and also your address, as he intends to write to you; and he always inquires about you, and asks to be remembered to you. I am sending you herewith a series of views of the Swiss Village which was the most picturesque part of our National Swiss Exposition last year. It has now all disappeared; not a stone remains but this set of pictures, published by the Journal de Genéve in order to preserve the memory of this utopian and ephemeral village will for a few moments bring back to you in its similarity the impressions of our little country which you carried away with you. I hope that your next sabbatical year, which is approaching, will bring you back to us, with all your family, and the children singularly transformed!—Until then, may the European war which is pending not put an end to our little country by some disastrous impact. The horizon is very dark on our old continent. You would be amused to see and hear with what energy and exaltation our children sympathize with the unfortunate Greeks and the people of Crete, and the sad way in which the *Great Powers* are treated under our roof!—that is, however, the very general feeling in our country. I hope that those of the Great Powers which surround us have not telepathic information of our sentiments toward their behavior, for they could well revenge themselves on us by subjecting us to the fate of Poland. Of course we sympathize equally, but a little less ardently, because of the distance, with Cuba against Spain and generally speaking we sympathize likewise with all rebellion going on in the world. We were extremely interested in the success of your lectures at the Lowell Institute—I am keeping the titles of your 8 lectures as a ready-made plan in case I should some time or other have to give a general course on this subject.—But, my dear James, what a lot of your time I am wasting by my interminable and wearisome letter! Our best wishes to your family, and to you my profound affection.

Th. Flournoy

FLOURNOY TO JAMES (dictated)

Geneva, April 6, 1897

My dear James,

My letter of a few days ago crossed with your fine volume of *Essays* [*The Will to Believe and Other Essays*] that you were kind enough to send me. I want to express to you my deep appreciation and congratulate you on this work in which your friends and followers will joyfully find you again, all of you, in your lively originality. I have read avidly several of your essays that I had not seen before, (The Will to Believe, On Some Hegelisms, etc.); and I have rediscovered with pleasure, in their original language, some old and very dear pieces, the reading of which in Renouvier's French translation in the "Critique philosophique" was formerly for me a veritable revelation and an initiation into moral philosophy. So much foolish stuff is published in our day that it is a refreshing treat to see a book like your Essays appear, and I hope they will have all the influence they deserve on the bewildered youth of our time. Thank you!

Your
Th. F.

Geneva, March 27, 1898

My dear James,

For several months we have heard nothing of you nor have I given you any signs of life. It is not that I have forgotten you; just the opposite, for this winter very particularly I have constantly lived and talked with you in thought because of the fact that I have reread and meditated on the greater part of your *Principles of Psychology,* in relation to my course on normal psychology. How often I have been on the verge of picking up my pen to have a little chat with you! But always the leap which separates the desire from the realization was too frightening for my weak-willed and relaxed nature, which retreats before action and unceasingly finds pretexts to postpone until tomorrow, above all when it comes to *writing.* I am taking advantage of a moment of relaxation now; I was so tired these last weeks that I cut off the end of the semester, a fortnight ago, left for Nice where I paid a visit of several days to my wife's parents, who spend their winters there. This escape to the Midi sunshine of the Côte d'Azur did me a great deal of good, in spite of its brevity, but upon returning to Geneva I found winter once more, and this morning it is snowing again in great big flakes. All my family are well, thank heaven, and we have had no serious illness this year; I don't mention grippe and influenza which reign in our country and have made the rounds of all my children. My wife still suffers, understandably, psychic repercussions from the tragic death of her brother a year and a half ago. She succeeds, however, in facing the diverse fatigues and concomitant demands of a full nest such as ours. Last summer, while our five girls were in the mountains under the care of their grandparents, I took my wife and my "boy" [7] for the cure at the sea-baths in Jersey, and all three of us came back greatly

7. In English in the original letter.

benefited by this delightful and interesting sojourn in the
"Channel Islands." But we had scarcely returned home when
I had to give, in the middle of the summer, a series of 5
lectures in the "Vacation Courses" which are given at the
University for foreigners, especially Germans, who come each
summer to learn French in Geneva. I got through this un-
timely effort somehow and devoted the 5 lectures to Psychical Research. Mrs. Piper was given her rightful place. Unfortunately, I knew nothing of her new feats under the control
of George Pelham!—A little later I had to give two public
lectures on *Fatigue* and the *Emotions,* and I have been only
too well aware all this winter of the lasting effects these
things leave for so long after them! My course this semester,
as to quality, has been very mediocre, and my laboratory still
worse. This is why I have arranged to have nothing to do
with the University during the summer session. I don't know
yet how I shall use the several months of vacation which I
find I have before me until next autumn. I have begun observations with a few mediums; whether it is that these mediums are of an inferior quality or that I do not know how to
take advantage of them because of lack of experience and
skill, my results are hardly worthy of publication. I have
spoken of my poor self too extensively, which you would not
be wrong in interpreting medically as an unfavorable symptom. The children grow and develop in a sufficiently satisfactory
manner so far. Alice takes her religious instruction and will
be "received" at Pentecost; Blanche has much taste and some
musical aptitude for the violin; Henri cultivates the 'cello,
woodwork, natural history, and his school, by fits and starts,
with an irregularity and a lack of perseverance which are
entirely pardonable at his age (he is going on 12); Marguerite
(14½) and the two younger ones present nothing outstanding
to mention. We have followed with greater excitement than
perhaps is suitable to the citizens of a small neutral country
the tragic events of this year; Greece and the Armenians have

no warmer friends than we, although the several representatives of these two nationalities I have had the occasion to see in my laboratory have been, with rare exceptions, only pretty sad specimens. In our opinion, Dreyfus is innocent beyond a doubt, it goes without saying, and we see in the darkest colors the future which the military and clerical coalition is preparing for France, a coalition which predominates there more and more. In our country, the general state of things is hardly better; for the recent vote of the Swiss people, by an enormous majority, has just placed the railroads in the government's hands and so revealed a weakening of individual initiative and energy, even a national neurasthenia, I would almost say, the existence of which nobody suspected to such an extent. Our country is in a sad condition and will probably have to go through hard times until finally a spark of good spurts forth from this excess of evil. We shall see! There is only the Spanish-American conflict and the fate of Cuba which, at present, leaves us rather indifferent—as this is happening too far from us, and above all the Zola case, which has so exhausted all our reserves of emotional capacity by an excess of wild excitement that for some time there won't be any left for anything else!

I have had several people read your *"Essays"* who were much encouraged by them,—and to others who couldn't read English I gave the invigorating essence which corresponded to their spiritual state (particularly your "Is Life Worth Living"). It is not only in America that you do good to many unknown persons, without your knowing it! Why on earth are there so few psychologists and philosophers who can really *understand* psychology and philosophy, and use them effectively for the good of others as you know how to do!

I take too much of your time with my verbosity. I have only enough space left to ask for some news about yourself and your family and to send you our good wishes. I almost wrote at the time of the terrible hurricane which hit Boston last winter but we hoped that Cambridge and especially Irving Street did not suffer from it. Your two eldest sons are now grown gentlemen who must by now have chosen their careers. Have you encouraged them to follow in the steps of their father? Miss Margaret must have become a very highly respectable young lady, and little Francis probably begins his scientific education. Give our best regards to them all, and especially to Mrs. James a thousand affectionate greetings from my wife, who thinks of her often, with all my respects too.

It will soon be your sabbatical year when we shall have the pleasure of seeing you in Europe on your holiday. Believe me, my dear James, with deep affection,

Th. Flournoy

If you have the opportunity, please remember me to M. Münsterberg. Your friend M. Ritter occasionally asks me for news of you; he is well, as are also M. Chantre and M. Gourd.

JAMES TO FLOURNOY

Cambridge, June 17. 1898

My dear Flournoy,

Your *delightful* letter reached me many weeks ago, and now that the College work is over, and a little detachment of mind, and feeling of vague new possibility is stealing over me, one of the first acts of my redeveloping freedom is to write to you—for you after all, are the point in the old world where I feel most *at home.*—All sorts of things have been happening. You wrote that your household had been so excited over Armenian, Grecian and Parisian atrocities as to have preserved no capacity for taking an interest in Cuban affairs, which are so far away. May I venture to hope that that sluggish state of mind has passed away, and that the young ladies and Henri now leap at the newspaper with palpitating hearts for news of American victories? Seriously speaking, this whole business has thrown a most instructive light on the way in which history is made, and has illustrated to perfection the 'psychologie des foules.' The basis of it all is, or rather was, perfectly honest humanitarianism, and an absolutely disinterested desire on the part of our people to set the Cubans free. Spain had certainly forfeited all rights. On this, various interests worked for their purposes in favor of war. The explosion of the Maine, and the diplomatic negotiations ensued, together with the preparations for possible defense and attack, and by that time Congress was entirely mad, supposing that the people was in the same condition, as it probably was, in less degree. Congress, unfortunately, by our constitution has the right to declare war, and in the psychological condition in which it was, that was the only possible direction of discharge. We were winning the most extraordinary diplomatic victories, but they were of no use. We were ready (as we supposed) for war and nothing but war must come. It is the worst blow at the *prestige* of popular government that I have *erlebt*. All the while, as I say, perfectly sincere philanthropism lay at the base, with no such fears as paralyzed the philanthropism of Europe at the time of the Armenian massacres. Our Congress was *absolutely* sincere in disclaiming any desire of conquest or of annexation.—But see how in the twinkling of an eye a Nation's ideals will change! With Dewey's sudden victory, an 'imperialist' party has arisen here, which, as it will command all the crude and barbaric patriotism of the country, will be a hard thing to resist. After all, it is on that pure instinctive masterfulness and ambition, that sense of a great destiny, that the greatness of every great nation is based; and we have it in great measure. But one must 'live up' to a great destiny, and alas our education as a nation, so far, little fits us for success in administering islands with inferior populations. Spain deserves to lose them, but do we deserve to gain them? Whatever happens, in any event, will happen not, as a result of any particular reason, but as the result of passion, and of certain watchwords that nations have learned habitually to obey. We have some pretty good ones of the latter sort, which will make for reason. But the *great* passion undeniably now is the passion for *adventure*. We are in so little danger from Spain, that our interest in the war can only be called that in a peculiarly exciting kind of *sport*. And after all hasn't the spirit of the life of all the great generals and rulers & aristocracies always been the spirit of sport carried to its supreme expression? Civilization, properly so called, might well be termed the organization of all those functions that resist the mere excitement of sport. But *excitements!*—shall we not worship excitement?—and after all, what is life for, except for opportunities of excitement?! It makes all humdrum moralizing seem terribly dead and tame! And it beautifully corroborates the 'chance' theory of history, to find that the critical turning points in these great movements are purely accidental. A victory often depends on the weather. Without the Maine explosion we should still very likely be at peace—that was the last item in the summation of stimuli, and that explosion was possibly due to the free-will of one of the molecules in the dynamite magazine! Etc. etc.

Next summer, I may hope to see you, for my sabbatical year again falls due; and we shall very likely go to Europe. I am appointed "Gifford lecturer" on "natural religion" at the universiy of Edinburgh in Scotland, for 1899–1901—two courses of 10 lectures each, in successive years, an honour, and very handsomely paid. I am also elected Correspondant de l'Institut (Acad. d. Sc. Morales & Politiques). Heavens knows why. I suppose it might prove in some ways convenient were I to inhabit Paris, but I never shall stay there for more than a week.

We have let our little country place, and shall make Cambridge our headquarters for the summer. My boy Harry who is developing very finely (more in character and intelligence than in genius) is going to visit his uncle [Henry James] in England for a couple of months, and I am going to spend

August and September in a journey to California, where I have some lectures to give. We are all *very* well, and I hope that the summer finds you all in similar condition. Your letters are always a rare delight so be liberal with them. Much love from both of us to Mrs. Flournoy and all the younger Flournoys. Item from me to yourself.

W. J.

Geneva, December 11, 1898

My dear James,

Your affectionate and interesting letter of June 17th came the very day we left for vacation to spend a month at Les Praz, a charming spot located 2 kilometers from Chamonix on the way to Argentière. Laziness and indolence overtook my good intentions and by dint of procrastinating I find myself at the end of my vacation without having succeeded in conquering my epistolary inertia and taking up my pen. You understand this very psychological phenomenon and you forgive it! Once I was back in Geneva and involved in endless obligations of all kinds, the weeks just flew—and now it is definitely the last moment to write if I want my message to reach you in time to wish you all a "happy Christmas" [8] and to send our best wishes of all kinds for the New Year. Among these wishes there is naturally a very selfish one—which is that nothing will prevent the realization of your plan to come to Europe, and especially to Switzerland, next summer, as your letter gave me to hope.

Your invitation to give the "Gifford Lectures," on which I congratulate you and even more your Edinburgh audiences—will, I dare hope, make you double your sabbatical year and spend two whole years instead of one in our old world, and

8. In English in the original letter.

we look forward joyfully to having a good share of your stay in Europe.—I am ashamed of not having congratulated you six months ago, most warmly & sincerely, on your nomination to the Institut de France, which made us very happy. No one was more deserving of this flattering distinction than you—and I was on the point of expressing to you immediately all our joyous statisfaction by a few words on a card, but the unhappy realization that a *card* was insufficient and that it was deserving of a real *letter* made me wait to find the time—and I didn't find it! Always the same story. Your friend Ritter, whom I met at that time, rejoices with me at this honor which is as brilliant as it is deserved. If only all members of the famous "Institut de France," Frenchmen as well as foreigners, were as worthy as you are of this brilliant halo of scientific glory!—I received your "lecture" on immortality ["Human Immortality, Two Supposed Objections to the Doctrine"] and the one which you gave before the Philosophical Club at the University of California; [9] and I thank you for them. I used these lectures immediately and many times for my courses and public lectures and I did so with a lack of shame and with a practical good sense you certainly won't blame me for. I take great care, by the way, to render unto Caesar the things which are Caesar's, and whenever quite naturally one of your ideas or expressions comes to help me out of an embarrassing situation by giving clear and happy shape to my confused thoughts, it is always with gratitude and eagerness that I take refuge behind your name.

I enclose a copy of the *Gazette de Lausanne,* which gives a summary of a lecture I delivered recently in a series of popular philosophic and religious lectures, a series which has been offered for several years; the write-up which is as good

9. This reference is to "Philosophical Conceptions and Practical Results," delivered at the University of California at Berkeley on August 26, 1898, and published six years later in the *Journal of Philosophy,* Vol. I (1904).

as you can expect from a journalist—is very incomplete and inexact on several points; the citations which I quoted from you didn't escape the reporter entirely though, in spite of the fact that he didn't write down your name everywhere I borrowed from you (for example, your idea of the brain as the transmitter of consciousness).—

Your ideas in your letter on the Spanish-American War were of great interest to me. If on the one hand the States have seemed to us sometimes to have taken a little advantage of the rights of the stronger vis-à-vis unhappy Spain, it is obvious on the other hand that in doing so they simply fulfilled the laws of history, as they did against the Indians; and on the whole we applaud the triumph of a republican and Protestant nation representing liberty and modern civilization over the old monarchical and Catholic despotism which certainly fully deserved the catastrophe into which it is finally sinking. Only, what future surprises does the American Army have in store for us, having once tasted these first successes?

I am saying nothing of the Dreyfus Affair, which, after so many dark days, at last gives us some hope; moreover, it passed into second place, recently, before the Picquart business. We notice since yesterday a marked lessening of tension on seeing Colonel Picquart snatched at the last moment from the anger of the High Command by the Supreme Court of Appeal.—I just spent a few days in Paris, at the kind suggestion of Richet, to attend several seances of Eusapia Palladino. I had the pleasure of meeting Mr. Myers there, whose presence gave much zest to the first séance, because Eusapia was obviously bent on convincing him, after the unfortunate séances at Cambridge two years ago. And indeed she quickly succeeded. We had excellent séances from the point of view of the control; in addition to holding her hands, knees, and feet, there was enough light to distinguish things clearly, and this control by sight added to that by touch made any kind of hesitation or suspicion impossible. In these conditions of perfect control, the curtains moved, a zither placed at a distance gave out sounds several times and finally transported itself onto the table. Mr. Myers was touched, pinched, hit by the invisible hand of "John," etc. There were no light phenomena or visible apparitions of hands etc. as Richet recorded on other occasions;—but though less brilliant and extraordinary, the phenomena were all the more convincing by their clearness and evident reality. Mr. Myers declared himself convinced and I don't hesitate to agree with him. The last séance, which Myers did not attend, was devoted to convincing Camille Flammarion, who had had a whole series of experiences with Eusapia but in very unfavorable conditions (too many people, bad control etc.). This time, I believe that Flammarion was satisfied, although the phenomena were rarer and less solid (some movement of the curtains, and Flammarion "touché" on two or three occasions) because Eusapia was very fatigued and indisposed; but the light was so good and the control of the hands and feet so excellent that no doubt was possible. Here at Geneva, I suspect the existence of true "physical phenomena" (table movements without contact, transportation of objects) with two mediums—but I have not yet succeeded in verifying these facts with absolute certainty: there is evidently some element of fraud, and there is too much darkness in the room.

My course (in which I treat Abnormal Psychology and Psychical Research this year) draws an encouraging number of people,—but the laboratory is on its last legs. It creeps and drags like a heavy cannon ball which I pull along like a convict. I have scanned the horizon, for a long time in vain, looking for a young man who might wish to take charge of it. It is evidently an error in judgment to want to found a psychological laboratory, being devoid as I am of all natural capacity for this kind of thing, and in a milieu too restricted and limited for such a superfluous luxury. Our small university and my personal incompetence do not allow for such an establishment.

My family is well. Our eldest, Alice, has been for three

months in a "Haushaltungschule" in the canton of Thurgovie, from which she will return at Christmas. Henri has entered the College [of Geneva] where he works moderately and wisely avoids intellectual overstrain! All six of them give us on the whole more satisfaction than trouble and we are grateful for them. My wife sends many affectionate good wishes to Mrs. James, to which I add my respects and for you, my dear friend, the expression of all my devotion.

Th. Flournoy

JAMES TO FLOURNOY (dictated)

Cambridge, May 30, 1899

My dear Flournoy:—

The last lecture of the college year was given this morning, and the first use my mind, set free from the trammels of the intellect, makes of its liberty is to turn to the sphere of the affections, and first and foremost I send a line of affectionate greeting to you. I got and enjoyed very much your midwinter letter and am glad to know that all so far has gone well with the Flournoy family and that you have been leading so active a life in the way of lecturing. I have had in that respect a rather quiet year, having resolved to confine myself to my college business and decline all invitations to lecture outside. My colleague, Münsterberg, has been less prudent—he told me the other day that he had already delivered this year sixty outside addresses, for only ten of which he had received any pay—he has given others since, so the number by this time, I think must be well up in the seventies. He will also have to "*ranger*" himself before long. He is becoming more of a metaphysician and less of an experimentalist—not altogether, as it seems to me to his benefit or to that of the higher philosophy. I don't know whether you have seen his recent volume of essays called "Psychology and Life." They do not impress me very favorably.

I hope that you have received the recent product of *my* Muse, "Talks to Teachers," which I ordered the publishers to send you. It is very popular and commonplace stuff, but I confess that I have a partiality for the paper "On A Certain Blindness." I hope that you will some time read that.

The James family has passed a thoroughly good winter, all of its members being happy and well, with the exception of a slight cardiac trouble in myself, which makes me wish to go this summer to Nauheim near Frankfort to take the cure. My Sabbatical year has come again, and Mrs. James and I with probably little Peggy and possibly the youngest boy, will spend most of it in Europe. We sail for Hamburg the 15th. of July to go straight to Nauheim. After that, as straight as may be to England, where I must settle down and work over the so-called Gifford Lectures on the Psychology of Religion which I have to give in Edinburgh in January. It is thoroughly sad for me not to look forward to being near you in Switzerland some part of the summer. Our intimacy seven years ago was one of my most delightful experiences, and I think that we must lay our course this time so as at least to take in Geneva. I trust that some mode of meeting will there be possible. Especially do I wish to see those young ladies and the extraordinary change in the way of beauty and fashionable appearance, which these critical years will have wrought. Probably they have forgotten even the name of James!

My two eldest boys are developing finely and are going to spend the summer in the Rocky Mountains in the service of the United States Forestry Commission. There is a bare chance of its developing into a profession for Billy. Next year they will remain here at the University.

I dare say you have not been following with any extreme interest the course of things in the Philippines—a sad issue to a war which on the whole was originally undertaken from philanthropic, or certainly disinterested motives. The United States now is swallowing all its ancient ideals. It all shows the power of the war-demon when once let loose. But I will make no further reflections, not even on the Peace Congress or the Dreyfus Case. Writing is unsatisfactory, but I shall hope to grasp your hand and see you face to face before many weeks are past.

With warmest regards to both Madame Flournoy and yourself from both of us, believe me,

Affectionately yours,
Wm. James

After July 15th., our address will be care of Brown, Shipley, & Co., (Bankers,) London.

Geneva
July 1, 1899

My dear James,

I have been so busy recently that I have postponed from day to day the pleasure of writing and thanking you for your kind letter and for your *Talks to Teachers.* I read the last two essays the very day the book arrived,—but alas, I have had to put the rest aside until my vacation, in spite of my desire to read them all at one stretch! Now I fear that this note, intended to wish you a good, happy voyage toward our old Europe, will arrive too late and find you no longer at home. Nevertheless, we send you all our good wishes for your crossing, for your cure at Neuheim, for the preparation of the Gifford Lectures—and above all, very selfishly, we hope that we shall soon have the joy of seeing you, Mrs. James, and your younger children.

We sympathize greatly with you for the fatigue and excitement of your departure, in spite of the fact that Americans are generally so accustomed to events of this kind. Still, it can't be with a completely light and easy heart that parents like you and Mrs. James separate themselves for so long a time from their elder sons! I hope that you will always receive excellent news from them!

For a long time I have wanted to write to tell you that among the many students and others whom I have had read your *Essays* (Will To Believe, etc.), a young man has been found who thinks of nothing but translating your work into French. He is Monsieur J. Sulliger, who has spent several years in America and knows English very well. He makes his living by giving lessons as a tutor here in Geneva, and he intends to write to you to ask your permission to translate into a small volume three or four of your essays. He is, I believe, capable of doing this in an intelligent manner, that is to say to render them in an appropriate manner for French readers, giving the charm and piquancy of your pages in English. Moreover, I think that he should send the translation of one of your discourses to you so that you may judge for yourself if it satisfies you. He is in the German part of Switzerland at the moment on vacation. I have sent him your address (Brown, Shipley & Co., London), and if he pursues his project and writes to you about this, I recommend him to your kind attention.

Our vacation will begin in a few days and we shall again spend a few weeks near Les Praz, near Chamonix (Haute Savoie), during July and until about the 5th of August. We were very comfortable there last year. We had a good winter and are very well. Our children are neither eagles nor geniuses (not any of them), but they get on reasonably well and we have more satisfaction than anxiety with them. The "demoiselles," whom you honor with your remembrances, have not forgotten you at all, and all of us look forward greatly to seeing you soon! My laboratory has been discontinued since the fire which destroyed a part of our University six months ago, so that while awaiting the reconstruction to be completed, I have my duties as "Director of the Laboratory" reduced to a minimum. I do not complain! I am occupied with the printing of the story of a medium who speaks the language of the planet Mars (!!!!!), but it will not be finished before autumn. I shall see you soon, my dear James, a thousand good wishes from us all. I appreciated very much your last two "Talks to Students." I find you again in them as I did in your *Essays,* and I am impatient to be able to reread them with the rest of the volume, in a few days, under the pines! Best wishes to you and yours, especially to Mrs. James. How much we look forward to seeing you again!

Your Th. Flournoy

JAMES TO FLOURNOY

Villa Luise, Bad-Neuheim

Hessen, Aug. 29. 1899

Dear Flournoy,

We got here four weeks ago and found your good letter awaiting us. I am getting somewhat "adapted" to the "hinsch-leppendes Leben" which was very repulsive to me at first—"don't walk fast, don't go up stairs, don't this, don't that! lie down before and after everything," etc. etc.—In short make as much of a sick man as possible of yourself. The park is lovely, and the country round about is fertile, well ordered and has interesting spots to visit. The results on the heart are so far not very marked, subjectively—but they say you *feel* the relief more after the cure than during it. In any case, I have had a big dilatation, & my mountain promenades, alas! are over. It is a process of dying to this world without any increased hopes of another! Mrs. J. has told Madame Flournoy of her flying trip to Vevey. I am in such desperate straits with my Edinburgh lectures, which are advertized to begin on January 15th., and on which I can do no work at all under these "Kur" conditions, that I fear I must start by the shortest way for England (viz: *via* Holland or Belgium) as soon as

I am released, and consequently not go round by Geneva and Paris, or see you. That will probably be for next summer, when I shall certainly have to return hither again. I hope that you have had a good holiday in the mountains, and that the whole family is well. I suppose that Henri is six feet high, or more. I condole (?) with you on the loss of your laboratory, and hope that it was not insured.—I suppose that you have no time for anything but the Figaro just now—I find that it takes up most of mine. The side of the accusation seems to crumble more and more daily. Bertillon is an exquisite Opera-bouffe character. One would suppose that no cause could survive with such personages to witness for it. Yet the spirit of caste and the prestige of their generals may make the judges blind.

Believe me, with most affectionate regards, dear Flournoy, yours always faithfully,

Wm James

JAMES TO FLOURNOY (dictated)[10]

34 De Vere Gardens W, London
Nov. 13, 1899

My dear Flournoy,

I don't think I have written to you since that happy day we spent at Geneva. Yesterday I returned to you by post the three books which you lent me, and in thanking you for their use I add a word about our condition. We are exceedingly comfortably and cheaply situated here in my brother's vacant London apartment, he for the time, having gone to live in the country. The conditions would be most perfect for working on my lectures, if my health were only *im Stande*. But unfortunately, for no special reason that I can discover, my

10. This letter is in the handwriting of Mrs. James.

heart took a very bad turn a month ago and I have been practically confined to the house, unable to do any writing, and indeed forbidden to do any talking ever since. Dr. Bezley Thorne, the best English heart specialist, hopes to improve me by another course of Nauheim baths, *à domicile,* and a very rigorous diet. But what the outcome will be, Heaven only knows. It is rather discouraging for I should like to get out these 2 volumes of Gifford lectures before turning my back on this world's vanities. But "man appoints, God disappoints," to use a little Cambridge negro's version of the French proverb, and I shan't fret over the event, whatever it turns out to be. Of all vanities, when you come to look penetratingly at them, lectures on the philosophy of Religion by mortal men may take the first prize.

I have seen my compatriot Baldwin and James Sully once, also Myers twice and find him considerably aged. He is investigating a first-rate trance medium whom he has brought here—I fancy quite as good as Mrs. Piper.

Our week in Switzerland leaves a shining trail of glory in one's memory. What a dear country! England is a great country, and a good country, but too much heavy humbug and sham about it, due to the curious admixture of social feudal survivals with modern democracy. The great impression one gets is of its wealth.

How charming a vision was that of Mrs. Flournoy and your girls! Also the noble Henri. I wish that our children could grow up together, but there seems little likelihood of that.

I hope, dear Flournoy, that your book is approaching its end, and that the fatigue and *pech* of its composition are already fading away. With warmest regards to you all from both of us. I am always

Affectionately yours
Wm James

P.S. I hope that Mrs. Flournoy got my letter with a packet of school circulars, and that they may help her. A. H. J.

FLOURNOY TO JAMES

Florissant, November 28, 1899

My dear James,

Your Postal Card [11] makes my cup of remorse overflow and upsets the balance of the nerve centers that control my writing; it has been unstable for a long time. I just sent to M. Pillon the volume by *Gilard.* I did not immediately open your package of books, not suspecting that it contained things other than what I had lent you; and when I finally opened it, a few days ago, I left *Gilard* on my table in order to warn you of this mistake. Then—the days passed! You can imagine how this happened because of inertia and the disproportion between duties and strength of action. I hope that M. Pillon will not have needed this volume this past month, and that you have not exhausted your brain to find out to whom you sent it by mistake! Please excuse my laxity and idleness.

The sad news which Mrs. James's letter brought, as well as yours, telling us of your health, distresses us greatly. I sympathize profoundly with the ordeal which the obligation of caring for oneself, keeping a strict routine of rest, and an endless watch on diet and activities must entail for an active, overflowing nature such as yours. Above all, at this time when you planned to work on your "Gifford lectures", this necessity for perpetual restriction must be particularly tiresome. "A soldier's finest movement is immobility," said some French general or other; these words come back to me often in thinking of energetic people whom circumstances oblige to rest, as with you this year, when they wish to be busy!—But ardently I hope that you will recover rapidly and regain all the strength and spirit you need for your fine work, thanks to the care with which you are surrounded and your home-administered Nauheim cure! Because—in spite of your mood from Ecclesiastes and your disillusion about the Philosophy of Religion—

11. Not extant.

you have before you a magnificent task for which no one is better qualified. I have no doubt whatever of your real success, I mean to say that your words will do your audiences in Edinburgh great good, until the time when your pen will benefit all your readers in the civilized world. We impatiently await a card telling us that you feel better and on the road to recovery and that you've been able to take up the work that you desire so much to do. A charming card from Mrs. James, a few days ago, told us that you are very pleased with Miss Peggy and her school, and we hope that you have good news from your sons.

Here there is nothing new; I should have liked to complete my volume before the New Year, but I do not know if I shall succeed, it is going so badly. In order to appease my local friends and acquaintances, I have republished an article from the Revue Philosophique, which brought thunderbolts of sharp criticism from many spiritualists here; and at the request of one of our regional reviews, I have published in it the first chapter of my little book; I am sending it all to you herewith, but do not tire yourself reading these valueless pages. My University courses give me more satisfaction. I have a good audience, which is increasing and includes over a hundred people, which is rather rare here with us; I certainly have more facility for speaking than for writing. After the New Year, I am going to give a course at Lausanne also (one lecture per week) at the Ecole Vinet (a public high school for girls). I shall soon be able to put on my visiting cards: "Psychologue pour dames et demoiselles." It is not precisely what one had planned in youth, but a man has to learn to content himself with what he gets and the lesson of humility is one of the principal ones to get out of this life. I don't need to tell you that your name is one of those and even the one which comes up most often in my course, and that I even pilfer without scruple from your *Talks on Psychology*, etc. for my lectures this winter. I profit from the fact that there is still no legislation on psychological property. It is certain that I should go bankrupt if you came to claim all that I owe you!—I gave your address to M. Ch. Ritter, who probably has written you from what he said to me. My wife is extremely appreciative of the school prospectus and information which Mrs. James was kind enough to send her. We've not yet made any decision, having not had time to think about it, because we are in the middle of resuming lessons, courses, occupations of all kinds by parents and children. It is not just the Americans who have need of the "Gospel of relaxation." Since all is relative, we too, with our few occupations, have too much to do for our feeble strength, physical and mental!—I leave you, my dear friend, with a thousand good wishes for your health. Please give Mrs. James all my respects, with the affectionate compliments of my wife, and best wishes to Miss Peggy, when you see her, from us all,

As ever yours,
Th. Flournoy

FLOURNOY TO JAMES

Geneva, December 12, 1899

My dear James,

To begin with, please thank Mrs. James for her good letter to my wife, who will reply soon. I do not need to tell you of all our good wishes for your improved health and our hope that the sojourn at Malvern may achieve the results desired and give you the strength and freedom which you need for your work.—This is a business card. M. Sulliger, of whom I spoke to you this autumn as having translated and desiring to publish several of your *Essays*, is about to obtain the right to publish "Is Life Worth Living?" in the *Grande revue* controled by Labori, with a short preface by Francis de Pressensé. It is not yet accomplished, and you must never sell the skin of the bear until you have killed it, but I believe that he will succeed. Only he must have your authorization and he is to write to you about this. These lines are to support his request to you; as far as I am concerned, I should be very happy to see the translation of your Essays presented to the French public under the egis of *Pressensé* and *Labori,* two of the foremost of that valiant and courageous minority which represented Justice and Truth, so little recognized in France, throughout the Dreyfus Affair!

If you have no objections, a word from you on a Post Card will suffice to permit M. Sulliger to go ahead.[12] I will write again at length during Christmas vacation, for which I sigh! Best wishes for your health and with affection,

Yours,
T. Flournoy

FLOURNOY TO JAMES

Geneva, Dec. 24, '99

My dear James,

Here it is Christmas Eve—and on this holiday which holds a greater place in the families of the Anglo-Saxon race than in our Latin countries where the New Year is the most important celebration—we think with sadness and sympathy of your separation from your sons and all those whom you have left on the other side of the Ocean; we think above all of the state of your health, which constitutes for you such a great test of resignation and patience, for Mrs. James a permanent cause of care and solicitude, for all your friends an object of heartfelt wishes and deep concern. The letter from Mrs.

---

12. Flournoy's strong desire to see James's works published in French caused him to support the request of Monsieur Sulliger for permission to do so. Unfortunately, the man proved to be unscrupulous, causing considerable embarrassment to both James and Flournoy.

James—please give her all my thanks—gave us much distress by telling us that the doctor speaks of sending you into the environs of Hyères, because that must of necessity upset your project for the *Gifford lectures* and obstruct your plans in a most discouraging manner; mainly for you, it indicates above all that your heart did not respond to the Nauheim Cure and "Nachkur" with all the benefits expected. I still hope that the improvement which was delayed has commenced to manifest itself and that perhaps your doctor will now hold more reassuring prospects and permit you to take up again your work projects and the Edinburgh lectures. On the other hand, would it not be better, actually, to renounce completely for this year all studies and English fog in order to place yourself completely and solidly in the beneficial sun of the Cote d'Azur? Whatever may be your decision, we sympathize with you deeply,—if only sympathy were able to have some real effect and sincere good wishes act at a distance with power!— As my wife wrote to Mrs. James on receiving her letter, if you decide to go to the Mediterranean coast and our proposition suits you, we shall be happy to take Miss Peggy under our roof; we have a guest room in which she will be very much at home—without that comfort which is certainly much greater in America and in England than in our countries;—and I don't need to tell you that we shall take care of her as well as (not to say *better* than) we do our own children, conscious of our responsibility and happy in the confidence which you would be showing us in giving her into our care during your sojourn in the Midi! Peggy would cause us no trouble at all, and her coming would give all of us, big and small, very great pleasure; thus, if this idea suits you at all and fits in with your arrangements, do not hesitate, I beg you, to accept our heartfelt offer in all the simplicity with which we suggest it.— Thank you a thousand times for the volume by Starbuck, which the New Year vacation will permit me to read. All our good wishes, my dear James, for Christmas, and may the New

Year bring you the renewed health and strength you need. Please assure Mrs. James too, of our devoted affection.

As ever yours,
Th. Flournoy

JAMES TO FLOURNOY

Lamb House, Rye
January 1, 1900

My dear Flournoy,

Your letter and book [*Des Indes à la planète Mars*] both arrived duly the other day. My wife has already written to Mrs. Flournoy in regard to your generous invitation to our daughter, so I will say nothing of that except to join my thanks to hers. I have read the first 75 and last 75 pages of the volume and turned over the intervening leaves. My reading was interrupted with loud exclamations of joy. Upon my word, dear Flournoy, you have done a bigger thing here than you know; and I think that your volume has probably made the decisive step in converting psychical research into a respectable science. The tone and temper are so admirable, the style so rich and human, the intellectual equipment so complete, that it is a performance which must strike every reader, whatever his antecedent prepossessions may have been, as of *first-rate* quality. Don't think I am simply wishing to please you by what I write; it is the unfeigned expression of my extreme delight as I read.

I have told Myers and the other researchers that monographic studies of psychic personages would be far more effective in gaining official recognition for this department of science than the great statistical enterprises which the S.P.R. is carrying on—here the proof *saute aux yeux*. I am sure that Myers and my friend Hodgson will be as much delighted with it as I am.

Myers himself is making a monographic study of an excellent medium (unpaid) whom he saw in London and who on the whole seems as good as, and in some respects is better than, Mrs. Piper. Richet has one in Paris whom he hopes to subject to thorough observations and who is even better yet, as it would appear; so that at least these studies are in a good way to be considered serious. The great thing about your writing is your charming style. You and Delboeuf are the only worthy successors of Voltaire! Your book has only one defect, and that is that you don't dedicate it to me. As I am passing off the scene, have resigned my Gifford Lecture-ship, and shall certainly be unable to keep my Professorship at Harvard, and shall very likely die with my great Philosophy of Religion buried inside me and never seeing the light, it would have been pleasant to have my name preserved for ever in the early pages of your immortal work. You groaned during its production, but how quickly you must forget those labour-throes in the pleasure you take in the living child.

And now for myself: I am gaining strength very slowly. I don't see how I can become much better unless I get to walking again; but walking is the one thing that will not go—more than five minutes at a time affects the heart very un-pleasantly. In order to get an out-of-door life consistent with passivity I am going to Costebelle near Hyères, in France, where Myers also expects to be, and where Richet has very generously offered both of us his 'Chateau de Carqueiranne.' [13] It sounds as if it came out of Capitaine Fracasse, doesn't it? We expect to leave in about a week. When I once get there I will send you my news. And meanwhile, with heartiest good wishes for a happy new century and plenty of them to both of you and your descendants, I am ever affectionately yours,

Wm James

13. J. M. Baldwin in *Between Two Wars* (Boston, 1926, I, 86ff.) gives an account of James and Myers at Richet's chateau.

JAMES TO FLOURNOY (dictated)[14]

Hotel Costebelle
Costebelle-Hyères
April 19, 1900

My dear Flournoy,

Thank you for your kind letter to my wife. We have se-
cured sleeping-car berths for *Monday* night, April 23d—nothing was to be had for Saturday or Sunday. Our train is due
at Geneva at 3.47 Tuesday afternoon, but we both beg you
sincerely not to come to the station to meet us. Nothing can
be more simple than the process of reaching your house, and
if we see you at the Gare we shall lose the delight of that
first vision of your welcoming face heading the rest of the
family and framed in your own doorway. Such moments are
too rare in this life not to be economized and arranged for.
So pray wait for us at Florissant where we ought to arrive
soon after four.

You understand, dear Flournoy, that you are not to treat
us as "Company." Let us, for a few days share your own family
life. I am in no condition to talk to strangers, especially in
French, and shall have to lie down and keep to myself a good
deal of the time. With you I hope to have much profitable
communion. So, hoping that the days will duly revolve, I am,
wth affectionate regards

Yours always
Wm. James

JAMES TO FLOURNOY

Luzern, June 30 [1900]

The wife arrived last night in good condition, full of enthusiasm about her stay with you and gratitude for the moral
privileges as well as the material comforts she had enjoyed.

14. This letter appears in the handwriting of Mrs. James.

I am taking the liberty of sending you by the same post a box of American candy for Ces Demoiselles at little Hampton. I hope it may not incommode you to carry it, and that it will arrive at Geneva in time. A note comes from Suliger this morning—of course I shall gladly authorize him to do whatever he likes.—Well, goodbye! I hope that travel & change will soon wash away your fatigue! We go on Monday to the *Hotel Sonnenberg bei Luzern* for a week, and if the altitude, &c., suits, we shall very likely spend all July there. It is a delightful spot. I have entirely renounced the idea of going to Sweden.

W. J.

JAMES TO FLOURNOY

Hotel Sonnenberg, bei Luzern,
July 6, 1900

Dear Flournoy,

I hope that the Journey was happy, and that you are enjoying England, and already getting out of the physical depression which the change of air and level will undoubtedly have caused.

The immediate cause of my writing is, however, not to say this, but to speak of a little correspondence I have had with M. Sulliger. He tells me that you have agreed to pay ½ the expenses of publication of his translation of 4 of my essays, Eggiman paying the other half, and he says that if I am unwilling to pay anything he will have recourse to you.

This mortifies me very much, for I *am* unwilling to be "responsible" in any way for this partial appearance of a volume which *might* later find publication at Paris in an unabridged form. Moreover, there has been a certain crudity in the letters of M. S. which disinclines me to the personal partnership with him—though of course I have not intimated this to him in my replies.

I have finally left the matter entirely open, saying "I have no legal rights, and you are absolutely free to do what you like about the Essays, on your own responsibility, without any authorization from me."

This leaves me without any complicity whatever.

As regards your contributing money, my dear Flournoy—I have no idea whatever what the required sum may be—I can only repeat that the thought of it pains me. But once more, not making myself responsible in any way, I cannot be responsible for that, and it must lie entirely between you and M. Sulliger.

It is no doubt a piece of neurasthenic perversion of sensibility, but I confess that translations of my own writings always give me a kind of horror, and the best thing for me is in no way to cooperate. I haven't read a single page of the German translation of my Essays or of the Italian translation of my Psychology.

Enough!—of a disagreeable subject. We have had on the whole an excellent time on this lake—and are now some 350 meters above it. I still improve, and have good hopes.

Love to you *all,*

W. J.

FLOURNOY TO JAMES

Felpham, Bognor

[Sussex, England]

July 8, 1900

My dear James,

I received your letter, over which I am distressed and dismayed to think of the bother that this beast Sulliger has caused you at a time when you are just beginning to improve and when you need rest and tranquility in order to complete your recovery. I did not expect such whims on his part as asking you to rewrite or modify one of your Essays and to co-operate in his translation!

And yet, I should not be surprised at what comes from such a psychasthenical one as he is. I fear that he is in one of those moments when all tact and sense of reality seem to escape him. The "crudity" [15] which you have found in his correspondence is one of his striking traits. I have letters from him which are astounding in this respect, in the circumstances in which he addressed them to me; but I thought that in his relation to you, he would have, somehow, a little greater sense of propriety! I offer my excuses to you and ask you to pardon me for having put you in touch with him, and, things being as they are, you have done well to reply to him as you did, in not according him the authorization requested.— A short account of my relations with him will be the best means of explaining all this to you. Sulliger, of whose existence, family, and even name I was ignorant, presented himself to me six years ago when he returned from America, where he had lived for several years in a more or less miserable condition. He told me that he was interested in philosophy and psychology and was looking for a way to earn his living by giving private lessons and tutoring in mathematics, English, German, etc. The information I gathered from him and my subsequent relationship with him revealed that he came from a very humble but respectable family (his father was employed on the railroad; his sisters manage a shoe store, etc.) and that he, himself, was a decent chap, industrious but quite nervous and a bit unsteady, and above all, beyond his class because of his intellectual aspirations, yet unable to earn his living by a trade and desirous of making his way in a literary or philosophical career. You certainly have met among your students many of these poor devils, maladjusted to their surrounding circumstances, too bright and ambitious to be content merely with earning a living, not solid enough cerebrally, nor sufficiently aggressive to succeed in the brilliant path of

15. In English in the original letter.

poets, philosophers, inventors, social reformers, etc. on which
they wish to enter! One doesn't know what to do with these
unhappy people whose families don't understand them and
who are a cross to their humbler associates. It was out of pity
rather than personal attachment that I have several times
procured for Sulliger small jobs or benefits to help him survive, and it was thus that two years ago I had him translate
your "Is Life Worth Living?" into French, having no time to
do it myself. Thus I killed two birds with one stone. I gave
him a little remunerative job (I paid him 40 francs for the
translation) and I had a French manuscript of your essay,
which I could lend to various people (students, etc.) who
didn't know English and for whom your essay would, and
actually did, do a lot of good. Sulliger, who is really interested
in philosophy, at this time read all your essays and naturally
thought of doing a translation *for publication.* I think that
he had a number of ideas at the same time: to put into French
some essays which he was especially enthusiastic about; to
make himself known to the public by signing his name as
translator; and eventually to earn something from it. Since he
seemed to me as capable as anyone else, by his intelligence
and his command of languages, of doing the translation, I
encouraged him in his idea, and as the financial aspects embarrassed him, I told him one day (somewhat in these terms,
which I naturally did not write down, but with this exact
sense), "When you've done your translation and have the
authorization from Mr. James, if you don't succeed in finding
a French publisher willing to publish your work, then I shall
help you by recommending you to Eggimann, whom I know,
and we'll find the means to publish your translation without
your being worried over the financial aspect of it." But this
poor fellow's imagination ran away with him when he wrote
you that I would pay *half* the expenses and Eggimann *the
other half,* because I have never spoken to Eggimann of such
an arrangement. It was my idea to confine myself to assuring

Eggimann that he would recover his investment if he published the work. I am, in fact, convinced that the sale of your
essays in French would cover the expenses and that I wouldn't
be taking too great a risk, even in the worst case, in arranging
to cover Eggimann in a possible loss! Several times I have
rendered Sulliger small services in giving him money when he
was very hard pressed and he accepted aid with such an
imperceptible degree of gratitude that I would have felt very
ill-disposed toward him had I not seen that it is a certain
flaw in his character; but in the case of this translation, it is
not simply the money which I thought of giving him out of
charity, but also the respect which I enjoy from Eggimann
(all modesty apart!) You see, my dear James, that if you are
pained by the thought that I would contribute financially to
the translation of your Essays (and I understand, certainly,
that you have been distressed since Sulliger presented things
to you in such a way), all this doesn't deserve such anxiety,
and I hope that you will be willing to forget all about it in
realizing that: 1) I should hardly expose myself to any financial inconvenience, my influence being limited to persuading
Eggimann to publish a translation made by the unknown
Sulliger; 2) even if I had to spend anything, it wouldn't have
been *for you* or for your Essays that I would have done it
(despite the fact that in reality, if I listened only to my own
personal feelings and desires, I wouldn't hesitate to make a
great sacrifice to see a work as admirable and morally beneficial as your "Essays" published in French) but *for this poor
wretch of a Sulliger,* out of pure natural pity and charity
toward one of these unhappy "déclassés" overwhelmed by life.

Now, the affair is settled, and it is evident that since you
have not given him your authorization, I am not going to
lend my hand to a publication to which you do not agree;
therefore, if Sulliger publishes anything of your work, be sure
that I won't have any part in it and that he will do it entirely on his own and under his own responsibility (but I do

not think he will do it). This poor Sulliger is one of those people who spoil their own destinies. I do not understand where this disconcerting idea could have come from (I can assure you it is not from me), the idea of having you retouch your Essays and share in the expense. On two occasions, already, on which I helped him out (an investigation into the schools of Geneva and some work on Luccheni), he failed by his own fault. He was born under an unlucky star and it is most discouraging to try to help him.

I hope that the possibility of a complete translation of your Essays, in Paris, will be realized soon because this would mean a great boon for innumerable readers. I had the opportunity of convincing myself of this recently in Geneva where several people spoke of your Essay which appeared in Labori's Grande Revue, and quite spontaneously told me how much the article meant to them. None of these people was struck by the quality of the style of the translation, neither for good nor bad, which is certainly not so bad as you thought; not to mention that when it comes to a philosophical article, the reader doesn't pay much attention to the style but concentrates on the ideas. This is the remark that two of the readers of your article made when I asked them their opinion of the style of the translation. They remembered nothing of the style but kept in mind the contents only.

Please forgive me this interminable and dull letter, my dear James. I have not the courage to begin again in order to condense and shorten it. I haven't written a single word since I left home, and I think of nothing—the sea air and the drowsiness from bathing paralyze my mental processes. My wife seems to be less affected than I, and she will write soon to Mrs. James, whom she thanks very much for her kind and affectionate letter. We find ourselves very well situated in our small, quiet "lodging" [16] and are delighted not to be in

16. In English in the original letter.

Bognor itself where there are too many people. The children have already benefitted greatly and have, even Hélène, shining faces and magnificent appetites. Only the weather leaves something to be desired: clouds, strong cold wind, and little sun. Our eldest children are very well established at Littlehampton where we have visited them. Your magnificent box of delicious American candy has had proper and lasting success there. I hope for you, also, that summer arrives definitely, giving some warmth to our frozen Europe. We hope that you have good news from all your children and we are very happy to know that you are well on the way to health and strength. Give Mrs. James affectionate greetings from my wife, my dear friend, with all my respects, and accept my kindest regards.

Your always devoted,
Théodore Flournoy

Hotel Sonnenberg
Luzern, July 11, 1900

Dear Flournoy,

How sorry I am to have troubled you about this matter of the translation! All I wished was to acquaint you with the situation, and to express a regret which would disengage me from all complicity, in case you (in the goodness of your heart) should see fit to impoverish the remainder of your days and diminish the inheritance of your children, by helping Mr. Eggimann out with his rash speculation. But I see that you are taking the matter very seriously, and even tragically and I fear that you may scold poor Sulliger in a way which he doesn't deserve. I pray don't say anything harsh to him. He has done nothing wrong. My state of mind is just what I described: I care little to see myself appear in French, but I am *absolutely* willing that he should do as he pleases in the matter, *provided I bear none of the responsibility.*

If I am to be responsible, I had rather it should be for the entire work, to be published in Paris; and I am sure that I do not wish to be *pecuniarily* responsible for that— not by reason of avarice, but *par amour propre d'auteur*, rather, which forbids one to *buy* his way into publicity in foreign parts. A translation ought to come to one as an unsolicited compliment.

I regret that this absurd and fantastic feeling should traverse in any way M. Sulliger's plans, of the carrying out of which I shall be the most cordial spectator. I appreciate your description of him, having known so many others of that unlucky type; and if I were to put money into the project, should far rather pay him as translator than help the publisher out.

Please don't scold him!

After just 8 days without sun, moon, stars, warmth, or dryness, the weather today has changed and the glorious landscape lies all iridescent and opalescent before the balcony on which I write. *What a country* is *die Schweiz!*

You must expect to feel terribly heavy and depressed in the English climate for a month; but you will probably be proportionally elated when you come away.

A charming letter from Miss Flournoy and Miss Blanche Flournoy yesterday! Excellent english, with quiet exoticism to give a flavor of originality—like Montaigne!

With renewed regrets at the trouble I occasion, and with warm regards to all, from both of us,

I am always truly yours,

Wm James

JAMES TO FLOURNOY (postcard)

Lake Lucerne Boat
July 24, 1900

This is to let you know that we are about to turn our backs on glorious Switzerland tomorrow, and face towards England

via Paris. My thoracic condition has been very bad for a
fortnight, and I feel perplexed. *Sur ces entrefaites,* an invitation from a friend who lives in Paris arrived, so that determined us to turn our faces towards lower levels, and (eventually) towards England. We may be only a few days in Paris,
so our safest address is always care of Brown, Shipley & Co.—
I hope you are feeling *cannibalischwohl* by this time. I will
soon communicate with you again. Love to you all.

W. J.

JAMES TO FLOURNOY (postcard)

Nauheim, Villa Luise
Aug. 27. [1900]

—You see where I am!—the solemn mockery is about to
recommence. I will inform you of its progress, upwards or
downwards; as the case may be. I hear of you at Paris through
the Secretary of the Institut Psychique whose appeal to the
public in the Bulletin seems to me a model of "emphase" &
"pathos" about nothing definite. The only thing lacking in the
program is that they should publish a daily newspaper! They
have put my name on the Council in spite of my formal re-
fusal, twice over; and I am quite angry.—I do hope that you
are greatly rested and refreshed by England, & stimulated
and amused by Paris. I long to hear your account of the
proceedings there.

Ever affectionately,
W. J.

FLOURNOY TO JAMES

Florissant, August 27, 1900

My dear James,

I was dreadfully sorry to learn from Myers in Paris that
your doctor was sending you back to Nauheim. After your

first two unhappy attempts at that water cure, it seemed to me that it was a defiance of good sense to condemn you to a third try. May your doctor's high intuition triumph over what seems to be good sense, and may you gather in, this time, with accumulated interest, the benefits resulting from the three cures! I shall be anxious to know what effects you feel from it. Meanwhile, your card arrived a moment ago indicating that you have resigned yourself to the circumstances with that calm resignation which is one of the traits of your stoic and heroic character. What does Mrs. James think of all this? I am sure it is not joyfully or with a light heart that she sets off again for Nauheim, about which, until the present, she has had only unhappy memories; and this new separation from your little Peggy, at the very moment when you had hoped to remain in England, must have been very hard. I sympathize more than I can say, my dear friend, with you and Mrs. James. I was so happy at the time of your last Swiss sojourn to think that you were really better and on your way to a quick recovery! My wife will also be very much distressed over this turn of events. She was so hopeful of seeing you again in good health in England. She is to leave Felpham today and will return the day after tomorrow, but I fear with the frightful weather we are having that she will have a rough crossing with the children!

I returned to Geneva on Saturday, happy to have finished with Paris and the Congress and almost regretting that I had not instead spent ten more days at the seashore. It is true also that if I had freed myself from this obligation I should regret it now! In any case, congresses are a thorn in the flesh and a source of painful impressions for natures such as mine, in which inhibitions and the tendency to stop dead in one's tracks predominate. I am incapable, therefore, of telling you whether or not this Congress was a success. Janet (and Richet) did his utmost for the affair, but he had the poorest possible support from Ribot, Binet, and the whole reception

committee. It was obvious that all the French were bored to
death playing host to the Congress. Too many projects, too
prolonged, not enough time for the discussions which, with
one or two exceptions, were cut short and without interest.
The main part of the Congress was, I believe, the presentation
of Spiritism in the form of several projects by Denis, Delarme
(the leaders of French spiritism), van Eeden, Montonnier
(experiment with Mrs. Thompson), etc. which very much
scandalized the narrow-minded anatomophysiological group;
however, it didn't raise any discussion in sittings. As for the
Institut Psychique International, that great humbug of the mys-
tically minded will have lived as long as roses or two-headed
monsters live. It was solemnly presented to the Congress in
a dignified way by Ochorowicz, and supported by Richet; I
waved my little censer for it too,—and, in the evening, the
Institut received sumptuously all the members of the Congress
in its own quarters, a superb apartment put at their disposal
by some opulent Russian prince. It was as glamorous as a
soap bubble that is about to burst. The next day, at the
meeting of the organizing committee which was to draw up
the constitution and rules of the budding Institut, they came
to the conclusion . . . that it was necessary to postpone everything until the Institut possessed a capital of from 300,000 to
500,000 francs—that is to say, as I see it, putting it off indefinitely. To sum up, a firstclass funeral following a fairy bap-
tism. Console yourself for being unwillingly one of the god-
fathers of this illustrious still-born child by realizing that you
are in good company; the final ridiculous outcome of this
colossal hoax is shared by so many accomplices that there is
just enough absurdity spurting on each member to allow us
to laugh ourselves silly over human stupidity! The Institut
could live only on misapprehension; it was dead as soon as
people began to suspect it a little. In the thought of the
initiators, Yourievitch, Murray, etc. it was a matter of a collective enterprise devoted to rigorous scientific study of *spirito-*

occulto-supranormal phenomena; but for that it was necessary that at its head there should be leaders of indisputable scientific reputation such as Janet (and I had given it my support only on this strict condition, as did many others)—and not people who are suspect (such as Rochas, etc.). On the other hand, Janet consented to devote himself to it only with the very fixed idea that it would not be concerned with occultism, spiritism, etc. This contradiction in both internals and externals became evident through the discussion about the name, some members wishing Institut PSYCHIQUE, this word alone being capable of interesting the general public and adding money to the treasury of the Institut—other members demanding the name Institut PSYCHOLOGIQUE, in order to stress a concern with psychological studies in general, to the exclusion of the occult field. But the general public will never bring its offerings to an institution whose aim is not to satisfy the public curiosity on psychic, occult facts. "Überhaupt," it is not through an institution created at one stroke, with fanfare and trumpets, that science progresses generally; and it needed the megalomaniac naïveté of a slavic brain, over-excited by the atmosphere of Paris, to give birth to this grandiose dream of an establishment in Paris where, at the expense of all the nations, mediums coming from all four corners of the world would be hospitalized until the official experts in charge of investigating them could finally proclaim what is true and untrue about the mysteries of the after-world!

But I impose upon your patience, my dear James, and you have probably received more exact news about the Congress from your friends in London and Paris. I returned from it very tired, so weary that I had to give up going for a few days to Salvan to see our little Ariane as I intended to do.—Please give my best regards to Mrs. James, and accept my most ardent wishes that Nauheim, this last time, will do you the good you have so long expected from it. Believe me always your very devoted

Théodore Flournoy

JAMES TO FLOURNOY (postcard)

Hotel Hassler
Piazza Trinita de'
Monti, Rome
Nov. 17 [1900]

We have been settled in this hotel, just on top of the Spanish steps, and I should have announced the fact to you before, but I let myself go to my wicked laziness. Rome is simply delicious, the mixture of greatness with unpretendingness and shabbiness is unique. I am walking better, and shall probably before long be able to do a good deal of sightseeing. I think there is no doubt that the animal extract treatment of which I told you, is doing positive good, although this is only the 12th day and from 60 to 90 days are required. We are well lodged, my work on the lectures proceeds satisfactorily, and all things promise well. Is it true that you are to give a lecture at the Institut Psychique International this winter?

Love to you all.
W. J.

JAMES TO FLOURNOY

Rome, Dec. 5. 1900

—We move tomorrow to the Hotel Printemps, Via Veneto, where I hope we shall stay permanently. We shall get more sun. Rome is glorious—I should like never to leave it. A perfect feast for the eyes & imagination.—I have had in 5 weeks three acute indispositions which have kept my strength down, but I verily begin to believe that my arteries etc. are softening under the influence of the lymph-injections. *Qui vivra verra!* I hear of much rain with you as well as here, but I hope you are all well. My wife is very well. Your late card was enjoyed.

W. J.

III

Progress in Psychical Research

1901–1905

The death of Frederic W. H. Myers in Rome in January, 1901, was a sad event for William James. For nearly twenty years they had been closely associated in their work in psychical research. During the previous spring, they had vacationed together at Richet's chateau in the south of France. While the Jameses were staying in Rome in the winter of 1900–1901, Myers arrived at their hotel hopelessly ill, and James was with him when he died. Dr. Axel Munthe, the attending physician, gives an interesting account of the scene in *The Story of San Michele* (pp. 372–73). He describes James as sitting outside the door of Myers' room, pencil and notebook in hand, waiting to receive the message which Myers had promised to send after death. This incident is understandable as part of the scientific investigation which Myers and James had long been making in relation to the "spirit-return" theory. Concerning the theory, James wrote the following year to James Ward: "I don't accept all Myers's opinions as 'gospel truth'—quite the reverse. But I think Myers's *problem*, the 'exploration of the subliminal,' to be the most important definite investigation open of late in psychology, and I think Myers's way of going at it on the whole admirable" (Perry, *William James*, II, 649).

For some time, Flournoy had wanted to see James's works translated into French and proposed doing the Gifford Lectures himself. James felt that no one could do a better translation, but protested against Flournoy's putting aside more important work for such an undertaking. James showed little enthusiasm over being translated at all. He wrote, in part: "It is no doubt a piece of neurasthenic perversion of sensibility, but I confess that translations of my own writings always give me a kind of horror, and the best thing for me is in no way to cooperate. I haven't read a single page of the German translation of my Essays or of the Italian translation of my Psychology" (Letter to Flournoy, July 6, 1900).

After an unfortunate arrangement with a Swiss acquaintance of Flournoy, Frank Abauzit, a capable scholar, of an old Geneva family, did *The Varieties of Religious Experience*, as *L'Expérience religieuse*, Paris, 1909, with a preface by Emile Boutroux.

Mentioned first by James in the letter of April 24, 1902, Wincenty Lutoslawski weaves in and out of the correspondence for the next few years, a tragicomic figure. "He is," wrote James, "a most loveable man (within safe limits) but sadly psychopathic. Really, I think, a genius." Flournoy was less charitable, viewing this "strange mentality" with considerable uneasiness, especially after Lutoslawski confided that he felt himself to be the Messiah foretold by Adam Michiewicz and others. Flournoy confessed that their Polish friend's conversation suggested incipient paranoia, and that he seemed "not yet quite up to the messianic role." Born in 1863 and dying at the age of ninety-one in 1954, Lutoslawski was one of the most colorful, brilliant, and eccentric figures in the whole galaxy of their mutual associates. A Polish patriot who "bluntly preached the assassination of the Tzar" while lecturing in Geneva, he was also a Platonic scholar, linguist, educator, reformer, and exponent of Yoga. He first visited the United States in 1893 to attend the Congress of Religions at the Chicago World's Fair and soon presented himself to James, who eventually introduced him to Flournoy. There were amusing anecdotes in the James family about his occasional visits to the Irving Street home in Cambridge, including one of his unconventional behavior during his early morning Yoga exercises. But something about the man demanded respect and admiration; he was intellectually gifted and had a nature, as Flournoy concluded, "singularly rich, genial, and affectionate."

In the spring of 1905, James took a vacation trip to the Mediterranean, stopping in Spain, Italy, and Greece. Since the Flournoy family at the same time were staying in Rome for several weeks, there were hopes of a reunion, perhaps at the Congress of Psychology meeting there in late April. A tragic event ended such a plan. Blanche, aged twenty-two, the Flournoys' second daughter, was taken ill and died shortly after returning home. On his way back from Athens, James stopped in Rome to see certain young Italian philosophers. Although he had originally declined an invitation to attend the Congress, he was persuaded by Professor Sante de Sanctis to give a paper, partly in place of Flournoy, and he took the opportunity to discuss his theory of consciousness. Years later his son Henry wrote of the occasion:

It was obvious that the appropriate language in which to address a full meeting of the Congress would be French, and so he shut himself up in his hotel and composed "La Notion de Conscience." His experience in writing this paper threw an instructive side-light on his process of composition. Ordinarily—when he was writing in English—twenty-five sheets of manuscript, written in a large hand and corrected, were a maximum achievement for one day. The address in Rome was not composed in English and then translated, but it was written out in French. When he had finished the last lines of one day's work, James found to his astonishment that he had completed and corrected over forty pages of manuscript. The inhibitions which a habit of careful attention to points of style ordinarily called into play were largely inoperative when he wrote in a language which presented to his mind a smaller variety of possible expressions, and thus imposed limits upon his self-criticism. (*The Letters of William James,* II, 219–20.)

After a two-week rest on the French Riviera, James went to Geneva to see the Flournoys, stopped briefly in London, spent one day at Oxford to see Schiller especially, and sailed early in June. Not until three years later did he return to Europe, to give the Hibbert Lectures at Oxford.

JAMES TO FLOURNOY (postcard)

Rome (Albergo Primavera)

Jan. 18, 1901

F. W. H. Myers arrived here 2½ weeks ago *very* ill, his worst symptom being an altogether anomalous one of Cheyne-Stokes respiration, which neither heart, kidneys nor sclerosis of arteries accounted for, and which caused him intolerable dyspnoea whenever he fell asleep. Five days ago, after no exposure, a double pneumonia set in, & he died last night. His book [*Human Personality and Its Survival of Bodily Death*] alas is unfinished, but can be finished by Hodgson, as the material is ready. His demeanour throughout the illness has been superb, showing how a really living belief in immortality will help a man.—I hope that your Ariane has entirely recovered, and that there is no longer any danger of more diphtheria!

W. J.

JAMES TO FLOURNOY (postcard)

Albergo Primavera, Rome

Jan. 19, 1901

Would it be possible for you to find, and lend me by the post, a little volume, the life of Hudson Taylor,* (I think?) missionary to the Chinese? I think there is something in it which would be good to quote in one of my lectures. These drag their interminable length along—2½ of the 10 yet to be written. Still, *es geht!*—The Myerses are bearing their shock well. They remain here until Tuesday. I do hope that the health of your house is good.

                                                                W.J.

*I read it when I was with you last Spring, you then had it.

JAMES TO FLOURNOY (postcard)

                                              Albergo Primavera, Rome
                                                         Feb. 1, 1901

Ex ungue leonem! ex pede Herculem! You probably don't know yourself how gigantic a thing your little "effort" on the Theosophists is,[1] or what an impression it gives of a mind with *room* in it for everything to lie rightly placed! Also of good humour! "Nay! I do not think I flatter!"—I wish to Heaven that you would write more abundantly.—Three months of the winter have been conquered—a great achievement. I fancy we shall now have no more cold. Can't you run down here?—since you say you are tired? We shall probably stay for 3 weeks more? Love to you all!

                                                                W.J.

JAMES TO FLOURNOY (postcard)

                                              20 Charlotte Square
                                                        Edinburgh
                                                      May 22, 1901

I shall send you the newspaper reports of all my lectures, notwithstanding their imperfection, since it is *possible* they may afford some suggestions for your own, next year. I lend my MS. to the reporter, and he concocts his *compte rendu,* by stringing passages together, with the intervening connection left out, etc. All illustrations & documents are left out.

1. The reference was probably to Flournoy's article, "Lettre sur la théosophie à Genève," which appeared in *Semaine littéraire,* January, 1901.

Half of the report of the second lecture which I send with this was *omitted* in delivery! The "applause" was supplied *a priori* by the reporter—of course you understand these conditions, and will not *judge* the lectures by these reports.—I feel encouraged: the audience very sympathetic, and now that I am taking digitalis I expect to get through successfully. Edinb. & Scotland are magnificent.

W. J.

I am also sending you Brainard's Life, a very interesting document. Keep it!

JAMES TO FLOURNOY (postcard)

Bad-Nauheim Villa Luise,

July 24, 1901

Your card of the 19th just arrives. I had written a card from here to your Geneva address, 2 or 3 weeks ago. It seems never to have reached you. I have been doing well enough, and take my 13th bath today. They weaken one, and the climate here is depressing, but I think I shall get some good out of it all. We had a visit of 3 days from the Abauzits— he a vigorous intellect & character, very sociable, & she very good and sweet. I should think that he ought to make a good University career. Your account of Pardigon is *alléchant*— I wish we might visit you, so as to see the Var in its summer tropicality and luxuriance. But don't *overdo* the bathing!— Salt water can weaken one.—Our son Harry has been with us & is very satisfactory. He is now gone to Paris. I have been reading Murisier, Payot: la Croyance, & Marie Bashkirtseff's Journal & lettres—the last by far the best and most important! [2] We are here for at least 2 weeks more. Thence to the Hartz—& then to England. Love from us both,

W. J.

2. Maria Constantinova Bashkirtseff (1860–84), Russian writer and artist in Paris, was celebrated for her correspondence with Guy de Maupassant and for her *Journal*, 1890.

JAMES TO FLOURNOY (postcard)

Nauheim, Aug. 14. 1901

In two hours we say good bye to this sweet little place. I have continued improving steadily ever since I've been here, and feel glad that we have come. To night we sleep at Strasburg, then I go for a week to the higher air of the Vosges—I sorely need the tonic. Alice will, I think, go to England without waiting for me as there is much to be done there before we sail. Lamb House, Rye,[3] will be the best address. I am filled with subliminal excitement at the thought of going home.—I am sorry that your trip to the Mediterranean seemed to be so little of a success. The heat must have been an unfavorable element. But you are evidently in a neurasthenic condition; and having myself experienced so much relief from galvanizing my spine, I can't help wishing you might give electricity in some shape a trial. Why not consult Widmer? Excuse this impertinent advice. Love to you all. I will write again ere we sail. Yours ever,

W. J.

JAMES TO FLOURNOY

Rye [England]
Aug. 29. 1901

My dear Flournoy,

This is a last dying farewell to you in the midst of our voluminous packing. We go to London tomorrow morning, and the following morning to Liverpool and the vasty deep. There is no news to tell of except that my wife has sprained her ankle, which is a slight impediment to our operations. It is a solemn moment, this; but I am full of a delicious inward excitement about returning, for in spite of its fatigues and complications, "be it never so humble, there's no place

---

3. The address of James's brother, the novelist Henry James.

like home." And in all seriousness we hope to see you there some day also!

The Archives [4] arrived 2 days ago. It looks both imposing and interesting, and I shall read it in all the *recueillement* of the mid-Atlantic. Count me as a faithful subscriber—of course the pecuniary burden of publishing it will be no small one to you personally.

Madame Flournoy's letter gladdened us the other day, although its content was in some respects no very glad one. I hope that the fair Alice is quite well again, but I fear that she will never be *entirely* well until she comes to Cambridge, Massachusetts.—As for yourself, I against [*sic*] suggest the experiment of electricity. I have run down a little myself since leaving Nauheim. The life there is so protected that it disguises the real situation. But I am full of hope still.

Well! Good bye, and may God bless and keep you all. Assuredly our intercourse with the whole Flournoy family has been the brightest thing in all our two years' exile. I have never know[n] so *gleichgesinnt* a *Mensch,* dear Flournoy, as you are, with myself.—So we ought to hold together! Yours ever affectionately

　　　　　　　　　　　　　　　　　Wm James

I have been reading with much interest Encken's Wehrheitsgehalt der Religion, which in spite of its length *lässt sich leicht lesen.* I should think you might find it suggestive for your lectures.

---

4. This was a copy of the first issue of the *Archives de Psychologie de la Suisse romande,* founded in 1901 by Flournoy and Claparède in the hope of stimulating original research in Switzerland. Because of the interest and collaborations of foreign colleagues, after the fourth number it was called simply *Archives de psychologie.*

JAMES TO FLOURNOY (dictated)

95 Irving Street
Cambridge, Mass.
Dec. 26th, 1901

My Dear Flournoy:

You have a right to some dissatisfaction that I should have let so many weeks go by without giving you any news of the James family. I have to thank you in the meanwhile for both letters, post cards and printed communications.[5] Yesterday the second number of your "Archives" came with its very extended continuation of your work with Miss Smith.[6] It looks highly interesting but it must have been a terrific piece of labor, and I am glad that you have got it off your hands.

Poor Hyslop's work [7] on Mrs. Piper, combined with the loss of his wife, so weakened him that the microbes of tuberculosis found him an easy prey. He is now in the country taking an open air cure in an almost arctic cold and leading otherwise the life of a vegetable. His report is intolerably ill written and I have not been able to read the whole of it, but I must confess that it makes out a stronger case for spirit return

5. Not extant.

6. After publishing *Des Indes à la planète Mars* in 1900, Flournoy continued his research on the case of "Mlle. Héléne Smith," and compiled the results in an article "Nouvelles observations sur un cas de somnambulisme avec glossolalie," *Archives de psychologie*, Vol. I (December, 1901).

7. James H. Hyslop (1854–1920), American philosopher and psychologist, was one of the strongest supporters of the Society of Psychical Research, publishing many articles in the *Proceedings*, especially on the Boston medium Mrs. Piper whom James had discovered. Concerning James's skepticism, Professor Gardner Murphy wrote: "Dr. Hyslop did in fact raise a couple of hundred thousand dollars, and . . . the organization goes on prospering in spite of all dour promises. The 'net worth' is today a half million dollars" (letter to the editor, April 23, 1963).

than anything I have yet seen. I am struck particularly by his criticisms of the hypothesis of telepathy. He is a very manly fellow, who has had a very hard life, and I am afraid that this is the end of him for worldly purposes.

I hope that since the publication of this big job of yours you find your nerves in better condition. *I* went to complete *smash* after my return home but have resumed the injections I had at Rome and with much better results than then. The skin and arteries softened almost immediately, and the nervous prostration, which at Rome did not improve, began immediately to improve greatly. I reached equilibrium in four or five weeks and since then have been *in statu quo* but am now vastly better than at any time in two years past.

I have done two-thirds of my lectures for next spring; and, as in the last ones I felt myself on more familiar ground, the old spirit of mischief revives in my breast and I begin to feel a little more as I used to.

Home is very pleasant, but after all what slight relations does one have with any earthly thing! I am surprised at the little I have to say at my old friends when I meet them. Surprised also at the constant interference of my enjoyment of American nature by mental images of nature derived from the last two years in Europe. Europe is the privileged part of the terrestrial globe and Switzerland the privileged part of Europe! Nowhere have man and physical geography together worked out such results for they are quite beautiful.* But I will not become either a philosopher or a prophet: I am only writing this to let you and Mrs. Flournoy know from both of us that we are faithful to your memory.

I hope that the next letter will bring as good news of you all and that you in particular will, before this year is over, become emancipated from all that nervous depression.

Ever affectionately yours,
Wm. James

Pray pardon my sending you this shabby sheet. I am forced

to use a stenographer, having postponed the writing of a number of letters which I find myself unable to accomplish without too much delay.

* You must thank the stenographer for these words—I don't just recollect what I dictated, but it was not what appears.

JAMES TO FLOURNOY

Hatley St. George
Torquay, England
April 24th. 1902

Dear Flournoy,

You see that we are on this side of the Atlantic again. We landed at Liverpool just two weeks ago, and have been to Edinburgh to get an honorary degree, at Birmingham to see Lodge, president of the S.P.R., about its affairs, at London to see my brother [Henry James], and here on this wonderfully beautiful Devonshire coast, to see some old American friends, the Godkins, he an eminent publicist and journalist, now struck with hemiplegia. My health is admirably better, and the wife also is well. The heaviness of english civilization oppresses me, and if I were free I should go *stracks* for Switzerland again. But lack of time and the expense prevent it so I stay here. We shall in a week be at Rye again and stay till I go to Edinburgh to begin my lectures on May 13th. The book is all in type, and you will receive a copy, I hope, by the middle of June.

I am curious to know how your own lectures on that subject went off, and whether, after your own researches and reflexions, you will approve of my results. Such as they are they are indicated rather than developed, and 99/100ths. of the volume are descriptive and documentary, not constructive.

I hope that your own neurasthenic symptoms have been relieved, and that the academic year has on the whole gone well. That Madame Flournoy and the young people are well and flourishing, *das versteht sich von selbst*—at least I hope so! Have you seen Lutoslawski? And could you establish a good personal *rapport* with him? He is a most loveable man (within safe limits) but sadly psychopathic. Really, I think, a genius! It is sad to write to you from this comparative nearness, and yet to have no hope of seeing you or Switzerland again. The world is of an inconvenient size.

This is just a line to let you know that we still live and love you all. When you feel like it, but not before, write a line to the care of Brown Shipley and Co. London, S.W., to let us know what the fortunes of the house of Flournoy are.

Yours ever affectionately

Wm James

FLOURNOY TO JAMES

Florissant, May 6, 1902

My dear James,

Your letter gave us much pleasure,—and at the same time the torture of Tantalus: to think that you are so near and yet so far away! I would have answered sooner but for a spell of depression and ennui which I've had trouble getting rid of.—

Perhaps the letter which I wrote five or six weeks ago and which must have arrived after your departure from America has been sent on to you, as well as the card from my wife thanking you for the picture of New York which you had sent to our Hélène, no doubt at the very moment of your sailing. If all that didn't reach you, it doesn't matter, for it was nothing very interesting. The main purpose of my letter was to recommend to you the Reverend Cox, pastor of the American congregation in Geneva for the past 3 years, who is returning to America and plans to study at Harvard for a year. His thinking is more open and philosophical than is generally the case with church people, and if you have an opportunity to give him your support, encouragement, and advice, I think you will be doing a good deed and not an unproductive one!—

I am very glad that your book is about to appear—and, meanwhile, perhaps you would be kind enough to send me, as you did last year, some of the resumés of your new lectures appearing in the Edinburgh papers. If it is any trouble, don't do it, for I don't want to bother you; but you cannot imagine what pleasure and profit I got from your first series of lectures. I tackled this subject this winter, in the last fourteen lectures of my course, but I confined myself to the research—more statistical than philosophical—of Leuba,[8] Starbuck & Co. (Cie.); fatigue and lack of flexibility kept me from rising higher, and I felt unequal to my task and to the expectations of the audience, for this subject had attracted a throng, and my audience grew bit by bit until there were 200 people, a good third of whom were not students; it is always sad and humiliating not to respond, as one would wish, to what is expected! My wife and I spent ten days at Nice in March. We returned to find Hélène ill with typhoid fever, fortunately a very light case, and she is completely well now. Our three eldest passed the month of April with my wife's parents at Nice. They all return tomorrow and we shall be very happy to see them. No news of Lutoslawski, who set out again two months ago for Cracow; I enjoyed my contacts with this strange mentality, so spontaneous and full of flights of enthusiasm,—but I evidently made the opposite impression upon him, feeling that I had to play, with respect to his grandiose projects, the trying and thankless part of a cold shower. I don't know at what point he is in his enterprise of the *University of Michiewicz*; he had hoped to find among us Swiss

8. James Henry Leuba (1868–1946), a Swiss philosopher from Neuchâtel, was for many years professor at Bryn Mawr College. His main interest was in the psychology of religious phenomena.

the enthusiasm and help which he had not succeeded in find-ing among his own compatriots,—and I had a great deal of trouble making him understand (if he did understand, which I doubt) that it was not for us to dash into an affair for which he had not yet obtained the support of the Polish people living in Switzerland! He must have found me odiously skeptical, timorous, and prosaic; but I should certainly have been full of remorse had I seemed to encourage all his utopian dreams; as long as he remains in the airy heights of specula-tion, all goes well, and he certainly has genius, as you say,—but, when he comes down to our sublunar world of bankers, checks, the Federal Code of Obligations, and political neu-trality, etc.—you just can't help trying to bridle his imagination which is too forgetful of empirical reality. At the beginning he had an enormous success with his course (which I was never able to attend, unfortunately), but then he made a regrettable error with his immoderate language: for example, he bluntly preached the assassination of the Tzar—or at least (I wasn't there) his auditors so understood him—and that didn't please either the non-nihilist Russians in his audience, or the Swiss who set store by their neutrality! He announced a course for this summer semester, but did not reappear and no one has had news of him, to my knowledge. I have a great admiration and real sympathy for him, and dread for him the disappointments and strokes of misfortune, which however he is man enough to stand up to heroically!—We are very happy to know that you and Mrs. James also are in good health, and we send you, with all our good wishes for your lectures in Edinburgh, our most affectionate and devoted regards.

Your
Th. Flournoy

Edinburgh, May 16th. [1902]

Dear Flournoy,

Yes! *all* your letters, and Madame F.'s recent card have been received, most gratefully. I am sorry for the "typhoid-ette," and for the fatigue which you yourself complain of, but I hope that the girls will come back from Nice so full of enthusiasm as to make the balance incline wholly in the right direction.

I wish that we might have prepared our lectures in collaboration—we could probably have helped each other to a more solid work, *aere perennius!* As it is, the public will have two half rations, at any rate a half ration from *me.* I sent you the Scotsman report of my 1st lecture, two days ago. The second, this morning, is too trivial to send. Nevertheless, I enclose it. The book ought to be out by the middle of June, and you ought to receive a copy immediately. I take it that your courses are over for the year, and that you have no pressing need of this stuff of mine. Nevertheless, if you do wish my material promptly, I can send you the proofs of the book, the 1st half now, the rest *au fur et à mesure* of the delivery of the lectures.

What cold weather! Hardly any sun for six weeks. I [am] tired to death of this unnatural life, not being well yet, and eager to end it and get home again. We cannot sail, however, before June 24th. I am interested in what you write of poor Lutoslawski—a tragic destiny, I fear, and, in spite of all his generous impulses, a man liable to lapses from philistine morality of a bad sort. He is a *clean* man, however, and that is much.

Good bye, & good luck to you all. Our address from next Wednesday onward is 5 Athol Crescent, Edinburgh. Answer, if at all, my question on a post-card.

Yours ever affectionately,

Wm James

FLOURNOY TO JAMES (postcard)

Geneva, May 30, 1902

Your proofs [9] received—I feast on them at every moment of leisure, and I am so delighted by them that I have already begun to . . . translate them! Seriously, have you already promised or given anyone hope of the rights of translation? If *so,* all right, because it is absolutely necessary for your book to appear in French, and without too much delay. If *not,* I do not ask you yet to grant me that right, because I must think it over carefully and experiment several days before knowing if I am cut out for this work. But it may be—if the heat and sun continue—that I shall write you soon in order to submit a sample of my style as translator, and to request from you an official authorization to translate you!

A thousand regards,

Th. Fl.

Your "The Value of Saintliness" is a pure masterpeice!

JAMES TO FLOURNOY

5 Athol Crescent

Edinburgh, June 2 [1902]

Dear Flournoy,

Imagine how delighted I am at receiving your post card this morning—the first real *praise* that I have yet had for this work—and from such a quarter, you, who, having worked at the subject yourself, *know* "what's what" in it! What my friend Howison [10] said is true—"What your genuine philoso-

9. *The Varieties of Religious Experience: A Study in Human Nature,* being the Gifford Lectures on Natural Religion delivered at Edinburgh in 1901–1902 by Willam James.

10. George Holmes Howison (1834–1916) had taught logic and the philosophy of science at the Massachusetts Institute of Technology at the time James began his teaching career. In 1884, Howison was appointed Mills Professor of Philosophy at the University of

pher most craves is *praise*, rank coarse praise—Harris (the ancient editor of our Journal of Speculative Philosophy) calls it 'recognition,' but it's *praise* which we all need and work for." Since your praise, I feel that my book is *certain* to be a success. But don't continue reading the proofs, for in one week you shall have the volume. I receive this morning my advance copy which looks very well indeed.

Now as for your wildly enthusiastic project of translation—I cannot possibly believe that on reflection you will think such a *corvée* desirable, and I am sure that your abilities and your precious nerve-strength ought never to be employed on such inferior work as translating productions, no matter how eminent, written in foreign tongues. You might *find* me a translator, and possibly look over his proofs, but even that I should be sorry to think of your doing. What I fear is the difficulty of finding a *publisher*. There have been I know not how many would-be translations of my 3 psychologies into french, but not one of my translators be able to find a publisher who will take the risk. Alcan invariably refuses. This book is much more risky, being both larger, and appealing to a smaller public, but not being even possibly a *livre de classe*. Your *desire* to translate—you with your original literary talent—is better than the finished translation of an inferior man, and is the finest "recognition" that my labours can possibly receive. Even more than by making a translation could you help me by writing a notice of the book, if ever you felt inspired to do that. I have no doubt that Ribot would be too happy to have you do it for the Rev. Philosophique. But I don't *ask* you to do it, except as a "derivative" and substitute for the

California at Berkeley, where he had a long career. It was at Howison's invitation that James delivered the famous lecture at Berkeley on "Philosophical Conceptions and Practical Results," which was his first explicit statement of his philosophy of pragmatism. Perry (Vol. I, Ch. XLVIII) gives an account of James's friendship and professional association with Howison.

awful translation which even now I fear you may be in some danger of being tempted to begin. Best love to you all! and innumerable thanks from

W. J.

FLOURNOY TO JAMES

Geneva, June 5, 1902

My dear James,

Thank you for your letter. I am going to do a review of your book for the *Revue philosophique* and I'm going to warn Ribot about it. But I fear that the article will be very weak and far from what it should be! My psycho-physiological state is actually the reverse of what is needed for making such an original and personal effort. That's why I am not giving up the idea of translating you—although I am still not decided and do not yet request your official permission. It seems to me that this work of translation or adaptation into French would be just within the capacity of my present strength. I am enclosing a few pages—the beginning of your chapter on saintliness—so that you can judge them not from the point of view of the French (they still require much correction in order to flow easily) but from the point of view of the liberties I have taken with your text. Do you find that it doesn't conform literally enough to the original, or would you authorize an even greater latitude? Would you be averse to my departing still further from the word-for-word translation, provided I render what seems to me to be the essential meaning of each paragraph and the sequence of the whole? I should need to be free to shorten and condense certain sentences, in order to slow down and lengthen others—so as to make a translation or an equivalent which would be easily read. I repeat that I am making only a preliminary attempt, and it is possible that I shall give it up—in the same way, you are absolutely free to say *no* when I do ask official authorization. From the practical point of view, it would give me less trouble, and more pleasure, to translate it myself than to *find* you a translator whose prose would have to be revised and corrected, perhaps with great difficulty! As for a publisher, the experiment I made with my book, *Des Indes,* printed and published at my own expense, allows me to foresee that, without a publisher, the translation of your volume would pay its way and end with a profit which we would share equally. Once the volume was printed under my responsibility, Alcan would certainly ask nothing better than to put his name on it, as was the case with my book,—and I do not doubt that he would accept your volume in the "Library of Contemporary Philosophy"—which is in any case not indispensable for the success of the sale.

You see that I haven't given up my idea in spite of your letter, since I am already foreseeing the various practical possibilities! It goes without saying that you do not run any risk, except those of profit!

My best regards to you,
Th. Flournoy

JAMES TO FLOURNOY

Edinburgh, June 9th. 1902

Dear Flournoy,

I send back your specimen of translation, which I really think it was rather absurdly modest of you to send, as if a consumate master of style like yourself needed to give proof of what you could do.

I still seriously doubt whether it would not be a *crime* in you to undertake such a job. Once in the middle of it, it would become a nightmare, and yet you would feel in some way pledged to it, and unable to let it drop. Get Madame F. to represent to you the danger of such an obsessive idea as translating. *All* your energy ought to be saved for more direct work of your own.

If nevertheless, you do begin to translate, I not only authorize you to feel free in the way you describe, but I *wish* you to feel absolutely free to abridge, invert, expand, paraphrase in *any* way, solely from the point of making the french reader content. I detest too literal translations, and you, of all men, should not be tied down.

Moreover I should hope you would add notes of any kind, explanatory, restrictive, contradictory, even defamatory, if your heart so inclines.

But I hope you *won't* translate the book!

I sent you a copy which you ought already to have received.

The last lecture went off today—about 400 auditors, very silent and attentive, and tremendous enthusiasm at the end. But *how* glad I am it is all over! Hereafter I will make no such contract again. I am *deadly* tired and going home to my own normal conditions, to get well.

Your applause is the best reward I have had thus far, by a great deal. Blessings on you all. Good bye!

W. J.

FLOURNOY TO JAMES

Geneva, June 12, 1902

My dear James,

I have safely received your magnificent volume [*The Varieties of Religious Experience*]; in fact, I have received it in duplicate—one copy from the publisher, and the next day one from you with your affectionate dedication. I send you my heartfelt thanks. I was extremely touched and honored by your mentioning me in the preface and in the course of the book; my poor documents were unworthy, alas, of such mention,—and the support of your unfailing kindness to me was needed to confer such distinction upon my work!

My warmest congratulations on the fine appearance of the book,—and for the happy ending of such a prolonged period of concentrated, arduous work.—Your letter, which I received this morning, tells me that you have finished your labor—and brilliantly, too! How happy I am to know that you are free and unhampered in the delightful feeling of relief from such preoccupations! My wife joins me in congratulating you, and she understands the joy and relief that Mrs. James must also experience! We hope the great fatigue that you naturally feel will soon disappear and that you will take, after so many years of endless tension, several good months of real holiday and of luxurious idleness!—I wrote to Ribot, who replied that all was in order and that he was awaiting my review of your book. I am busy with it, but I am having a devilish amount of trouble, as usual, with my drafting and I shall be terribly far from doing it in the way that a work like yours really deserves. As to translating it, I should not think I was wasting my time and effort in bringing your book within the reach of the French public, which greatly needs to read things well thought-out and treated in this way; but at present I have stopped after 40 pages, in order to write my review for the Revue philosophique, which requires quite different mental processes. The question of knowing if I shall carry out my wish to translate your work is thus postponed—and all will depend on my state of nervous fatigue and what I shall do this summer, etc. So please feel free to give the permission for translation to anyone who may request it; however, if you should receive requests which make you hesitate, I would be grateful to you for letting me know by post card and that would make me decide *yes* or *no*. And if I decide before other translators make you offers, I shall get in touch with you immediately to request (or relinquish) the definitive authorization.—What are you going to do now? Do you leave for your "home" [11] at once? Won't you come over to the Continent and to Switzerland? What happiness that would be for us!—We expect to go to Pardigon in July, as we did last year.

11. In English in the original letter.

I need warm air and sunshine. My nervous state is not exactly good. The smallest incidents of daily life affect me with an intensity not usual with me, and I border on a state of neurasthenia, which I hope the summer will help me to escape.

Again, my congratulations and thanks to you—from my heart.

Th. Flournoy

JAMES TO FLOURNOY

R.M.S. "Ivernia"

Friday, June 13th, 1902

Dear Flournoy—I received No 2 of your Archives last January, I believe, but, being fully absorbed with my Gifford lectures until April, I was unable to read *any*thing serious during that time, so I bro't it with me. Bad luck again, and for the past 4 weeks total inability again to use my mind on anything— no reading whatever was possible. But the repose of the steamer is already getting me right, and I have read your supplementary account of "Hélène" with extreme interest, and unbounded admiration for your great literary talent. It completes an invaluable monograph which puts into our possession for all time a term of compassion, which all future discussers of "psychic" individuals will have to take account of in their conclusions. I need hardly repeat that your conclusions seem to me to be the only legitimate ones to draw. But what a wonderful extension the case gives to our notion of subconscious activities and to cryptomnesic activities as instanced by your interpretation of the Indian romance and of the Chesseny names. I am much struck by your remarks about the effects of too long influence of one sitter upon a medium—& (between ourselves) I much fear that the long Hodgson Piper cooperation is a case in point. I really suspect that many perhaps most of the present developments there are due to his suggestive influence. But I do wish that *someone* could continue work with Miss Smith. Some of her phenomena have grazed so closely upon the supernormal that one would like to see whether she ever does pass the barrier, as I believe it can be passed. Your jovial treatment of your critics, and in general your humorousness, are beyond all praise. All that you have to say about method, etc. is simply splendid, classic, masterly. Oh! if my book ever *did* have the good fortune of a french translation what an unheard of additional good fortune would it be if the translator had a power of writing equal to your own! But this is not meant as a plea to you to disregard my previous dissuasions, for I still feel convinced that from your own point of view you could embark on no more calamitous adventure.

June 20—We landed safely yesterday—and find all well at home.

Love from us both to you all!

W. J.

JAMES TO FLOURNOY

Chocorua (N.H.), June 25th. [1902]

I write this line to say that I am ordering my London bankers to send you a set of proofs from the stereotype plates of my book, which arrived after my departure and are no use to me. If you *do* translate my book, it might be mechanically convenient to have it in this loose form. The proofs I sent you previously were not revised.—I came straight up here from Cambridge to resume the interrupted recuperative process in the midst of this wildness and simplicity. Best greetings

W. J.

JAMES TO FLOURNOY

Chocorua, N. H.

July 23 [1902].

(Address till October 1st)

Dear Flournoy,

Thank you for writing your notice of my book so ultra-promptly. I am sure it is a splendid one, erring only by too much praise. Ribot, who wrote to acknowledge the volume, said that you were going to review it, and added: Il est en de bonnes mains. The book seems to be *ganz objectivgefusst*, for I get the most diverse reactions on it, and God's friends and his enemies both find in it fuel for their respective flames. An enthusiastic clergyman wrote me yesterday that I am of the company of Isaiah and Saint Paul. I have just replied: "Why drag in Saint Paul and Isaiah?" (You know the painter Whistler, when some admirer told him that there were only two painters, himself and Velasquez, said "Why drag in Velasquez?")—I was very sorry to learn from your postcard that you were still so fatigued. Have you tried my remedy of galvanizing the spine? It works every time, and lasts for weeks and weeks—the *effects*, I mean, last. I hope that Pardigon will have its good effect. I am just reading Ostwald's Vorlesungen über Naturphilosphie, a perfectly splendid book.—

What I write to you about most particularly is this. I want to send my son William to Europe for a year. He has his Harvard A.B. and is so mixed in with Clubs and Societies and Athletics in Cambridge that another year there would result in nothing but wasted time. He will probably be a doctor. At any rate he wants to pass next year studying Physics, Chemistry, and Anatomy being weak in the 2 former studies, and in the latter a zero quantity. I naturally incline towards Geneva, if good general Courses in Physics and Chemistry, with some laboratory work are given there. I suppose that human anatomy is given anyhow, though I confess I am confused between the medical advantages of Geneva and of Lausanne. Can you give me any information? The alternative would be a German smaller University, but I know not which, and on general grounds I should much rather have him acquire a home feeling in Switzerland and such a command of the french language as a year in french Switzerland would give.

He is a boy of fine moral character and personal tastes, but rather tardy in his intellectual activity. Strange enough, at the age of 20 he is already surfeited with social success, having been elected Captain of the University boat crew, whose annual race with Yale university is one of the 2 chief athletic events of the year. He hates the whole business, and wants to get away.

In my sylvan simplicity here, I am getting much better, and beginning to walk a little as in old times. But my "spirit" is rather broken by what I have been through, and I doubt if life will ever seem as rosy again. With love to you all,

Ever yours affectionately

Wm James

FLOURNOY TO JAMES

Geneva, August 26, 1902

My dear James,

Your letter of July 23rd reached me in Pardigon, and climbing the wooded and perfumed hills of that terrestial paradise, I imagined with "Mitfreude" your walks up hill and down dale in your rustic solitude of New Hampshire. I hope that in the course of time Chocorua will revive, and for good this time, the person you were 4 or 5 years ago and make you forget the bad years in Europe, Nauheim, Carqueranne, etc. Our sojourn in Pardigon was delightful,...[12]

---

12. At the request of the Flournoy family, a passage describing the illness of Mme. Flournoy's mother has been omitted.

The news that your son William may come to spend a year in Geneva pleases us greatly. I hope—without wishing to influence your decision—that you will prefer Geneva to Lausanne or to Germany. I shall send you as soon as I can the programs of our two universities. The courses and the laboratories of physics, chemistry, and anatomy are very good here. The winter semester opens October 15th—courses actually commence on the 22nd. Upon arriving and until he has found a pension or lodgings to his taste, it goes without saying that your son will live here at Florissant,—and that later he will come as often as he desires and feel completely "at home!" [13]—Geneva is certainly superior to Lausanne (modesty apart!) in terms of intellectual activity—lectures, courses, etc.—and, I think also, as to the University and laboratories. On the other hand, Geneva has the reputation, unless I mistake, of being more corrupt—as it is a larger city and close to France—but I do not think that a well-tempered American character, such as your son's, runs any great risk of giving way to bad influences and would not know how to resist the temptations of gambling at the Casino, etc, etc. There is at the University a good proportion of students (Genevese, Swiss, and foreign) who are perfectly steady and industrious, and your son will quickly make his choice of friends. If he takes it into his head to go to meetings of the Société de Zofingue [14]—following the example of his father, who was a *hospes perpetius!*—he will find there a good number of fine, distinguished young men.—But he will not find many compatriots at the University; last semester out of 1075 students or auditors there were only seven Americans and seven Englishmen!—

Several days ago, I received the proofs for the *Revue Phi-*

13. In English in the original letter.

14. A student society in which William James had been active during his year at the "Academie," 1859–60, and which Flournoy joined in his student days, a decade or so later.

losophique,—but, alas, I was profoundly disheartened by my review of your book, and I make my apologies to you; its dullness and insipidity bear witness to my weariness in June, —I should have liked to do it over but time didn't allow. I am very ashamed and humiliated to have done this article so poorly.—I have just learned that Abauzit found a publisher for his translation, and he tells me he will come here soon. Perhaps he might want to translate your Religious Psychology [*The Varieties of Religious Experience*] also; in any case, he would be much more capable than I am, when I see how poorly I reviewed your book! I am still not decided as to this translation, not having thought of any work during the last two months, and not being psychically disposed to set to again, although the sea baths have done me much good. I hope that all your family is well; my wife wrote to Mrs. James from Pardigon. Have a good time, and may you return to full health and youth amid your forests!

As ever yours
Th. Flournoy

JAMES TO FLOURNOY

Chocorua (N. H.)
Sept. 17. 1902
Address: Cambridge (Mass)

My dear Flournoy,

Your first-rate letter came only the other day, and we thank you heartily for the information about the University and the problem of our second-born. The Programs of courses also came, a few days later. It is very good of you to offer to take him into your house on his first arrival, and we all accept with enthusiasm. I suppose that the best thing for him, at any rate for the first couple of months, would be to find a family where he could board, and hear some intelligent conversation at table, so as to get his french as soon as possible into working order. If you know of any such place, or can hear of any, pray help him to it. He is a good clean fellow, of gentlemanly instincts; and athletic, especially in rowing. For his age he has had a good deal of experience in the way of travel, (Californian & Oregonian forests, and the Sandwich Islands) but he is not distinguished for intellectual vivacity, seeming to develope rather slowly in that direction; and I confess that I can make no distinct prophecy of his professional future. More *distastes* than tastes —a common complaint! He ought to spend a winter of hard study at Geneva, and it ought to have a good deal of effect in maturing him. Physics he ought certainly to take, though only a general course. I think he ought also to make his initiation into human *anatomy* this year, for the purpose of getting into a medical atmosphere, before he finally makes up his mind whether to go on. He has had one general Course in Chemistry, but he did no very serious work at it, the rowing having interfered too much. He *ought* to have more chemistry; but it may be advisable, when on the ground, to substitute something else for that. At this distance, not knowing the laboratory hours etc., I can't decide; but I shall depend on you, my dear Flournoy, to give him the needed advice, which your early medical education and present position will make so easy for you, and whatever courses he takes, I am sure that the year will be profitable. Possibly even you might lubricate slightly the way into the Société de Zofingue for him! It seems queer to me to be sending a 2nd W. J. to Geneva, 40 years later, to be my homologue there, under auspices so much more favorable in every respect. I have never lost the affection for Switzerland which I acquired then, nor the "home-feeling" there, and I hope that our William will now be affected in the same way.

I am glad to learn that Pardigon did you good, and hope that you may not lapse into as bad a depression again. It evidently is a subjective thing, not affecting the quality of your work. The second part of Mlle Smith was of as high a quality as anything you have done.[15] As for the translation of my Varieties, I still have great scruples about your undertaking such an amount of drudgery. If you could re-edit it altogether with alterations of your own, it would be different—you would then have the stimulus of doing something original, and I should be quite willing to sacrifice part of my text. The book seems to be a great success, judging by the numerous letters of thanks (many from strangers) which I receive. Don't feel responsible to me for your review in the Rev. Phil. I am sure it will be a just one, tho' possibly too friendly, and that is all that's required. We have spent a happy summer in our sylvan Nature, here. I am able to walk, and even to climb hills, like a normal man. I think I have been too active, for I have lost ground for 3 or 4 weeks past, but I am confident of getting up again. We go to Cambridge in the last days of the month, I have only 3 lectures a week for ½ the year, so am safe.

I esteem it an immense advantage to have such kind friends for my boy at Geneva as your family will prove to be. But pray don't feel, either you, Madame Fl. (or ces demoiselles!) or Henri, too *responsible*—everyone must paddle his own canoe, and be saved or damned by his own efforts and destiny. B[ill] sails on the 24th, and will turn up at Geneva about the 12th. He will write to you of his approach, and unless he hears from you to the contrary, he will accept your magnanimous invitation by driving straight to your house.

[W.J.]

15. The reference is to Flournoy's article on the medium "Hélène Smith," "Nouvelles observations sur un cas de somnambulisme, etc.," in the *Archives*.

FLOURNOY TO JAMES

Geneva

Nov. 4, 1902

My dear J.,

Your son Billy is the most charming young man that I have ever seen, and we were very happy over the two or three days that he spent with us at Florissant. We should have been delighted to have him stay longer, but he was wise to leave and get settled in his pension for the beginning of his courses. He probably has written you that, after having seen many lodgings, he decided on Madame Goetz's pension where he will certainly be very well taken care of in every respect, better even than in many families with a man at the head, because there are not very many homes in which the men take as much care as do Mme and Mlle Goetz!

The death of my father-in-law has been a cruel blow because my parents-in-law were about to come to spend the winter near us; their apartment was all ready to receive them! My mother-in-law is with us for part of the winter. I am in the depressed state which always marks the beginning of courses!

Ever yours,

Th. F.

JAMES TO FLOURNOY

Lakewood, New Jersey, U. S.

Jan. 27, 1903

My dear Flournoy,

I have received more than one post-card from you, I believe, since I myself wrote, the last one being a Christmas greeting, in which you also incidentally said that you had abandoned the notion of translating my book. I absolve you gladly from any and every responsibility in that direction! I felt gratified by the enthusiasm which you showed, when the book first came into your hands, for "propagating the gospel in foreign parts," but I also felt that that unspeakable kind of drudgery was not the sort of work that you ought to engage in, and I warned you to that effect, ungracious as the warning may have seemed. I am positively *glad,* now, that you have thrown up so irksome a job, without getting more deeply involved in it. If you had gone further, you would have ended by maledictions upon me and my unlucky book together. I hope as it is, that you have not wasted too many hours, and that, in case another translator should ever present himself, you can endow him with what you have written, so that your labor may not be wasted. To tell the unvarnished truth, I always feel indifferent as to translations of my writings, and have never taken any trouble to get them made. I have felt on the contrary like apologizing to the translators for giving themselves so much unnecessary trouble. I should have been proud of *yours* on account of the superior french *style,* which I should then have appropriated as the native garment of my thought, but otherwise I don't care a jot. The book has sold extraordinarily well in english, for a book that costs over three dollars. The 10th thousand is already being printed; I get enthusiastic letters from strangers, and the reviewers, although, *without a single exception,* they all use the word "unsatisfactory," having eased their conscience by that term, they proceed to handle me with sympathy and praise. If you are going to put in any labor on that kind of thing, Flournoy, you ought to prepare your own lectures for publication. Cox has told me that your last lecture in that course was the most inspiring thing he ever heard in his life. I like Cox very much, and thank you for sending him to me. He is through and through a *man.* I am glad he only spends a year in our Philosophy-department, for he ought to be engaged in parochial work, and preaching; and too much philosophy acts as a kind of narcotizer of the active faculties.

We have heard a great deal about you from Billy who writes long and frequent letters, and dear Mrs. Flournoy's letter to my wife, telling of her mother's illness came just before I left home a week ago. You have indeed had a year of gloom and sorrow—these losses multiply as we grow old. I seem to be losing all my old friends—if not by death, by decrepitude and dropping out of active life. I hope that Madame Burnier will soon be restored *ad integrum,* for she made on me no impression of being old.

I wish, my dear Flournoy, that I had Bill's last letter near so that I might copy verbatim the passage in which he speaks of his enormous debt to you. He owes literally all the happiness and admirable companionship which he seems to have begun to enjoy the very moment he arrived in Geneva, to the kindness you and yours felt towards him, and to the confidence you reposed in him. You launched him in the university, you introduced him to the élite of Genevese youth, who have treated him like a brother, you advised him at every turn, in fact you brought about immediately a relation to the environment on his part, which normally could only have been reached after six months at least—and we are correspondingly *grateful.* I wish we could in some way repay the debt. The only thing I can think of is to ask you to come and spend as much of next summer or any later summer, as you can, bringing Madame Fl. and as many of the second generation as possible, with us at our little place in New Hampshire. It isn't Switzerland—bien s'en faut—but it is pleasant all the same.

I sent you the other day, for your amusement, a syllabus which I had just had printed for my class. It is, I fear, unintelligible without the context which the lectures gave; but it will show the kind of thing that now is occupying my attention. I am very tired, but naturally, not neurasthenically, but, as my lectures end on February 21st I can go away and do what I like. Alice wants me to take a mediterranean steamer & spend two months dans ces parages. But that is too far and too wasteful, so I shall probably go somewhere in our southern states.

I am paying a short visit at my friend Chas. A. Strong's, who teaches Psychology at Columbia University in New York. He is a clear and patient thinker, and I recommend his forthcoming book "Why the Mind has a body" to your attention. It will be instructive. His father in law, John D. Rockefeller, the richest man in America, and possibly in the world (rumor places his fortune at 1,000,000,000 of dollars made by the most abominable piratical methods, but all *business,* no stock speculations or finance) is staying with us, and is a curious psychological study. The most powerful human organism I have ever seen, cunning, flexible, a volcano of passion under absolute self-control, a devout Christian of the narrowest sectarian type, not an interest in any subject except *business,* & the endowment of universities which he has taken up as a fad or hobby in middle life. He has created Chicago University, which is now a really magnificent institution. God help us when men of such power have such narrow ideals!

I have been re-reading Bergson's books, and nothing that I have read in years has so excited and stimulated my thought.[16] Four years ago I couldn't understand him at all,

16. Henri Louis Bergson (1859–1941) was probably the most important philosophical and personal attachment which James made in this last decade of his life. There were many reasons why James and Bergson should have been attracted; in addition to their philosophical views of which Bergson's theory of *durée réelle,* for example, coincides on many points with James's conception of the "stream of consciousness." Both were men of profound humanity and possessed a degree of artistic sensibility not usual among philosophers. Both were masters of prose style, Bergson eventually winning the Nobel Prize for literature in 1928. For a discussion of their relationship see Perry, *William James,* Vol. II, Ch. LXXXVI.

though I felt his power. I am sure that that philosophy has a great future. It breaks through old *cadres,* and brings things into a solution from which new crystals can be got.

Good bye dear Flournoy. Love to you all.

Wm James

JAMES TO FLOURNOY

Cambridge, April 30, 1903

My dear Flournoy,

I forget whether I wrote you my applause or not, on reading your chapter on Religious Psychology in the Archives.[17] I thought it a splendid thing, and well adapted to set the subject in the proper light before students. Abauzit has written to me for authorization to translate my book [*The Varieties of Religious Experience*], and both he and W.J. junior have quoted you as assured of his competency. I myself feel confident of it, and have given him the authorization required. Possibly you may supply him with as much of your own translation as you have executed, so that the time you have spent on the latter may not be absolutely lost. "Billy" also says that you have executed a review of Myers's book [*Human Personality and Its Survival of Bodily Death*], finding it a more difficult task than you had anticipated. I am highly curious to see what you have found to say. I, also, wrote a notice of the volumes, and found it exceeding difficult to know how to go at the job. At last I decided just to skeletonize the points of his reasoning, but on correcting the proof just now, what I have written seems deadly flat and unprofitable, and makes me wish that I had stuck to my original intention of refusing to review the book at all. The fact is,

17. "Les Principes de la psychologie religieuse," *Archives de psychologie,* II (December, 1902), 33–57. In pamphlet form, this article was subsequently published in Russian, Italian, and German.

such a book need not be *criticized* at all at present. It is obviously too soon for it to be either refuted or established by mere criticism. It is a hypothetical construction of genius which must be kept hanging up, as it were, for new observations to be referred to. As the years accumulate these in a more favorable or in a more unfavorable sense, it will tend to stand or to fall. I confess that reading the volumes has given me a higher opinion than ever of Myers's constructive gifts, but on the whole a lower opinion of the objective solidity of the system. So many of the facts which form its pillars are still dubious! Bill says that you were again convinced by Eusapia, but that the conditions were not satisfactory enough (so I understood) to make the experiments likely to convince absent hearers. Forever *baffling* is all this subject, and I confess that I begin to lose my interest. Believe me, in whatever difficulties your review of Myers may have occasioned you, you have my fullest sympathy!

Bill has had a perfectly splendid winter in Geneva, thanks almost entirely to your introductions, and to the generous manner in which you took him into your own family. I wish we could ever requite you by similar treatment of Henri, or of *ces demoiselles*. He seems to labor under an apprehension of not being able to make you all believe how appreciative and grateful he is, and he urges me to "make you understand it" when I write. I imagine that you understand it anyhow, so far as he is concerned, so I simply assure you that *our* gratitude here is of the strongest and sincerest kind. I imagine that this has been by far the most profitable and educative winter of his life, and I rejoice exceedingly that he has obtained in so short a time so complete a sense of being at home in, and so lively an affection for, the Swiss people & Country. (As for *your* family, he has written more than once that the Flournoy family seems to be "the finest family" he has ever seen in his life.) His experience is a good measure of the improvement in the world's conditions. Thirty three years ago [18] *I* spent 9 months in Geneva—but in how inferior an "Academy", and with what inferior privileges and experiences! Never inside a private house, and only after three months or more familiar enough with other students to be admitted to Zofingue. Ignorant of 1000 things which have come naturally to my son and yours in the course of education. It *is* a more evolved world, and no mistake!

I find myself very tired & unable to work this spring, but I think it will depart when I get to the country, as we soon shall. I am neither writing nor lecturing, and reading nothing heavy, only Emerson's works again (divine things, some of them!) in order to make a 15 minutes address about him on his centennial birthday. What I want to get at, and let no interruptions interfere, is (at last) my 'system' of tychistic and pluralisic "philosophy of pure experience."

I wish, and even more ardently does Alice wish, that you and Mrs. Flournoy, and all the children, or any of them, might pay us a visit. I don't *urge* you, for there is so little in America that pays one to come, except sociological observation. But in the big slow steamers, the voyage is always interesting—and once here how happy we should be to harbor you. In any case, perhaps Henri and one of his sisters will come and spend a year. From the point of view of education, Harvard is first rate. Love to you all from us both,

Wm. James

FLOURNOY TO JAMES

Geneva, June 25, 1903

My dear James,

I am ashamed to be so delayed in my correspondence with you, still not having replied to your good letter of April 30th,

18. Actually, it was 43 years earlier, in 1859–60, that the family of Henry James, Sr., spent nine months in Geneva. They had also spent a few months there in 1855 when the boys attended a boarding school. See Le Clair, *Young Henry James,* Chs. VI and XI.

followed some time ago by the *Boston Evening Transcript* containing the whole collection of oratorical lucubrations released by the centenary of Emerson,—in the midst of which your discourse looms up like a vigorous oak tree surrounded by underbrush. You have an unequaled talent and art for putting your finger exactly on the important point and for making the essential trait spring into full light—the dominating characteristic, as Taine would have said—whereas all the other lecturers lose themselves in the confusion of secondary things. I am very impatient to read your article on Myers—on whom nothing remained to be said from the psychological point of view, after your previous article, "Myers's Service to Psychology." The compulsion to write several pages on his posthumous work has disturbed me greatly these past months, and I was horrified on rereading, in the printed proofs, the two articles (which, by the way are almost identical in part) I produced on this subject for the *Proceedings of the Society for Psychical Research* and for our *Archives de Psychologie.* —Apropos this last, Claparède told me that you had paid your subscription; we were extremely touched, but a little embarrassed; because in sending you our modest Archives, we had no intention of making you a *paying* subscriber. I urge you, dear friend, not to renew your subscription for the following copies—if there are any!—and to permit us to send you our little review as a tribute we should like to make worthier of the one to whom we send it and to whom we owe so much!—

I saw Abauzit who passed through Geneva at Pentecost, and who was very much encouraged by the subscriptions which he had already collected. I believe that his translation of your book will be a great success, and that he will easily cover his expenses (which is magnificent for a work in French!).

In May, I gave 3 lectures on religious psychology, spiritism, etc., at Montauban, where I was invited by the Faculty of Theology. What interested me most there was—Lourdes, where

I spent twenty-four hours. Just at that time, there were five pilgrimages there (from Switzerland, Bavaria, Belgium etc.), about 20,000 pilgrims, so that I had a wonderful show! I even attended a "miraculous" healing: a young girl of 18 who arrived stretched out on a mattress and totally incapable of moving her legs (according to what was told me) raised herself up a little the first day, sat up the second day; on the third day, while I was there, she walked alone, followed by the enthusiastic crowd;—but her poor little face, pale and emaciated, which I would have judged that of a 12-year-old child, and all of her puny aspect, strongly suggested the idea of hysteria; and I very much fear that when she returns home the paralysis will take hold of her again. But still, it is really something to have walked, even for only a day or two, and nobody can tell what blessing and light the memory of this pilgrimage to Lourdes will perhaps have for this poor child all her life!—I visited Lourdes with my parents in 1865: I was 11 years old, and we were shown the wild grotto, on the bank of the Cave where the Virgin had appeared seven years previously; there was in this miserable hamlet only one shabby inn where we had dinner;—but it is all stamped on my memory with the clarity which the impressions of travel make upon us at that age; it is interesting and exciting to me to contrast the difference after nearly 40 years: a city of large hotels; the mountain torrent pushed back to make room for an asphalt promenade where the swarming, clamoring crowd shout litanies before the miraculous grotto; a basilica with electric lights, and the whole well-regulated exploitation of human faith by a skilled clerical organization . . . and all this colossal transformation resulting from the hallucination of a little shepherd girl. Zola's book on Lourdes, and the article by the 2 Myers on the miracles of Lourdes, came back to my memory.

—I was interrupted and so I drop Lourdes! We miss your son Billy very much; we had become accustomed to having him call every Sunday evening, and we treasure happy memories of this very amiable and charming young man to whom we remain truly attached. There is something so frank, hale, and vigorous in his physical and moral character that one is immediately attracted to him, and I should like it very much were our Henri to resemble him. At the moment, the latter, who has grown too quickly, is quite mild, quiet, dull; —but his exams, which he is in the middle of at present, don't go too badly, and this is all we can ask of him at the moment. We have received two charming letters from Billy since his arrival at Marburg, and he seems to me to be profiting seriously from the scientific resources of the place;—however, the German character, language, and the type of students do not seem to fire him with much enthusiasm!!

We are very appreciative of the insistence with which you, and Billy, have pressed us to make you a visit in America. But alas, it is far away,—and our strength as aged, decrepit and declining Europeans restricts us to less ambitious schemes! Until our offspring, more energetic than we are, we hope, spend their vacations on the other side of the Atlantic, we limit our desires to this side, to the Mediterranean; we are to return in eight days to Pardigon where we have gone for the past two years. In walking about the hills perfumed with lavender, laburnum, and pines, I shall imagine that these are the forests and mountains of Chocorua and I shall expect— in vain, alas—to see you come into view at some turn of the footpath. I hope, dear friend, that you are already rested from your university year and that, in the relaxation of nature, you are going ahead rapidly in your philosophy of tychism,[19] the main outlines of which I sometimes amuse myself by

19. Flournoy had received the previous January a copy of the syllabus which James prepared for his "Philosophy 3" course, in which he set down in outline form one of the most comprehensive statements of his philosophy. To Francois Pillon, on June 12, 1904, James also gave a concise statement of "tychism"—"My philosophy is what I call a radical empiricism, a pluralism, a 'tychism,' which

guessing at—from all that I know of you. Its early publication is one of my most ardent wishes.—My wife has had a letter started for a long time to Mrs. James, but when will she have the leisure to finish it???!

With our best wishes to you all for a good summer. Believe me, as ever your affectionate,

Th. Flournoy

JAMES TO FLOURNOY

Chocorua, N. H.
(July 28, 1903) [20]

Dear Flournoy,

Your letter of a month ago, the "Proceedings" with your article on Myers's book, and No. 7 of your Archives have all recently arrived. We are profoundly touched at your so extremely kind words about our second-born, and are extremely glad that he proved so *sympathische* an *Erscheinung* in your household. His own opinion of the household you already know, and we can never be too grateful to you all for the welcome you gave him, and for the home-feeling which he consequently so soon acquired in Geneva. The absence of any corresponding feeling in Marburg on his part

---

represents order as being gradually won and always in the making. It is theistic, but not *essentially* so. It rejects all doctrines of the absolute. It is finitist; but it does not attribute to the question of the Infinite the great methodological importance which you and Renouvier attribute to it. I fear that you may find my system too *bottomless* and romantic. I am sure that, be it in the end judged true or false, it is essential to the evolution of clearness in philosophic thought that *someone* should defend a pluralistic empiricism radically" (*Letters*, II, 203–4). It was not until 1907, however, that James published his famous *Pragmatism. A New Name for Some Old Ways of Thinking.*

20. Dated in Flournoy's hand.

is very striking, and is, I think, matter for considerable regret. We shall see him again now in about six weeks, and doubtless he will have many stories to tell.

I find your article on Myers masterly. Knowing how hard you take such tasks, I felt sorry to hear that you had accepted this one, and still more so when you wrote me that it had embittered months of your existence. But the article is as powerful and frolicsome as if no effort lay behind it, and I must say that the big law-giving tone of it *ought* to make a new epoch in the tone in which 'scientists' treat such subjects. Your defense of the subliminal self is particularly striking and important. I had great trouble in deciding what to say in my criticism of the book, and feel quite ashamed of my dry little article after reading your big and human production. Thank Heaven, it is all over for both of us and having so fully paid our debt to Myers's *manes* for all that he ever did for us, we can feel satisfied, and turn towards other things.

We are at our little place, and the summer, already far advanced, has on the whole treated us kindly. Peggy asks me to enclose a letter to your Marguerite, thinking she may be at home by this time, or with you, wherever you are. Harry has developed a taste for farming and is introducing some real work on our place. He has been all day spraying with arsenic & bordeaux mixture a field of potatoes which is our pride. Hodgson left us this morning after a visit of 10 days. It is a pleasure to see a man in such an absolute state of moral & physical health. His very face shows the firmness of a soul in equilibrium—another proof of the strength which a belief in future life may give one! Yet I am bound to say (*to you & between ourselves*) that I would bet a large sum that the present Piper performances to which he practically consecrates most of his energy, and which seem to me vastly inferior from the point of view of supernormal knowledge to the earlier ones, are almost entirely due to suggestion, largely from him and are dramatizations of a most silly sort. The difficulty of getting "tests" H. now explains by a theory that spirits also have subliminals, and that the subliminals are the parts of them engaged with communicating, mostly disintegrated, dream-like and anaemic. Yesterday he quoted this incident in support of the dream state. The daughter of Sheldon Amos (an English lawyer) came to Boston and had a 20 minutes sitting. Later the spirit of her father gave a lot of messages to Hodgson for her. He shortly afterwards showed them to the widow in London, who found some of them veridical. Among them was this: "Tell John not to cut the shrubbery." John was their gardener. A few days before Mr. Amos's death, he looked through the window and found John cutting down some shrubs of which he was fond. Soon he fell into delirium, and repeated incessantly the words that Mrs. Piper had given.

Thanks, dear F., for your extremely liberal offer about the Archives. I accept, with thanks. I also thank you for your quasi-co-operation with Abauzit's enterprise. I hope he won't suffer loss. Of course if he does, I will make restitution. He strikes me as a little too excitable a young man.

How well French Scientific & philosophic literature is developing!

I have just begun to write a little on my new book.[21] I am in pretty good condition as long as I don't allow myself to get fatigued.

My wife sends you all her love, and so do I.—sorry that it had to be *sent* and not demonstrated on the spot.

Ever truly yours,
Wm James

21. Since James published no books between *The Varieties of Religious Experience* in 1902 and *Pragmatism* in 1907, the reference must be to the latter.

Geneva, Dec. 22, 1903

My dear James,

All summer I have not succeeded in taking hold of my pen to thank you for your good and charming letter of July. Naturally, I had still less success during the semester. And now that it is Christmas vacation, these lines will not arrive in time even to wish you all health and happiness for the New Year! Be assured that—even though they come late because of my congenital inertia, which only gets worse with age—our good wishes for you and all your family are none the less sincere and profound. I hope that your health is entirely restored now, and that you are working with the energy and vigor of your best years on the metaphysical monument—Tychism, Pluralism—that all your friends are impatient to see appear. A letter from Kaltenbach, received some time ago, told me of your Friday morning "Seminar in Metaphysics," as well as the charming friendliness with which you received him. He described to me the joyful surprise which he experienced upon discovering that you are not "a cold, sober man, always deep in grave meditations and scornful of common mortals," as he has imagined you must be because of your celebrity. I had, however, painted you in other colors to Kaltenbach when he came to see me before his departure for America, but it seems that my words could not modify the preconceived idea he had formed about you—I do not know under what influence, for he did not study at our University—and he had to have the contact with reality itself, in order to overcome his error!—When I go uninspired on Monday morning to the laboratory to face a dozen Russians, not knowing either what to tell them or what to have them do, I dream with an inexpressible *Sehnsucht* of that seminar being held at the same hour (except for the difference of longitude!) at Harvard. I would give I don't know what in order to be transported there magically—as much to hear you as to get rid of my Russians there!—and I think that if there were any truth in occultism, the intensity of my desire would already more than once have split my personality and transported my double through the air to the other side of the Ocean, straight into your lecture room; look out, next time, to see if you can't see me floating somewhere in the shadow of a corner of your classroom, drinking in your words on the question of Pragmatism!—

We miss your son Billy very much this winter. We enjoyed so much, a year ago, having him come to our house, and we are not the only ones who miss him, for M. Naville speaks to me often of him, and none of his fellow students has forgotten him; L'Huillier, for example, whom I happened to meet a few weeks ago, told me with warmth and enthusiasm of his recollections of Billy's fine character and charming personality. What is he doing now? Is he getting his teeth into medicine with relish? Give him our very best regards. I hope that you are all reunited this winter and that, after so many and such long separations, Mrs. James, with her maternal affections, enjoys a happier time.

Our Marguerite returned in September delighted with her stay in England where she was very happy with the three families with whom she stayed (a merchant, a "clergyman," [22] and an officer), and she doesn't know which of these very different homes she prefers.

The laboratory weighs upon me so much that I have decided to make a change in my position at the end of this semester; I hope to have Claparède nominated prof. ordinaire de Psychologie (with the Laboratory)—and to keep for myself my little course, 2 hours per week, as prof. extraordinaire." If the Faculty or the Canton authorities do not agree with this, I shall retire completely from the University. But I hope that they will allow me to continue my course, which interests

22. In English in the original letter.

me (giving me just enough occupation) and in which I do not do too badly (I have 150 to 200 people, a large number for our Faculty), whereas the laboratory exhausts me, and is no success at all.

I began to read "Humanism" by F. C. S. Schiller when it appeared—unfortunately, I have had to abandon it because of my work this semester, which doesn't allow me a free minute. I am going to take it up again soon. This volume interests me since one finds in it your direct inspiration and influence, but refracted (and, I am afraid annoyingly warped), seen through a temperament which seems to me rather different from yours.—No news at all from Abauzit for three months; at the end of September he had translated about 100 pages of your book. The quality is as perfect as possible, but the quantity very small; the poor chap was very ill this summer, and had a sick child also, causing worry and loss of time. I believe that this translation, which we hoped to see appear in a few months, may be seriously delayed, but it will be, I think, a masterpiece of translation, exact as to sense, very free, and in good French.—Monsieur [Gaston] Frommel, professor of Dogmatics at our Theological Faculty, gives a course in religious psychology in which he discusses your volume— (he had hoped that the students would already have had the French translation of Abauzit!)—And at Neuchâtel, Monsieur Bovet (successor of [Ernest] Murisier, provisionally at least) gives a course on the philosophy of Monsieur James. You see that you are by way of stamping your impression very clearly on French Switzerland!—Adieu, a thousand good wishes,

Yours,
Th. Flournoy

JAMES TO FLOURNOY

Cambridge, Jan. 1, 1904

My dear Flournoy,

This is the first of January, and I don't wish to let it pass without a *signe de vie* on my part. I dare say that something from you is also on the way hither; but I know what a bore it is to you to write letters, and I pray you restrict yourself to post cards as much as possible. I understand the whole situation.

I am amazed at the strength which your "Archives" display, always important and valuable material. In truth, the world threatens to be inundated with psychological material; Janet's & James Ward's [23] new enterprises are to be matched in America by an enlargement of the Psychological Review, by a new Philosophical Archives, and by a new start on the part of the Journal of Neurology and Psychology. With all this quantity of material, the quality here in America remains pretty unimportant. We have plenty of privates and non-commissioned officers, but no major generals! It is curious to see how all the real work that counts in the world at any time is done by very few individual men. The others simply make background.

I have been pretty well this fall until three weeks ago an attack of influenza got me, and I still suffer great nervous weakness. I have done practically nothing in the way of writing my book, life having seemed of late to consist exclusively of interruptions and of doing things either to help, or to oblige, other people: but I shall end it now and insist, whatever happens, on keeping myself free, for the next six months,

23. James Ward (1834–1925), of Cambridge University, met William James in 1880, corresponding and exchanging visits for the next three decades. Ward gave the Gifford Lectures at Aberdeen in 1896–1898, publishing them in 1899 as *Naturalism and Agnosticism*. For his relation to James, see Perry, *William James*, Vol. II, Ch. LXXXVIII.

of other people's business. Billy is in the Medical School going over the same work he did last year, and, strange to say, having to work about as hard as if he had never touched the subject. He is a good boy, but I confess I cannot see him clearly in my mind's eye taking the form of a future practitioner of medicine. He is devoted to the memory of your family, and assuredly his winter in Geneva was a very good thing for him. Can't Henri find it for his interest to come and spend a year at our University? With us here, everything could be made easy for him. I shall send you in a few days a copy of Dewey's "Studies in Logical Theory." [24] It is a very important output of the University of Chicago. Don't feel yourself obliged to read it because I send it, possibly some young man may take more interest in it than you do.

Now, my dear Flournoy, I close this letter, which, as I said in opening, is only to commemorate the date of this blessed first of January. That 1904 may be a happy year for you and Madame Flournoy and every one of you is the prayer of Alice and myself. Believe me,

Ever your affectionate
Wm James

I am in the 4th week of confinement to the house with a poisonous catarrhal influenza. Only within the past 2 days has my strength begun to come back. I hope that you are free of these complications.

24. John Dewey, (1859–1952), American philosopher and educator, had corresponded with James since 1891. For James's influence upon Dewey see Perry, Vol. II, Ch. LXXXI, and James, *The Meaning of Truth*, pp. xvi–xix, also the biographical essay by Jane M. Dewey in *The Philosophy of John Dewey*, edited by Paul Authur Schilpp.

FLOURNOY TO JAMES

Geneva, April 14, 1904

My dear James,

Yesterday, two unexpected things happened to me. First a visit from Abauzit who told me that your son Billy was seriously ill following a bad case of grippe and that you yourself have had several illnesses this winter. We are profoundly disturbed by this sad news and send you our most sincere wishes that, since the end of March, the date of your letter to Abauzit, convalescence and health have definitely returned to your home. I like to believe that you have recovered your strength and are free from worry over the state of Billy's health. If I were not afraid of putting one more burden upon your life, already so full, I should ask you to send me quickly a few words on a post card, giving us news of you, because we are longing to know that you are all recovered.

It seems, alas, that influenza rages on the two continents at the same time, not sparing any country, because it is cruelly felt in Geneva too, and we have just witnessed the passing of many among our friends and acquaintances of all ages. We cannot complain at Florissant, although 7 out of 8 of us were nipped by the microbe; but at length we have recovered, save for a strong dose of fatigue and of physical and mental lassitude on the part of my wife and myself. My wife has, moreover, had her life complicated by her mother's illness which obliges her to visit Lausanne constantly, where she is again this week; I fear that my mother-in-law has not much more time to live.

As for poor Abauzit, of whom I have had no news since the New Year, he paid a heavy price to neurasthenia, which obliged him to quit his teaching for six months, on the order of Grasset, and go to Lausanne or elsewhere to take care of himself, meanwhile leaving his wife and child in the Cévennes. There is some good in this misfortune if this enforced vacation should permit him, as I hope, to continue his translation of your book. It is a work which interests him and which he does very well (he showed me a new chapter and I was extremely satisfied with it from every point of view) and which he will be able to carry on, I believe, without inconvenience because of his neurasthenia, after he has rested two or three weeks from the fatigue of his winter in Alais.

The second unexpected thing, arriving about the same time as Abauzit but from another point on the horizon, is a notebook of confessions or religious autobiography from Lutoslawski. You will form your own opinion about it, because I am sending it to you at the same time as this letter, since it is intended for you really more than for me, who am hardly worthy of it! I read it last evening at one single stretch, and I must say that this manuscript interests me greatly, teaching me many things which were obscure to me in Lutoslawski's past, and it caused me great relief and pleasure in that it gave me a much more favorable impression of Lutoslawski's mental state than what I had retained from his visit here at the beginning of January. At that time, various bits of his conversation seemed to me suspiciously like incipient *paranoia;* he gave me to understand that he *himself* was definitely the Messiah foretold by [Adam] Michiewicz and others of his heroes of Polish philosophy etc; and since in many childish ways and really very fanciful details, he seemed to me to be not yet quite up to the messianic role, I wondered if he wasn't irremediably crack-brained. His first post-cards from Naples and Port Said hardly reassured me on this. But really his stay in Jerusalem seems to have put him back on the right track, and his pages 39–42 apparently mark his return to less megalomaniacal ideas: he realizes that he was becoming a pseudo-messiah, and he is content more modestly just to be the founder of the University of Michiewicz! That is quite something, of course, but I am not . . . Polish enough to be assured of the success of his enterprise. My confidence remains at half-cock!—But, after all, we shall see what we shall see, and he has my warm wishes for his success; and the role of university founder makes me less fearful for him than that of Messiah!—In any case, our Polish friend's nature is singularly rich, genial, and attractive, and I feel greatly indebted to you for his acquaintance, for I owe it entirely to you. My impressions of the rest of his manuscript are still too confused for me to hazard a comment on them to you, or rather, to write you about them. If you were only here at hand to grant me the privilege of a few moments of conversation!—in Any case, I am going to reread the manuscript quickly before sending it to you with this letter; I naturally have a great deal of trouble assimilating his Catholic point of view mixed with theosophy as it is; I do not know if in the long run I shall finally see through the jumble and understand how a man who has direct, personal revelations (p. 43) still needs confessor and Pope. . . . The comparison between the Protestant pastor and the Catholic monk with which he ends (p. 60) made me conscious of the difference in our inheritance and how difficult it is for us to understand and appreciate those who are different from ourselves!—

I am taking great delight, during my moments of leisure, in reading The Gentle Reader by Crothers,[25] which your son Billy very kindly sent me at New Year's—for which I do not even know if I thanked him! Tell him how much I like the book. There are pages which seem to flow from *your* pen, and in any case seem to be inspired by *your* ideas, to such an extent that at times I ask myself if "Crothers" isn't your double! Evidently not, but at least there is between him and you, or rather your manners of writing and judging things, a kinship of humor which for me doubles the charm of this volume.—Once more, my dear James, all our wishes for the

25. Rev. Samuel McChord Crothers (1857–1927), Unitarian clergyman and essayist, was Minister of the First Parish in Cambridge and enjoyed a certain popularity at the turn of the century, especially with the book mentioned.

health of all of you. Tell us soon that Billy is well again; that
Mrs. James is not too fatigued; that your other children are
well; and that you, yourself, are full of life and vigor for your
work! And believe me always your most grateful and devoted

Théodore Flournoy

JAMES TO FLOURNOY

Cambridge (Mass.) June 14, '04

Dear Flournoy

I owe you for an excellent long letter (April 14th), to
say nothing of Mrs. Flournoy's rather sad letter of about the
same date to my wife, telling of her Mother's death. You all
have my warmest sympathy. One loses a mother only once,
and the light of the sun is different ever afterwards. You
show yourself too much concerned about my health, and that
of Billy. I had 2 attacks of influenza, one of them keeping
me for 5 weeks in my room, and Bill had a frightful attack,
with ulcerated throat etc, which took away all his strength.
We have both been well again for many weeks past. I say
"well," but in my own case the result of the year is extreme
fatigue, and the interruptions to work are so incessant that
I have written exactly 32 (!) pages of my immortal new work
since last October. It is rather pathetic; and I ought to get
out of the University. I resigned this year, but they refused
to accept my resignation; and the special difficulties of the
University this year made it more honorable for me to continue. But *next* year I shall get out for good, and then I hope
to do more writing. I admire the punctuality and richness
of your Archives. Long may it continue! Have you seen Hall's
new Journal of Religious Psychology? [26] Very *Hall*esque as far

26. Granville Stanley Hall (1844–1924), Professor of Psychology
at Johns Hopkins and later President of the newly founded Clark
University in Worcester, Mass., had been James's student and associate at Harvard.

as his part goes, but probably destined to make an epoch in that matter. Leuba comes out frankly against you and me. He sees no significance in mystical experiences. At the same time he doesn't show his hand at all as regards his rational religious philosophy. He is either excessively cautious, or still very much in doubt as to any general view of things. I saw him last summer but could get nothing out of him. If one's general philosophy permits a God, I don't see why one should be so averse to permitting non-rational relations with him. It is good at any rate that Leuba's position is now frankly defined. Abauzit seems to take his translation very seriously. Some specimens that he sent me were splendidly done. So free! I wish that he could recover his health. Which reminds me of Lutoslawski & his wonderful manuscript. He too is casting wistful eyes on America—this time as a free lecturer. I feel like discouraging him, and I have to admit that to some extent I am animated by selfish fears. I am too easily a prey to "cranks," and in my own badly neurasthenic condition, too much contact with them poisons me. Besides, L. would be sure to come to grief pecuniarily (in the first year at any rate) and I dread having to help him out. I feel partly responsible for his invasion of *your* peace. But I console myself by thinking that he would have known you and grown intimate with you at any rate, once established as he was at Geneva. He is a most loveable man, but it seems to me a mild form of circular insanity. I can hardly imagine him ever *settling* to anything. Meanwhile his gifts are enormous; and in Poland his power as a ferment must be very great. The trouble with men of his type, however intense their affections & elevated their emotions may be, seems to be a certain profound superficiality (if one may use such a phrase) which leaves them deficient in moral delicacy when that is most needed. Meanwhile, his autobiographic document is very valuable, and on the whole honorable to him.

Speaking of geniuses reminds me of Münsterberg, whose

facility is more like Lutoslawski's than like anyone else's whom I know. I regard his St. Louis scheme, which you have doubtless seen, as an almost insane piece of abstract schematization. But his talent in putting it through against resistance has shown a great organizing power.

I have taken particular pleasure in refusing to have anything to do with it. You are happily out of it too. Saint Louis will be so hot in September that I fear all the Europeans will die of it, and have to be sent home in their coffins.

In an hour I depart for Chocorua for the rest of the summer. I wish I could see some of you there. I shall hope, after a couple of weeks, to get at my writing again and to produce a few pages. I follow the war with *spannung* and am altogether in favor of Japan. I suppose that you also think that she *deserves* better than Russia, and that the insolence of the White race in Asia ought to receive a check. Billy has lost his 2nd semester, and I, who never believed that medicine was his proper vocation, think he had better stop. But what? That is the question for he is composed altogether of *dis*tastes when it is a question of choosing a life work.

I hope that your summer will rest & refresh you all. Of course life grows somewhat graver as we grow older & losses multiply themselves. Give my love to Madame Flournoy & to each & all of the young ones.

Yours ever affectionately

Wm. James

FLOURNOY TO JAMES (postcard)

Geneva, July 13, 1904

My dear J.,—I thank you and your family very much for all your affectionate messages—your letter, that of Mrs. J. to my wife, that of Billy received yesterday, and your article on Spencer, which I shall read at Pardigon beside the blue waves of the Mediterranean. We leave tomorrow—Henri has already

left, on Sunday, for Bornemouth, where he will try to learn
a little English during the 3 months of vacation. That is why
I limit myself to this little card. I shall write you after our
return in a month. We are all very tired and *on edge,* and
I long for the solitude of Pardigon to rest ourselves, for we
are practically exhausted.—I received the 2 big volumes on
Adolescence by Stanley Hall. I tried to read a chapter but
I found its style so boring that I had to give it up and postpone it to a better time. Why is it that you alone write in
a way that enables one to read both with profit and pleasure?
I also wanted to read an article by Baldwin, but my brain
refused to work. All good wishes and thanks to you all from
us all.

T.F.

I hope Abauzit goes right ahead this summer.

FLOURNOY TO JAMES (postcard)

Geneva, Oct. 9, 1904

My dear J.

Thank you kindly for sending your "Does Consciousness
Exist?" It is very difficult to transpose into French, in view
of the fact that the word "consciousness" is indispensable, for
lack of another word, to express "knowing, knower" [27] etc.
How fortunate are the English and the Germans to be able
to manufacture terms without any restrictive rules!—Is there
a real and essential difference between your "pure experience" [27] and the *Empfindung* of [Ernest] Mach, the *Phénomène*
of Renouvier, etc.? It seems to me not, and I believe that
"Consciousness," [27] *Bewusstheit,* Menstruum, etc., which you
fight with reason, have for a long time ceased to exist in
French thought—it was fundamentally the old theory of [Vic-
tor] Cousin and the classic manuals, quite out of fashion with

27. In English in the original letter.

us now, but prevalent, it is true among many Germans . . . I
hope that you had a good summer, that Billy has completely
recovered, and that you are all well.—Upon returning from
Pardigon, I had to get busy with the Congress of Philosophy,
whose meetings were in my opinion deadly dull; but it was
good weather and the festivities were successful—and that's
what is essential at a Congress.—I had the pleasure of making
the acquaintance of Strong, who is a charming man. He was
very worried over his wife's illness, which is keeping them
from leaving Divonne, and he doesn't know when they will
be able to sail for New York.—Abauzit has done ¾ of the
work, and I begin to hope that it will be finished and printed
by spring. All good wishes to you and yours. A real letter
later on.

> As ever yours
> Th. Flournoy

JAMES TO FLOURNOY (post card)

> Cambridge, Oct. 11. 1904

Dear Flournoy,

Let me praise you for the delicious words with which you
close your review of Schiller's Humanism,[28] in your last Archives. You are the only man now living (except Schiller himself—and he spoils everything by his bad taste in jokes and
his polemic brutality) who can write philosophy "human"ly;
telling the individual truth sincerely and without official or
professional pretension. That by itself is a *specialty*, and I
predict for your lightest word an ever-growing authority over
the younger generation. I do believe that truthfulness does

---

28. Ferdinand Canning Scott Schiller (1864–1937), English
philosopher and psychologist, was educated at Oxford and Cornell.
He was a tutor at Oxford from 1903 to 1926 and later a professor
of philosophy at the University of Southern California. He had a
wide reputation as an exponent of pragmatism, which he discussed
under the term "humanism."

have some effect in the long run. Your balanced position in psychic matters is particularly precious. You cannot be accused of partiality, yet you insist on keeping the door open.

Vive la Vérité!

I have read the rêve prophétique article with interest—it seems more like chance coincidence, at any rate it is safest so to count it.

I have had a visit fm. poor Hyslop today. He deludes himself with the belief that he can raise a large fund of money to endow psychical research with, and is trying to do so. He has all the heroic qualities of human nature and none of the indispensable ones. Alas! alas! Munsterberg's St. Louis Congress, the International Peace Congress, the Pan Anglican Church Conference, and the 5000 students of our University, all arrived simultaneously last week. You can imagine our social condition. All have flowed off or settled down by this time and we breathe freely. It was amusing while it lasted, and I managed to escape great fatigue. The two most interesting personalities whom *I saw* were [Wilhelm] Ostwald & [Adolf von] Harnack—absolutely different. I think I should on the whole prefer to live in a world of Ostwalds. Pierre Janet & his wife, Lloyd Morgan [of Bristol] & [Harald] Hoffding [of Copenhagen] remain here, Janet & Morgan lecturing in Boston, at the Lowell Institute. Would you yield to an invitation to come? if asked? Six or 8 lectures, in French, at 150 dollars a lecture? We are hoping to have both the Janets and Morgan in our house. Hoffding comes tomorrow to us, a dear *bon papa* sort of a man, whom everyone loves, in spite of his fabulous erudition. Have you read his little Philosophische Probleme? The most sensible, empiristic, individualistic philosophy I know—I value it greatly, in spite of its rather dull and ineffective manner of statement.

Good bye, dear F.! Love to you all—I know my wife sends it.

W. J.

Billy, after a melancholy year with medicine, has dropped

the whole thing and gone in for *Art!* He spends his mornings
at the life school in Boston. He smiles & makes jokes again
and is more like unto his old & natural Self than we have
seen him in two years. *I* never could apperceive him as a
doctor.

JAMES TO FLOURNOY (postcard)

Oct. 21. 1904

In writing to you the other day, I forgot to ask whether or
not I had ever *sent back* to you that MS. of Lutoslawski
narrating his religious history. I can't find it; and I don't
remember sending it back. Pray set my mind at rest! Best
greetings to you all.

W. J.

FLOURNOY TO JAMES (postcard)

Geneva, Oct. 31, 1904

My dear J.

I received your card concerning Lutoslawski's manuscript:
I do not know if you have sent it back to me, but it is quite
certain that I *have not received it.* I thought at any rate that
you would have sent it back directly to him. I have had no
news of him since spring; his last card was from Cracow.—
I don't know what he has done since then or where he is
staying now.—I wrote you a card on October 9th, (addressed
to Chocorua); and soon after I received your charming and
excellent letter, for which many thanks. Very touched and flat-
tered by your proposal that I come to give 6 or 8 very well-
paid lectures. It is not the desire which is lacking, above
all with the prospect of seeing you,—but, alas, I am too old
or too shy to face a foreign public.—I have never even accepted an invitation to give a lecture in Paris. I am one of
those unhappy people afflicted by congenital, general inhibi-

tion and misanthropy who suffer accordingly all their lives. I have succeeded in overcoming it for Geneva and Switzer-land—but I have no longer the strength to begin educating myself for foreign parts! Thank you all the same, and all my gratitude to you!—I have had news (old) of you from Kalten-bach, whom you received so cordially. Best wishes from the whole household.

Th. Flournoy

Congratulations and good wishes for Billy's artistic career! Henri is going to be a doctor.

JAMES TO FLOURNOY

Cambridge, Feb. 8. 05

Dear Flournoy,

In spite of New Year's attentions from both you and Madame Flournoy, I have held my peace until this late date, being a graphophobe, and having my attention entirely absorbed by other things. Now a lull has come, and I turn towards my Genevan friends. Madame F., who very kindly wrote to Billy, said that you were about to go in March to Rome. I too have plans of travel, and imagine that in one way or another, it will not be hard for us to meet. I have just finished my lec-tures, and after getting through with examinations (not enor-mous) and about 2000 pp. of "theses" to read and briefly criticize, I shall be entirely free. I have also written 8 new philosophical articles since last July, and best of all, do not feel in the least degree fatigued. All which seems to justify me in "letting myself out" a bit; so I have taken passage for the Mediterranean on March 11th. My present idea is to get off at Gibraltar, run up to Madrid to see the Valesquez's, and take the steamer a week later to Naples, thence immediately to Greece, arriving during the first week in April. I want to spend 4 or 6 weeks in Switzerland or France, according to where Strong is. I want to see Bergson; and I want to see *you.* Won't you have a letter for me at Gibraltar by March 20th. and another one at Naples by March 25th (for I may not get off at Gibraltar) both addressed to the care of Thomas Cook and Son telling me just what *your* plans are. Might it be compatible with them to go to Greece also for four or five weeks? I think that I shall not sail for home till the 10th of June, from Liverpool. I expect at Athens to fall in with 3 American friends, serious fellows, one of whom knows Greece well and will save us a lot of perplexity if we rejoin him.

Thus does one renew one's youth like the eagle!

The James family is well enough except for a frightful attack of 'parotitis' on the part of Harry—as bad as any thing can be, and complicated, as the doctor now thinks, with influenza. The turning point has been reached today, but he has suffered greatly. His mother nurses him and is naturally tired. Otherwise our winter has gone off well. My brother is now in the south, and has enjoyed himself greatly, on the whole.

I will write no more, since I hope to meet you so soon!

With love to all your family, believe me ever faithfully yours,

Wm James

I don't remember whether I wrote to say how very instructive I found your and Strong's discussion. Bergson's paper at the Congress I found tant soit peu *spitzfindig.*

FLOURNOY TO JAMES

Geneva, February 19, 1905

My dear James,

Your letter fills me with joy: showing me, to begin with, what a magnificent flourishing state of health you are enjoying, and, next, in telling me your fine plans for travel which will give me a chance to see you. I think that this note will reach you before you leave Cambridge; in any case, I shall send you a word in time at *Gibraltar* and at *Naples.* Our plans are to spend three weeks in Rome as a family (with my wife and our 4 oldest); we shall arrive in Rome about the 17th of March. We have already reserved rooms at the Anglo-American Hotel, Via Frattina. Then, the children will return alone to Geneva for their studies; and we shall remain another three weeks at Rome, my wife and I alone, until and including the Congress of Psychology, April 26th to 30th, for which I promised Sante de Sanctis to present a paper which he asked me to do on "Religious Psychology." We shall return to Geneva early in May and not budge again for a long time.

Your suggestion that I go along with you to Greece is very kind and attractive, and I thank you for it, but for many reasons I cannot dream of it; my more modest plans are limited to showing Rome and its environs to our children; it would not suit them or my wife if I left them in the lurch for a sojourn in Greece, after having promised them for such a long time this trip together to Rome! I, myself, haven't the energy available for any greater efforts than quiet walks in the Eternal City. I have been very depressed this winter, by the cold, rhumatism, etc.; I am much older and more dilapidated than you are, dear friend. But your example is a good omen to me, and when I think of the heart-rending state from which you succeeded in reaching the peak of good health and spirits, I do not despair of recovering my youth also—when I reach your age!—But if you stop a day or two in Naples before sailing for Greece, I shall certainly leap toward you from Rome in order to shake hands and spend some happy moments with you. A thousand good wishes for the prompt recovery of Harry, all our respects and affectionate good wishes to Mrs. J., remember us to all your children.—And Bon Voyage! See you soon.

As ever yours,
Th. Fl.

JAMES TO FLOURNOY (postcard)

Lausanne, 9 Avenue Eglantine

May 20, 1905

I was no better yesterday morning, so I spent the day in solitude, and the loss was not *yours!* Same thing again today— it is an obstinate case. I write now only to ask you not to forget to let Henri ask his friend for Lutoslawski's address. Love to you all.

W. J.

JAMES TO FLOURNOY

Grand Hôtel de la Cloche

Dijon, France

May 23, 1905

Dear Flournoy—

This is simply to let you know that I am out of Switzerland which I abandoned this morning. I have continued to lose sleep so badly that I think rather seriously of sailing on the 2nd from Liverpool, and skipping Oxford altogether, so as to begin all the sooner a course of "lymph compound." If the sleep improves, however, I shall of course stay, for socially, or rather philosophically, the Oxford program is extremely interesting. Schiller, Bradley, and a meeting of the Oxford Philosophical Society—a group of the younger teachers there, with Schiller reading a paper, and the atmosphere highly charged with "pragmatistic" electricity.

I re-read Abauzit's circular of his translation the other day, and it makes me feel decidedly as if I ought *not* to be his *parrain* with us. He is doubly eccentric from the American point of view—1st. as a typical *francais meridional,* 2nd. in his individual *tour d'esprit.* I doubt whether he can make a success in the class-room at all with us.

Will you kindly see that I get 50 reprints of my article ["La Notion de Conscience"]?

You can't tell, dear Flournoy, how good it has been to me

to see you both again, sadder, and a little older as we all are, but so true and good. Madame Flournoy must not forget, in the girl that has gone, what cause for exultation she has in those that remain, and in Henri. I can carry home so fine an account of them.

Believe me always, affectionately yours, and with love to Mrs. Flournoy especially,

Wm James

JAMES TO FLOURNOY

Cambridge, Oct. 1, 1905

My dear Flournoy,

I have kept you without news of my precious self and family for more weeks and months than seem exactly fair, in spite of the fact that the envelope which will contain this letter has stared me in the face on my writing table—all addressed—for I know not how long—since July at any rate. We have had a rather "mean" summer, with headquarters in Cambridge, (having let our country house, the children all but Harry being scattered) and Alice & I both caught a most virulent influenza 6½ weeks ago—both at the same moment!— from the debilitation of which we haven't yet recovered. The consequence is that no work whatever, save a little reading, has yet been done by me, and a rather arduous winter of work is ahead, the University having just opened, and I in no good condition to meet it, unless those famous lymph-injections of which I boasted to you, prove efficacious once more. I have just begun (10 days ago) to take a course of them and already feel a good effect. The children are all in fine condition, Billy furiously devoted to "Art," & already showing good capacity; and Peggy having just passed successfully her entrance examinations at Bryn Mawr College, a first class feminine institution, which she will not enter, however, for another year, since she and her mother have conspired to bring it about that she shall spend one year at least in idleness and social frivolity—*dancing,* as the *great* preparation for Woman's life!—and be more *blasée* and mature when she settles to her studies.

So much for *us!* May I hope that after your year of hard trial, you all, and especially Madame Flournoy, are beginning to feel a new sort of equilibrium, a more austere one, of course, establishing itself. It must have been an acrid experience—I can only understand it by trying to imagine what it would be for us to have our Peggy taken. Have you been to Pardigon again? Or to your own Swiss Mountains? Returning tourists have told me that Switzerland was never so "full" before—I don't see how you Swiss people who are not hotel keepers or railway or steamboat officials can stand the sight of all those tourists, every year!

We shall not make part of them next year at any rate. I told you there was a chance of my lecturing at the Sorbonne next winter, and coming over in the summer, but we have just decided that *es geht nicht,* and even if invited, I shall not be able to go *then.* We shall be at Chocorua next summer & spend one more winter at least, on this side of the Atlantic. The book that has interested me most of this summer has been Heymans's Einleitung i. d. Metaphysik (I think that is the title).[29] I dare say you have read it, and will agree with me in considering it a masterpiece of clear composition. I don't sympathize with his rationalistic way of using the Causalprinzip, but I relish immensely his radical assertion of the reality of 'psychic causality,' and the coincidence of his reasoning with Strong's is extraordinary. I have always told Strong that I failed to get the *working grasp* of his system which his imagination evidently possesses. I think that Heymans has given it to me, and I must say that I am well nigh converted. Bellanger: Les Concepts de Cause, etc. has also struck me as a valuable book. But I can't philosophize in a letter!

29. Gerardus Heymans, *Einführung in die Metaphysik,* 1905.

I have to thank you for a letter and several post-cards, and hope for more, but *only when the spirit moves!* Don't feel a duty! Alice and I both send our love to you all.

Yours as ever

W. J.

FLOURNOY TO JAMES (postcard)

Geneva, Nov. 18, 1905

My dear J.

While waiting for the time and spirit to write you a *letter*, I send this card to thank you most cordially for your kind pages of last month. I hope that you have recovered fully, also Mrs. James, from the influenza, and that the winter has begun well for you all. We did not go to Pardigon last summer; my wife made a short visit to Salvan, with her brother who had a chalet there; our daughters were invited right and left to their friends' homes; as for me, I did not budge from here, nor did Henri who was preparing his "propédeutique" (natural sciences—to enter medicine). He succeeded brilliantly, highest in all branches, and now he is studying anatomy with [Sigismond] Laskowski, etc.: In these respects we are satisfied. I have begun my courses and lectures again (in which I am studying *Bergson* with the students); and I always have an audience more numerous than is merited by the very watery sauce which I serve them!—But the empty place left by our dear Blanche makes us feel even sadder with the regular routine of winter activities, constantly recalling to us all that she was and did for us all only last year! Alas!

Poor Abauzit, in the process of a divorce, has instructed me to give you his compliments; he hasn't the courage to write you. His book will finally appear *soon*(?!)

As ever yours,

T. F.

Attached is a *Semaine littéraire* with an article on your brother.

IV

Fulfillment and Despair

1906–1910

In January, 1906, William James took a leave of absence from Harvard to give a series of lectures at Stanford University during the spring term. He planned the course in preparation for a projected textbook of philosophy in which he intended to outline his metaphysical system. The lectures were dramatically terminated by the San Francisco earthquake on April 18. The damage to buildings in Stanford and at the University was so severe that all courses were discontinued. Miss Lillian J. Martin of the philosophy department was distressed over the fate of relatives, and James accompanied her to San Francisco on an early morning train. Thus, he saw the city a few hours after the disaster had struck and recorded vivid impressions in letters to friends, as well as in an account which can be found in *Memories and Studies*, 1911. Within a few days, when train service east was re-established, Mr. and Mrs. James returned to Cambridge.

The material for the Stanford lectures James developed into a series of lectures which he gave that November at the Lowell Institute in Boston and published in 1907 as *Pragmatism*. In February, 1907, he repeated the series at Columbia University. That same month he sent in his resignation to the Harvard Corporation, effective in June, although his "half-course" was finished at the mid-year. In the fall of 1907, upon receiving the invitation to deliver the Hibbert Lectures at Oxford the following spring, James was, as he stated to Flournoy, very hesitant to accept. His health had grown worse, so that physical exertion, especially the effort involved in giving public addresses, brought on pain and difficulty in breathing. Yet, the invitation afforded him an opportunity to write out certain material which might not otherwise be set down, and despite the danger such a strain could bring, he agreed to do the lectures. They were delivered with success at Oxford between May 4 and 26 in 1908. Except for a short holiday in Belgium and Holland, James remained in England for nearly six months. The trip to Geneva which he wanted to take was too demanding, and he could not accompany Mrs. James and their daughter to the Flournoys' in August. Staying at his brother's house at Rye, James enjoyed the rest and quiet he needed, though increasingly he desired to get back to his own surroundings. "Murder! how I long to get home!" he wrote Flournoy in September. From the Hibbert Lectures came *A Pluralistic Universe* in 1909, and in the same year, *The Meaning of Truth*, his last publication, a collection of papers mostly already printed.

On August 25, 1909, James wrote to Flournoy urging him to come to Cambridge and give some lectures at Harvard, bringing Madame Flournoy for a visit the Jameses had long hoped for. Included in this letter was a note to Madame Flournoy from Mrs. James, expressing the warmest hospitality and great expectations of a visit from them both. Madame Flournoy had died three days before the Jameses wrote their joint invitation. The tragic irony of these circumstances was almost unbearable to Théodore Flournoy. As can be seen in the rest of his correspondence with James, her death was a blow from which he never fully recovered. On September 4, he wrote to the James family an account of his wife's illness and death. James's letter of condolence which was probably written between that of August 25 and his next, on September 28, is apparently not extant. However, the letter which Mrs. James wrote to Flournoy was published in a memorial volume to his wife, issued privately in 1910. It reads in part:

... I loved your wife; each time I saw her I loved her more and looked forward to an ever-deepening friendship ... She was so beautifully *living*, so entirely right in her lovely nature that even death for her must have been orderly, serene, a step forward and to no strange country. And what a beautiful life she had! ... I shall never forget nor cease to be thankful that I knew your wife. We had such good talks together and never lost time over insipid matters; the good and beautiful friend she was! (*Souvenirs de Marie Flournoy-Burnier, 1856–1909*, Geneva, [1910] p. 15).

In the spring of 1910, James had several reasons for going abroad, the most important being his health. He wanted to consult a heart specialist in Paris and to take once more the baths at Nauheim. He wanted especially to see his brother Henry, who was ill and over whom he was distressed. Consequently, he and Mrs. James went directly to Lamb House, Rye. Leaving Mrs. James to bring his brother to Nauheim later, he visited the doctor in Paris, who could do nothing for him but confirm previous diagnoses. At Nauheim, the effects of the baths were depressing, and he could not shake off the sense of fatigue he had long had. Hoping that the air of Switzerland might help him, he went to Lausanne and Geneva, seeing Flournoy for what proved to be the last time.

The Jameses, accompanied by Henry James, whose health had somewhat improved, arrived at the Hotel Beau Rivage in Geneva on July 4, James being too ill to be a guest at the Flournoy home in Florissant. However, there were visits and notes exchanged, as many as the situation would allow. Madame Flournoy's death and the extremely serious condition of James's heart cast shadows over these last few days of a twenty-year friendship. A month later, en route from London to Liverpool, James wrote his last few lines of affectionate

farewell, just before sailing, and with characteristic courage
said "... near home now, and not afraid of the voyage." Upon
landing at Quebec accompanied by his wife and brother,
James went directly to his summer home in Chocorua, New
Hampshire. Within forty-eight hours, his condition indicated
how extremely ill he was and what a tremendous effort he
had exerted during the last weeks of his journey. He died on
August 26, 1910. For ten years more, Flournoy mourned the
friend who had thought of them as "two men particularly well
faits pour nous comprendre."

JAMES TO FLOURNOY

Stanford University
Feb. 9, 1906

Dear Flournoy,

Your p-c. of Jan. 22nd arrives and reminds me how little
I have communicated with you during the past 12 months.
It would even seem that I have not told you of my engagement ("University exchange") to come here to give 3 hours
a week of "Introduction to Philosophy" for the 2nd Semester
of the year. I have been here just a month and on the whole
enjoyed it, until 5 days ago, when I was seized with an attack
of classic orthodox *goût* which is, I think, a little better this
morning, but which sends streams of anguish through my
organism whenever I dare to *move.*

Let me begin by congratulating Mlle Alice, but more particularly Mr. Werner, on the engagement which you announce.
Surely she is a splendid prize for anyone to capture. I hope
that it has been a romantic love-affair, and will remain so to
the end. May her paternal and maternal example be the model
which their married life will follow! They could find no better
model. You do not tell the day of the wedding—probably it
is not yet appointed.

Yes! Hodgson's death was ultra-sudden. He fell dead while

playing a violent game of "hand-ball." He was tremendously athletic and had said to a friend only a week before that he thought he could reasonably count on 25 years more of life. None of his work was finished, vast materials amassed, which no one can even get acquainted with as he had gradually got acquainted; so now good bye forever to at least two unusually solid and instructive books which he would have soon begun to write on "psychic" subjects. As a *man* Hodgson was *splendid,* a real *man;* as an investigator, it is my private impression that he lately got into a sort of obsession about Mrs. Piper, cared too little for other clues, and continued working with her when all the sides of her mediumship were amply exhibited. I *suspect* that our American Branch of the S.P.R. will have to dissolve this year, for lack of a competent secretary. Hodgson was our only worker, except Hyslop, and *he* is engaged in founding an "Institute" of his own, which will employ more popular methods. To tell the truth, I'm rather glad of the prospect of the Branch ending, for the Piper investigation—and nothing else—has begun to bore me to extinction. I think that the material records of the case (and Mrs. P. herself) will now go to England, where Mrs. Sidgwick and Mr. Piddington will work it over. They think they have some signs of communication between her trances and the automatic writing of Mrs. Verrall and a couple of other english mediums, and wish to see if it grows stronger when she comes nearer (this of course is *entre nous*). Mrs. Sidgwick and Piddington form a strong critical combination.

To change the subject,—you ought to see this extraordinary little University. It was founded only 14 years ago in the absolute wilderness, by a pair of rich Californians named Stanford, as a memorial to their only child, a son who died at 16. Endowed with I know not how many square miles of land, which some day will come into the market and yield a big income, it has already funds that yield 750,000 dollars yearly, and buildings, of really *beautiful* architecture, that

have been paid for out of income, and have cost over $5,000,-
000. (I mention the cost to let you see that they must be
solid). There are now 1500 students of both sexes, who pay
nothing for tuition, and a town of 15,000 inhabitants has
grown up a mile away, beyond the gates. The landscape is
exquisite and classical, San Francisco only an hour and a
quarter away by train, the climate is one of the most perfect
in the world, life is absolutely simple, no one being rich, serv-
ants almost unattainable (most of the house work being done
by students who come in at odd hours), many of them Japa-
nese and the professors' wives, I fear, having in great measure
to do their own cooking. No social excesses or complications
therefore. In fact, nothing but essentials, and *all* the essentials.
Fine music, for example, every afternoon, in the Church of
the University. There couldn't be imagined a better environment for an intellectual man to teach and work in, for 8 or 9
months in the year, if he were free to spend 3 or 4 months
in the crowded centres of civilization—for the social insipidity
is great here, and the historic vacuum and silence appalling,
and one ought to be free to change. Unfortunately, the Authorities of the University seem not to be gifted with imagination enough to see its proper role. Its geographical environment and material basis being unique, they ought to aim at
unique *quality* all through, and get sommités to come here
to work and teach, by offering large stipends. They might, I
think, thus easily build up something very distinguished. Instead of which, they pay small sums to young men who chafe
at not being able to travel, and whose wives get worn out
with domestic drudgery. The whole thing *might* be utopian;
it *is* only half-utopian. A characteristic American affair! But
the half-success is great enough to make one see the great
advantages that come to this country from encouraging public-
spirited millionaires to indulge their freaks, however eccentric. In what the Stanfords have already done, there is an
assured potentiality of great things of *some* sort for all future

time. My coming here is an exception. They have had psychology well represented from the first by Frank Angell, and Miss Martin; but no philosophy except for a year at a time. I start a new régime—next year they will have two good professors. I lecture 3 times a week to 400 listeners, printing a syllabus daily, and making them read Paulsen's text-book for examinations. I find it hard work, and only pray that I may have strength to run till June without collapsing. The students, though rustic, are *very* earnest and wholesome.

I am pleased, but also amused, by what you say of Woodbridge's *Journal:*—"la palme est maintenant à l'Amérique." It is true that a lot of youngsters in that Journal are doing some real thinking, but of all the *bad writing* that the world has seen, I think that our American writing is getting to be the worst. Dewey's ideas have unchained formlessness of expression that beat[s] the bad-writing of the hegelian epoch in Germany. I can hardly believe you sincere when you praise that journal as you do. I am so busy teaching that I do no writing and but little reading this year. I have declined to go to Paris next year, and also declined an invitation to Berlin, as, "international exchange [professor]." The year after, if asked, I *may* go to Paris—but never to Berlin. We have had Ostwald, a most delightful human *Erscheinung*, as international exchange at Harvard this year. But I don't believe in the system.

[W. J.]

JAMES TO FLOURNOY (postcard)

Cambridge, June 15, 1906

Just read with admiration your *first rate* article on Richet in the last Archives.—Your letter on the earthquake etc came duly a couple of weeks ago. I don't write at greater length for I am too "psychasthenic" at this vernal moment. But we

are otherwise all well, and I hope that you continue so. Billy
is at Paris painting in the Atelier Julian. Love to you all.

W. J.

FLOURNOY TO JAMES

Geneva, July 1, 1906

My dear James—Thank you for your card. I hope that by now
you are out of your phase of neuro- or psycho-asthenia, and
that a good vacation will wipe out all traces of fatigue from
your Stanford work and of the excitement of the earthquake.
We read with the greatest interest your article, which you
had the kindness to send us on your impressions out there;—
seeing the finesse, the humor, and the assurance of your descriptions, in which we could see you whole, as *man* and
philosopher at the same time, we shouldn't have supposed
that you were going through a period of psychasthenia!—

We are preparing to leave for the Valais in 3 or 4 days;
thus we are as excited and agitated as though we were going
to make a world tour! My wife is very tired and I hope that
the mountain sojourn will be restful to her. We have had an
excellent letter from your son Billy, and we cherish the hopes
of seeing him in Switzerland and of having him here to attend the wedding of Alice, which will probably be the 1st
of September. My future son-in-law [Georges Werner] is a
great friend of Reverdin, of L'Huillier, and of Chessex—all of
whom Billy saw often in Geneva, and he remembers well
having met Billy several times at The Brasserie or in student
gatherings. I hope that Billy is very satisfied in Paris, from the
point of view of art, although he did not give us his impressions on that.

What I am writing about *today* is the enclosed letter which
I received from a young man to whom I lent your *Talks to
Teachers* to read in the mountains during his vacation. He is

26 years old; very intelligent; unfortunately very deaf; this infirmity does not prevent him from being interested in everything, above all in whatever touches on pedagogy and morals; he is "licencié ès lettres" from our University and should receive his Ph. D. in a few months. He is the son of Dr. Ferrière, and the nephew of M. L. Ferrière who had lunch with you at Edouard Claparède's a year ago. (At this luncheon also was [Gaston] *Frommel,* professor of theology, who died very unexpectedly a month ago; the autopsy revealed a brain tumor. It was an irreparable loss to us all, for the University, and for French-speaking Protestants.) But to return to Ferrière, I believe that he is very capable of translating your *Talks to Teachers,* if you give him the authorization.—I have seen poor Abauzit, who has been in several times, going to see his little girl in Lausanne. The divorce is final. He seems very pitiable. He seems to have given up the idea of going to America (for which I congratulate you!). I hope he finds another wife, better suited to his nature.—A thousand good wishes to you all,

As ever yours,
Th. Flournoy

JAMES TO FLOURNOY

Cambridge, July 1st., 1906

Dear Flournoy, while I was at Stanford this winter, I saw much of a Miss Lillian J. Martin, Associate Professor of Psychology there, a woman of first-rate intellect and admirable character. In 1899 she published the results of three years' work with G. E. Mueller in Goettiengen under the title "Zur Analyse der Unterschiedsempfindlichkeit"—a very solid contribution to learning. But she looks beyond the "streng wissenschaftlich" in Psychology, and would like to acquaint herself with recent French work on the more concrete aspects of human nature. She thinks very highly of your "'Indes-Mars" book.

She is, in my opinion, a remarkably fine and "real" human being endowed with great earnestness, perseverance & courage. I therefore do not hesitate to recommend her most warmly to your kind offices & advice, in case she ever comes to Geneva. When she does so she will send you, along with a card of introduction from me, a note asking for an appointment. Pray preserve this present letter, so that you may be reminded of who she is.

Unfortunately she has yet to acquire a vocal & auditory use of the French language.

A card from Bill, at Paris (18 Rue Bonaparte) says that your Alice is to be married in September. I am glad it is not later, but sorry it isn't earlier still—these long engagements are tiresome things! My vacation has begun, & I am already a good deal rested from the fatigue of the year. The children are scattered, & Alice & I will spend the month of July in Cambridge.

I have undertaken to co-ordinate a lot of stuff that is now coming out through Mrs. Piper, purporting to be from Hodgson, in order to make a report.[1] There is a great amount of subliminal automatism involved, but I suspect that the residual doubt will always remain as to whether it may not be a very amnesic extract of the real Hodgson trying to communicate. It will be sad indeed if this undecided verdict will be all that I can reach after so many years. Ars longa, indeed!

Believe me, dear Flournoy, with love to yourself, Mrs. Flournoy, & the entire family, yours every faithfully,

Wm James

Excuse the type writing—a new acquisition, in which I am not yet expert.

1. In 1909 this voluminous report on "Mrs. Piper's Hodgson-Control" was published (*Proc. of the Soc. for Psychical Research,* Vol. XXIII, 1909), and a few months later, "The Confidences of a Psychical Researcher'" (*American Magazine,* October, 1909).

FLOURNOY TO JAMES (postcard)

Geneva, Jan. 2, 1907

My dear J. I must send you news, *de visu,* of your Billy whom we found the same as usual, that is to say as charming and as fine a young man,—but with a thick moustache in addition, which makes him eminently respectable and above all with the happy, open countenance of the artist who has found his way and who is not pulled down by the burden of studies antipathetic to his nature, as he was four years ago. His much-too-short visit to Geneva gave us immense pleasure.— He told us that you had given up the idea of coming to Paris next winter to lecture, which fact we regret very much indeed, because I had really hoped to see you on that occasion; he also told us that you have just finished up your university courses for good, on which I warmly congratulate you! Now you can write with complete freedom and give us the works we so impatiently await from you! A thousand good wishes for you and yours,

As ever yours,
Th. Flournoy

JAMES TO FLOURNOY

Cambridge, Jan. 2nd. 1907

Dear Flournoy,—this is a rather belated new year's epistle, but no matter, if it only find you able to receive our greeting and assurance of continued affection, even tho' communication in these days gets more rare. I find that letters, never flowing very easily from my pen, grow less and less spontaneous in these sexagenarian years. All is well with the James family—all but an increase of my arterio-sclerotic symptoms in the last six months. But after 9 more lectures at Harvard and 8, a month hence, at Columbia University in the City of New York, I am free from that particular *corvée* for eternity, and mean to lead a life without excitement or strain. It makes

me almost tremble to look forward to such freedom! Alice
has had a pretty good winter, rather unusually free from
headache, because the house has been so quiet. Billy being
in Paris, Peggy at College at Bryn Mawr near Philadelphia,
have made us feel very empty. But all, including Harry and
Aleck (or "Francis") are well, so we are free from Care. I
want to make you all enthusiastic converts to "pragmatism"
(something not necessarily connected at all with "radical empiricism") on which I gave 8 Lowell lectures to a fine audience
in Boston this winter (these are the lectures which I shall
repeat in N. Y.) I didn't know, until I came to prepare them,
how full of power to found a "school" and to become a
"cause," the pragmatistic idea was. But now I am all aflame
with it, as displacing all rationalistic systems,—all systems in
fact with rationalistic elements in them—and I mean to turn
the lectures into a solid little cube of a book which I hope
to send you by next October, and which will, I am confident,
make the pragmatic method appear, to you also, as the philosophy of the future. Every sane and sound tendency in life
can be brought in under it. At New York last week (where
I attended the meeting of the American Philosophic Association) I saw Strong, who, having lost his poor gentle wife,
has returned home. Binet's article (also his book) [2] on brain
and mind are charmingly written and get very close into the
roots of the subject, but they don't seem to me to go as far
as either Strong or Heymans, who are singularly alike. How
well your Archives keep up! And what a tremendously able
psychologist & philosopher Claparède is proving himself to
be, covering as wide a ground as he does in so superior a
way. My reading is more philosophical than psychological
in these days, but I have to confess that I meet no books
that come upon me with the force of revelations—& I have,
as we all have, to read so many—the immense majority—un-

2. Alfred Binet, *La Fatigue intellectuelle*, 1907.

opened. The world is getting too big. You are fortunate in living in Switzerland—you ought once to see New York! an earthquake *en permanence*. I wish never to go there again. Your friend Reverdin [3] was there at the Philosophic Association —bored, naturally, to death. He seems a very well-bred fellow but a little deficient in vivacity and made somewhat constrained by the foreign tongue. Rappard is much more a man of the world. But we like Reverdin very much. How tremendously interesting is the condition of France. Vive Briand! Vive Clemenceau! To think of court-martials abolished and Picquart Minister of War! Pure poetic justice *does* then sometimes prevail here below! Compare this french republic with that of 1793, and one sees that the pragmatic method has made progress. And now, dear Flournoy, give 1000 loving messages from both of us to yourself, to Mrs. Flournoy, to Madame Alice, to Henri, Marguerite, Ariane, and take our wishes for a happy new year.

Your ever affectionate,
Wm James

FLOURNOY TO JAMES

Geneva, March 16, 1907

My dear James,

The day after New Year's day, at the time I was sending you a simple, ordinary post-card, you were writing me a good,

3. Henri Reverdin (1880–   ) and William Emmanuel Rappard (1883–1958) were both students of Flournoy at Geneva and through his influence attended Harvard, both being members of the last course which James taught. Reverdin was professor of Philosophy at Geneva from 1919 until his retirement in 1956. Rappard taught at both Harvard and Geneva where he was also for many years director of the Institute of Higher International Studies. He was active in many public affairs also, particularly the International Red Cross and the League of Nations.

long, affectionate, and interesting letter—for which I have not
yet thanked you! For more than two months it has lain on
my table, and I have felt daily remorse for my laziness. Today,
when I start my vacation, it is finally possible to take up my
pen. I have had a very busy winter; in addition to my University courses, I had to give a good many lectures which
were requested of me here and there. Among others, I gave a
series of ten talks at the Athénée before our most select Genevese public; your son Billy was to send you a program;
but as he has perhaps forgotten, I am sending one to you:
you will see that you came into them much more in reality
than appears on the program, because you supplied the subject of three or more of the lectures. And I realized that it
would not have been too much to devote even double that
time to you. In other words, I have lived very much with
you in thought this winter,—and with all your publications,
which I have reread; if telepathy were really capable of being
put to use, you would have been overwhelmed with my questions and reflections; I almost wrote to you on this or that
point, on many occasions, but the increasing difficulty of writing and drafting and the delays caused by the distance always
held me back; and the announcement of the volume which
you have on the way and which will appear this autumn, you
tell me, has helped me to be patient. I quite understand your
being enthusiastic over the power and richness of the pragmatic method, which you handle as its genuine creator; for
the worthy Peirce [4] does not appear to me to have been more
than the starting push, the immediate cause, which would

4. Charles Sanders Peirce (1839–1914) was an intimate friend
of James from Harvard student days. It was he, actually, who
introduced the principle of pragmatism into philosophy, defining his
theory in the *Popular Science Monthly*, January, 1878. He originated
the word as well as the idea, though he later changed the name to
pragmaticism. See Perry, *William James*, Vol. I, Ch. XXXII, and
Vol. II, Ch. LXX and LXXVI.

have had no result without the real motive force, the power to convert potentiality into reality, which you have supplied entirely. And what would remain of the fragmentary pragmatist tendencies conceived spontaneously by Bergson, Boutroux,[5] Mach, etc., if you, together with Dewey and Schiller, had not provided them with a kind of nuclear center and coordination! I am very anxious to see your book, and who knows if, in case you should not find a French translator, I might not propose that I should make the venture? Because, from even the little that my dull brain and very weak philosophical faculties allow me to understand of pragmatism, of radical empiricism, of tychism, and of "pure experience," it has completely won me over, and it seems to me that I, myself, would have discovered it all if only I had had the grain of genius necessary to bring out clearly so many things vaguely and confusedly felt in the course of my life!

I began this week to read starting at the end (the chapter on Liberty), Schiller's new volume (Studies in Humanism), and I am enjoying it greatly. The case which you make for Binet's work (on soul and body, etc.) makes me very pleased for him, for I am much in sympathy with him personally, because of his modesty, his kindness, and his candor;—but I must acknowledge that these writings, which please you, seemed to me a farrago of nonsense and that goes for the fundamental ideas and their presentation! I must add that as little as I appreciate Binet and his *philosophical* writings, I value him very greatly as an *observer* and an *experimenter*. And when I think of the low opinion you often express for

5. Etienne Emile Marie Boutroux (1845–1921), whom James corresponded with but didn't meet until 1908, was professor of philosophy at the Sorbonne, 1888–1902, and from 1902 until his death was director of the Thiers Foundation in Paris. See Perry, *William James*, II, 560–69. As has been noted, Boutroux wrote the Preface to Abauzit's translation of *The Varieties of Religious Experience*.

the philosophical movement of the *Journal* of [J. E.] *Wood-bridge*—which I sometimes read, always with lively interest, and which I find extremely suggestive and lively—I conclude that it is very difficult to judge and understand those who are the closest to us in language and nationality!—

The news that you had given up your teaching, in order to devote yourself to writing, pleased me greatly; and we were very much interested in a letter from Reverdin to my son-in-law Werner, telling of your last lecture at Harvard,[6] discourses of the students, etc.

I am happy, though regretting it for the students at Harvard, about this decision, which will, I hope, contribute greatly to the improvement of your health and to your joie de vivre, to publish and to watch the success of your work and your ideas. (In our country, the enlightened public is each day becoming better acquainted with your thought; and the translation of your *Talks to Teachers* by [Justin] *Pidoux,* following so soon after the *Expérience religieuse* by *Abauzit,* is having a most favorable effect upon the diffusion of your ideas in French-speaking Switzerland. There is, moreover, a clear and odd affinity between our temperament and your mental processes generally: our public finds in you something that it needs and which it finds neither in French nor in German philosophers of the present day.)

Now and then we have good news of your son Billy from the Naville family. He also wrote a very nice letter to my wife several weeks ago. I hope that Mrs. James and your whole family spent a good winter. Here—nothing in particular. Alice

6. Concerning this last lecture, James's son Henry wrote: "The last meeting of his class ended in a way for which he was quite un-prepared. His undergraduate students presented him with a silver loving-cup, the graduate students and assistants with an inkwell. There were a couple of short speeches, and words were spoken by which he was very much moved. Unfortunately there was no record of what was said." *Letters* II, 220–21.

and her husband make a very attractive little home, which is a great source of joy to us and of diversion for my wife. Henri passed his second "propedeutique" (anatomy, physiology) very well last week and left yesterday for an expedition, with Professor Chodat (botanist) and some fifteen students, to Spain, Algeciras, and Tangier. After his return, I shall probably go to the Italian Lakes with my wife to recover from the fatigue of the winter.—We are increasingly deluged with Russians of all political hues; unhappily, this Slavic race is not very attractive to our own, and I have the impression that our country, for these foreigners, is not playing the civilizing and educational role that it should; Geneva is failing in its mission as far as that goes!—Adieu, my dear James. Thanks for all that you are doing for Reverdin and Rappard. Endless affectionate good wishes from us all. Believe me, your always devoted

Th. Flournoy

P. S. After 15 months of absolute silence, Lutoslawski informed me some days ago that he would be passing through Geneva at the beginning of April. He is in Poland, without other details!

JAMES TO FLOURNOY

95 Irving St.
Cambridge, Mass.
March 26, 1907

Dear Flournoy

Your dilectissime letter of the 16th. arrived this morning and I must scribble a word of reply. That's the way to write to a man! Caress him! flatter him! tell him that all Switzerland is hanging on his lips! You have made me really *happy* for at least 24 hours! My dry and business like compatriots never write letters like that. They write about themselves—you write about *me*. You know the definition of an egotist: "a person who insists on talking about *him*self, when you want to talk about *your*self."—

Reverdin has told me of the success of your lectures on pragmatism, and if you have been communing in spirit with me this winter, so have I with you. I have grown more and more deeply into pragmatism, and I rejoice immensely to hear you say, "je m'y sens tout gagné." It is absolutely the only philosophy with *no* humbug in it, and I am certain that it is *your* philosophy. Have you read Papini's article in the February *Leonardo*? [7] That seems to me really splendid. You say that my ideas have formed the real *centre de ralliement* of the p-g-st tendencies. To me it is the youthful and *empanaché* Papini who has best put himself at the centre of equilibrium whence all the motor tendencies start. He (and Schiller!) has given me great confidence & courage. I shall dedicate my book, however, to the memory of J. S. Mill. I hope that you are careful to distinguish in my own work between the pragmatism and the "radical empiricism" (conception de conscience, & etc.) which to my own mind have no necessary connexion with each other. My first proofs came in this morning, along with your letter, and the little book ought to be out by the 1st of June. You shall have a very early copy. [8] It is exceedingly untechnical, and I can't help suspecting that it will make a real impression. Munsterberg, who hitherto has been rather pooh-poohing my thought, now after reading the lecture on truth which I sent you a while ago, says I seem to be ignorant that Kant ever wrote, Kant having already

7. Giovanni Papini (1881–1956), Italian author, editor, and philosopher, was one of the younger men whom James wanted to see at the Congress of Philosophy in Rome in 1905. The article referred to is "Crepuscolo dei filosofi," *Leonardo,* February, 1906.

8. "La Notion de Conscience," the address which James gave at the 1905 Congress in Rome and which was published in Flournoy's *Archives,* Vol. v (June, 1905), and later included in *Essays in Radical Empiricism,* 1912.

said all that I say. I regard this as a very good symptom. The third stage of opinion about a new idea, already arrived:— 1st: absurd! 2nd, trivial! 3rd, WE discovered it! I don't suppose you mean to print these lectures of yours, but I wish you would. If you would translate my lectures, what could make me happier? But, as I said apropos of the "Varieties," I hate to think of you doing that drudgery when you might be formulating your own ideas. But in one way or the other I hope you will join in the great strategic combination against the forces of rationalism and bad abstractionism. A good *coup de collier* all round, and I verily believe that a new philosophic movement will begin!—I think you mistake my attitude towards Binet. I like his absence of pretension, his sincerity, his clear exposition, & his genuine wrestling with the problem, with no abstractive philosophical prejudices to interfere. I think that some of his distinctions and articulations let in light. But I think that in the ultimate resort, he is confused, and his result a failure. His article in your Journal, I tho't *much worse* than his book. But no one can judge of a foreign *style*—you find his form displeasing for reasons that are probably too delicate for my barbarian mind in things french. I think Woodbridge's Journal highly useful & suggestive. But they write a dreadful technical jargon, and very few of them have any clear ideas, *yet!* I thank you for your congratulations on my retirement. It makes me very happy. A professor has two functions: 1) to be learned and distribute bibliographical information 2) to communicate truth. The 1st function is the essential one, officially considered. The 2nd is the only one I care for. Hitherto I have always felt like a humbug as a professor, for I am so weak in the 1st requirement. Now I can live for the second with a free conscience.—I envy you now at the Italian lakes! But good bye! I have already written you a long letter, tho' I only meant to write a line! Love to you all from

W. J.

FLOURNOY TO JAMES

Geneva, July 17, 1907

My dear James,

Here it is more than a month since I received, and read straight off, your marvelous volume on *Pragmatism* and I still have not thanked you! I do not know how the time has gone! From day to day I have wanted to write to you and I have remained caught, pounded by the inexorable machinery of daily occupations.

I had thought of undertaking the translation of your book, but I have had to give up the idea, because I lack the strength and am too tired. I hope that someone will be found to do this translation, which is certain to be highly successful, just as was Abauzit's translation of your *Expérience religieuse.* He would be eminently qualified to translate your *Pragmatism,* which is much shorter and much less difficult to translate than your previous volume. And how they need this work in French-speaking countries! What simplicity and what clarity there is in your system and your style, compared with the over-refined and farfetched speculations of the French metaphysicians!—I am thinking of Bergson and his recent volume, *L'Evolution créatrice,*[9] which is inspired by a lofty and beneficent spirit, but which in execution is singularly confused and undigested; when one tries to divest his thought of the metaphors and superb images in which it is wrapped up, one can understand nothing; it's clear enough that he wants to save liberty, individuality, moral spirituality,—but basically he hardly succeeds, for this *élan vital* which is the source of all,

9. James esteemed Bergson's book highly, considering it as marking a turning point in the history of thought. Concerning the style, he wrote to Bergson: "You may be amused at the comparison, but in finishing it I found the same after-taste remaining as after finishing *Madame Bovary,* such a flavor of persistent *euphony,* as of a rich river that never foamed or ran thin, but steadily and firmly proceeded with its banks full to the brim. . . ." (*Letters,* II, 291).

and which engenders the plurality of beings in coming up against the resistance of no one knows what, singularly resembles the unconscious Thrust of the German monists; for them too, the absolute Idea, or the unconscious Will or Force, etc., is the primordial urge, the original *jet d'eau* which breaks into small drops or divides up into finite beings; and, in Bergson's theory, it seems to me, you hardly escape any better from determinism or from fundamental monism than you do with Fichte or Schopenhauer, Hartmann, etc. It is true that what interests one about a philosopher is not what he has *succeeded* in carrying through, but what he has *aimed* at and tried to do—not what he has *proved*, but what he *believes*. And seen in this way, Bergson is very attractive and stimulating. Only I have the impression that he is not so original as many people think he is; various indications make me think that he dipped pretty freely—even before his first work, "Les Données immédiates de la conscience,"—into the "Critique philosophique," and especially into the articles which that review published, between 1880 and 1889, by a certain Will. James.—I allow myself to tell you this, because this remark was made to me spontaneously by one of my friends, an amateur philosopher who knows your writings very well and who, on reading Bergson's L'Evolution créatrice, had the impression that you had been considerably plundered! (This amateur philosopher is Monsieur L. Cellérier, banker and son of Professor Cellérier, professor of mathematics at the Geneva Academy.) Cellérier finds that all the Bergsonian theory of *Duration* and of Consciousness is only a plagiarism of your *Stream of Consciousness.*—But why are you not here so that I could chat with you, because there is no doubt my pen is more and more difficult to control as I grow older!—

Our sea voyage (Venice, Dalmatia, Corfu, Sicily, Naples) at the end of April was extremely interesting; but physically it rested us very little, my wife and me, and the weather was too cold and not very favorable. This year is the coldest we have had in twenty years; summer has hardly begun, a good month behind time. In a few days, we leave for Zermatt and Chamonix until about the end of August; I fear that we shall freeze there.—

Reverdin has returned, but I have not yet seen him.

I hope, my dear James, that you are having a good summer, and that you are thoroughly resting yourself after that fine work on Pragmatism,—before passing along to the Metaphysics of Pluralism and of Tychism! All our respects to Mrs. James and to your children. Believe me yours semper idem,

Théodore Flournoy

FLOURNOY TO JAMES

Geneva, Dec. 18, 1907

My dear James,

These lines will not reach you even in time to bring you, as well as your whole family, our very warmest good wishes for Christmas and the New Year. For a very long time, I have wanted to write to you, but I am proof of the proverb: the less one has to do, the less one does! For a great many reasons, I have taken a vacation this winter and let Claparéde take over the courses and laboratory in my place. I had hoped, once freed from three public lectures which I had already promised to give in November, and not having to prepare any courses, that I should be seized with enthusiasm for writing letters, research articles, neglected work which has dragged on several years, etc. But nothing of the kind; here it is four weeks since I gave my lectures—and I have not succeeded in taking up my pen. My *graphophobia* grows each year and reveals, in its exaggerated forms, its obviously pathological nature. I have given up all bibliographical work. I groan and stupify myself over mediocre and uninteresting old documents picked up in the course of these last few years on mediums and spiritists in Geneva, because I absolutely must get something from them, but I succeed in getting nothing but discouragement and profound boredom. Evidently the heroic

Lutoslawski is right: I should change my nature from top to bottom, eat but once in 15 days, become enthusiastic over the messianic role of Poland, etc. But I lack faith; I have too good an appetite; and the Yoga exercises, the breathing exercises, stopping up first one nostril then the other, etc., which Lutoslawski recommended to me, seem to me so very childish that I feel my good will collapses into ridicule! I content myself with practising "physical culture"—that is to say modern hygienic gymnastics (we have a fine gymnasium, quite new, in Geneva)—and I benefit greatly without resorting to fasting or the eccentricities of the Yogis; and I hope that this will result in building me up psychically. But that's enough about me; I add, in order to finish up what concerns my entourage, that we are all well, thank heavens. During the summer we spent a month at Zermatt and at Praz (near Chamonix). Henri is studying medicine at Berne and comes to see us often. Alice is expecting a baby in March. My wife is not very well, and naturally for her, as for me, sad memories of the past remain on the surface of consciousness . . . —In September, I saw the worthy Abauzit twice. He was engaged in finishing the 2nd Edition of his translation of your "*Varieties* etc*,*" and he had resolved to translate quickly your *Pragmatism;* but, as usual, he has shown no further signs of life since the reopening of his courses at the lycée; I hope, though, that he hasn't given up his good intentions, and that at Christmas he will inform me that the translation of your *Pragmatism* is well advanced. I have often heard my friend Cellérier speak of the unfortunate circumstances concerning the translation of your *Textbook;* it appears, however, that the thing is now in a good way and that Peilhaube has found, to take charge of it, hands a little less deplorable than those of this unfortunate Berthier (or rather of his students). It is surely good to hope that your Textbook, so marvelously clear and concise, will not be lamentably disfigured in French!—I hope that you have not had to suffer from this terrible financial crisis which has shaken your country and which Europe feels also. Here, Genevan finances are in a very poor way now; fraudulent bankruptcy, suicides of shady bankers, disappearance of securities, and people ruined, for the past six months this has been the sole topic of conversation in Geneva; if we have escaped until now, we have many friends who have been hit, and we are not very proud of the moral state of our financiers, and, alas, in general, about the morality of our whole population! The fact that things are even worse in the large countries which surround us is not a very heartening consolation!

I hope that you had a good summer, and that you are working with joy and with good spirits in your retirement. All our affectionate good wishes, please, to Mrs. James and the children. How is Billy's painting career getting along? Will he return to Paris? And how are your own plans for Europe coming along?

Always affectionately yours,
Théodore Flournoy

JAMES TO FLOURNOY

95 Irving St., Cambridge.
Jan. 3. 1908 [10]

Dear Flournoy—Your new-year's letter got here true to time, but made me very sorry that you still have that devilish neurasthenic low energy to complain of. Why do you write *letters,* if it comes so hard? Delectable as your letters are both in form and matter, I would gladly accept nothing but post-cards myself, if that would save you from fatigue. I saw Revd. Cox yesterday—excellent, and now somewhat heroic, man!—who said that he had also had from you a letter, and it all made me feel as if you might be taking your new year's epistolation too conscientiously. Apart from my Roberts-

10. This letter is misdated "January 2, 1908" in *Letters,* II, 300.

Hawley lymph compound injections, which still work beautifully on *me*, I have no prescription to make in your case;
but I have similar symptoms, and know how hard they are
to bear. All the while, your real *soul* (manifested by all you
write) is one of the most vigorous ones alive!

I am just back from the Am. Philosophical Association
which had a really delightful meeting at Cornell University
in the State of New York. Mostly epistemological. We are
getting to know each other and understand each other better,
and shall do so year by year. Everyone cursed my doctrine
and Schiller's about 'truth'. I think it largely is misunder-
standing, but it is also due to our having expressed our
meaning very ill. The general blanket-word pragmatism covers
so many different opinions, that it naturally arouses irritation
to see it flourished as a revolutionary flag. I am also partly
to blame here; but it was *tactically* wise to use it as a title.
Far more persons have had their attention attracted, and the
result has been that everybody has been forced to *think*. Sub-
stantially, I have nothing to alter in what I have said.

I enjoy very much not having to hurry to my lectures.
Moreover the trustees of the Carnegie Foundation for pen-
sioning teachers have accorded me their maximum pension
of 3000 dollars which is a thousand more than I have got
for teaching since 1900.

I have just read the 1st half of Fechner's Zend Avesta, a
wonderful book, by a wonderful genius.[11] He had his vision &
he knows how to discuss it, as no one's vision ever was
discussed.

---

11. Gustav Theodor Fechner (1801–1887), the German experimental psychologist and professor of physics at Leipzig, was
a strong influence on James. His *Elemente der Psychophysik*, 1850,
propounded the thesis that the bodily facts and the conscious facts
combine in one reality. *Zend-Avesta* was published in 1851, but
James read the second edition, 1901, recommending it strongly to
Bergson.

I may tell you in confidence (I don't talk of it here because my damned arteries may in the end make me give it up— for a year past I have a sort of angina when I make efforts) that I have accepted an invitation to give eight public lectures at Oxford next May. I was ashamed to refuse; but the work of preparing them will be hard (the title is "the present situation in philosophy") [12] and they doom me to relapse into the "popular lecture" form just as I thought I had done with it forever. (What I wished to write this winter was something ultra dry in form, impersonal and exact.) I find that my free and easy & personal way of writing, especially in "Pragmatism" has made me an object of loathing to many respectable academic minds, and I am rather tired of awakening that feeling, which more popular lecturing on my part will probably destine me to increase.

Lutoslawski came and went, and seems now very well lodged in California. His Boston lectures were weak and amateurish (history of Poland) and altogether, tho his *energies* may have increased and grown more continuous, his mind seems to me to have deteriorated, Egotism & silliness are all! He got no Yoga pupils here. Alice constantly reproaches me for having "introduced" him to you. I tell her that as docent in your University, he was sure to get to know you anyhow.

You express concern about our financial crash, but it seems to have revealed almost no rottenness, being a simple tightness of money. So many people had enlarged their business and borrowed to do so, that when the word "pay!" went out to everyone at once, the banks couldn't get their dues quickly enough to avoid suspending cash payments. Things appear to be mending very rapidly. I am sorry that the *haute finance* of Geneva is not better! On the whole, our American corruption is not so much worse than the European in quantity, and

12. These lectures were published as *A Pluralistic Universe*, 1909.

better in quality, I am sure. I saw the great John D. Rockefeller last Sunday. He *gave away* 42 million dollars during
1907. I have been with Strong who goes to Rome this month.
Good, truthloving man! & very penetrating mind. I think he
will write a great book. We greatly enjoyed seeing your friend
Schwarz, the teacher. A fine fellow who will, I hope, succeed.
A happy new year to you now, dear Flournoy, and loving
regards from us all to you all.

Yours as ever,
Wm James

FLOURNOY TO JAMES

Geneva, April 21, 1908

My dear James:

I have followed your advice not to tire myself with correspondence only too well, seeing that I have not yet thanked
you for your good and very interesting letter at the beginning of the year and the *printed matter* which followed it,
and I shall not write you at length today! But I want, all the
same, to wish you bon voyage and to tell you how much we
rejoice in the prospect of seeing you as well as your family.
For I think that you are going to carry out your project of
coming in May to give your lectures in England, and afterwards to breathe Swiss air. I hope that this air will be warmed
up again by that time, because for the moment it is snowing
and we are freezing. Spring, which made an appearance in
March, has given place to winter again and it was necessary
to start the heater again on Easter Sunday! I dream of going
to live, like Stevenson, on some isle in the Pacific, with eternal
spring, bananas, no University, psychology, books, telephone,
nor ink—only your visit and not that of Lutoslawski. I had
one yesterday from Abauzit. He played dead all winter then
suddenly came alive at Easter vacation, with a spirit and
loquacity which have my admiration and envy (sometimes

also my despair when this lasts for many consecutive hours);
nevertheless, one pities the poor boy from the family point
of view. He was engaged in the autumn to a young woman
who was recommended to him and wore himself out all winter
going to see her each week, five hours by train from Alais,
where he gives lessons at the Lycée, and discovered, finally,
that she was really too neurasthenic and that he must renounce her! He then broke off, not without torment and pain
not so long ago. Yesterday he went to Lausanne to see his
little girl, who is now six years old and is in very bad health,
and is in a pension at the home of the Ceresole family, because
her mother cannot care for her, being herself too nervous and
for some time in a clinic!—but none of this detracts from
Abauzit's energy. He is going to translate your *Pragmatism*
this summer, if nothing happens to interfere with his project.

My daughter Alice Werner and her baby are perfectly well,
and this little family of hers is a great joy to us; they have
just bought a little piece of ground in order to construct a
villa to their liking. My wife has times of great fatigue and
has much trouble facing the exigencies of life. She is going
to spend a few days in Munich where Henri will attend the
summer session; he was at Berne this winter and we enjoy
very much having him with us during vacation. Marguerite
is in Paris staying with friends for a few weeks; The two
youngest children are full of life. As for me, I am withering
and growing mouldy at one and the same time over old notes
about uninteresting *mediums,* and I can't succeed in finding
anything of value; I am disgusted, disheartened, and on edge.
They nominated me "professeur ordinaire" a little while ago,
and I hope to have them finally nominate Claparède professor, who certainly deserves it, since the amount of work he
does is frightening. I have begun to read the *works of* Münsterberg, but they are over-refined for my taste. Pragmatism
means more to me. Following the separation of the Church
and State voted last year, the Church of Geneva is occupied

in trying to reconstitute itself, but it is a terrible mess; and, some days ago, I gave a public lecture in order to try to bring about a little unity and conciliation between the dissident parties. It was the 1st time (and without doubt the last) that I have intervened in the public life of my country! I had more success than I had hoped for, but that doesn't say much. We shall soon know if Genevan Protestantism is capable of living, or not, without State support.

A thousand good wishes from all of us to all of you—and we shall see you soon, I hope. Bon voyage!

As ever yours,

Th. Flournoy

P.S.   I hope the terrible fire in Boston did not affect any of your relations.

JAMES TO FLOURNOY

Lamb House, Rye, England

Aug. 9. 08

Dear Flournoy, I can't make out from my wife's letters whether she has seen you face to face, or only heard accounts of you from Madame Flournoy. She reports you very tired from the "Congress"—but I don't know what congress has been meeting at Geneva just now. I don't suppose that you will go to the philosophical congress at Heidelberg—I certainly shall not. I doubt whether philosophers will gain as much by talking with each other as other classes of *gelehrten* do. One needs to *fréquenter* a colleague daily for a month before one can *begin* to understand him. It seems to me that the collective life of philosophers is little more than an organization of misunderstandings. I gave 8 lectures at Oxford, but besides Schiller and one other tutor, only 2 persons ever *mentioned* them to me, and those were the 2 heads of Manchester College by whom I had been invited. Philosophical work seems to me to go on in silence and in print exclusively. You will have heard (either directly or indirectly) from my wife of my reasons for not accompanying them to Geneva. I have been for more than 3 weeks now at my brother's, and am much better for the simplification. I am very sorry not to have met with you, but I think I took the prudent course in staying away. I have just read Miss Johnson's report in the last S. P. R. Proceedings and a good bit of the proofs of Piddington's on cross correspondences between Mrs. Piper, Mrs. Verrall, and Mrs. Holland, which is to appear in the next number. You will be much interested, if you can gather the philosophical energy to go through such an amount of tiresome detail. It seems to me that these reports open a new chapter in the history of automatism; and Piddington's and Johnson's ability is of the highest order. Evidently "automatism" is a word that covers an extraordinary variety of fact. I suppose that you have on the whole been gratified by the "vindication" of Eusapia at the hands of Morselli *et al.* in Italy. Physical phenomena also seem to be entering upon a new phase in their history. Well, I will stop[;] this is only a word of greeting and regret at not seeing you. I got your letter of many weeks ago when we were at Oxford. Don't take the trouble to *write* now—my wife will bring me all the news of you and your family, and will have given you all mine. Your ever affectionate,

W. J.

Love to Madame Fl. & all the young ones, too, please.

JAMES TO FLOURNOY

Charing Cross Hotel [London]
Sept. 16, 1908

Dear Flournoy,

I should have written you before now to tell how happy the Flournoy's rendered my wife & daughter, and a little of what the latter have done since leaving Switzerland. I met them at Antwerp and we spent a delightful fortnight in Belgium and Holland, seeing the towns, and the pictures. What a marvelous school of painting, and how splendidly one can see the whole evolution of it brought together in those various galleries. Such realism and such technical perfection—I lump the flemish and the dutch into one.

We are not going to sail till October sixth. Altho' I pine for my own occupations & habits and have been ready to go back any time in the past 2 months, the wife and daughter, who seem to be of the same age in that respect, are still insatiable for sight seeing, and moreover our boy must be placed at Oxford, and our original date of the 22nd is too early for that.

I have had an enthusiastic account from Schiller of the interest shown in "pragmatism" at Heidelberg. I doubt whether he saw things in a *siccum lumen*—he is so enthusiastic himself. Nevertheless the truth is bound to prevail *some* time even in Germany, and I feel absolutely confident (as I never felt before about anything!) that my account of "truth" (which is the centre of pragmatism) is *true*.

Immediately on my return, I am going to send you a bottle of the "Roberts-Hawley lymph-compound" for hypodermic use, avec la prière de vous en servir consciencieusement pendant au moins 4 semaines. It grieved me very much to hear from my wife so poor an account of your neural condition. The symptoms are so like mine, and in general your mentality and mine are so similar, that I can't help suspecting and even hoping that this remedy may have analogous effects. I have had now an eight years experience of it and the results are perfectly uniform. In a week all symptoms begin to improve, fatigue diminishes, sleep improves, digestion ditto, courage & aggressiveness replace pusillanimity etc, etc. All without any positive stimulation. If the treatment is stopped after a short time, (2 or 3 weeks) the benefit gradually fades away. But if a full six weeks course be taken the good effects last three months more. I think that I have owed my power to do effective work in the past 7 years essentially to my semiannual dosage with this remedy. And, as aforesaid, I pray you, notwithstanding your probable inertia & scepticism, to give it a fair trial, *for my sake!!*

Murder! how I long to get home!

With fondest regards, not only to yourself, but to Madame Flournoy and all the young people, I am always my dear Flournoy,

Affectionately yours,
Wm James

FLOURNOY TO JAMES

Florissant, Geneva
Sept. 20, 1908

My dear James:

Your very interesting and affectionate letter revived my smarting remorse for not having quickly replied when you wrote me in August. I let the days pass and then I knew you were in Holland and I did not have your address. We were immensely pleased to see Mrs. James, and your charming daughter so gracious and full of health. It was a keen regret for us not to be able to profit more from their presence in Geneva—we had to contend with the competition of dressmakers and milliners on their side,—and, on ours, against the perpetual invasion of life by a thousand insignificant things; my wife never tires of listening to Mrs. James's stories,—she comes very near to worshipping her. I can't tell you how much we regretted your absence,—but I understand so well why you remained in quiet retreat at your brother's after your fatigues of Oxford!—I sympathize with your impatience to get back "home;" [13] travel is good, but it shouldn't last too long. I thank you very much for your concern over my health and for wanting to send me a bottle of your marvelous lymph. It would be ungracious of me not to comply, and I shall submit

13. In English in the original letter.

myself with obedience and an angelic patience to your prescriptions, without a skeptical attitude. If you could add in
the solution of water from the Fountain of Youth in a pinch of
your genius for writing (it would be passing lawful bound-
aries to ask also for a grain of your power of thought) that
would suit me perfectly.

My misfortunes spring from a growing incapacity,—at which
my wife herself, who sees it close to, is horrified—to write
articles. I lack something in the graphic centers. As soon as
I give up writing, I get along admirably. I always sleep very
well and I have an excellent appetite;—oral lectures give me
very little trouble, and I had much rather give thirty hours
of courses than write six pages. In order to put into written
form an hour's lecture which I have already given, it is necessary for me to work for an entire month for ten or twelve
hours per day. $\dfrac{\text{Speaking}}{\text{Writing}} = \dfrac{1}{300,}$ such would be my formula
of effort or of suffering. I fear that your specialist's lymph
cannot change this proportion, evidently constitutional with
me;—and if it only augments my total production, then I shall
really become a much too loquacious, verbose, and cheap
lecturer, which I already tend too much to be. I leave you
to judge.—I have had news of the Congress at Heidelberg
only through [Lorenzo M.] Billia, the philosopher from
Turin, who passed through Geneva the day before yesterday.
He found the Congress very tedious, much too German and
not international; he doesn't seem to know very well what
Pragmatism is. He knows only the young compatriots of the
late *Leonardo,* whom (except for Papini) he treats as *poseurs.*
You will see from this that this excellent man is not an excellent judge in these matters. I hope soon to have other more
serious echoes of the Congress, and it will interest me to see
if they tally with the enthusiastic opinion of Mr. Schiller.

We have often thought of you, and we followed in imagination Mrs. James on her trip back to you. I am very pleased

that your voyage in Belgium and Holland was so satisfactory. My wife and I were there 22 years ago, in a glorious September, and we cherish perfect memories of the cities, the museums, and the country. The abundant herds of cattle grazing in the misty light of the rich meadows; a perfume of flowers and of damp earth, floating in the atmosphere; we used to spend our mornings in the company of Rembrandt, Potter, Fr. Hals and Ruysdäel, and the afternoons wandering here and there along the canals or on the dunes; one would still meet a few natives, escaped from the paintings of Teniers, in the little secluded villages, Katuryck or Rhine, Leyde, Brock, Delft, Muyden, etc; and reading on the spot from *Maitres d'autre-fois* by Fromentin, completed our enchantment. We should like very much to return. My wife returned yesterday from Munich, where she escorted Hélène and left her in the best of circumstances for the winter. Henri recovers slowly from an accident of three weeks ago in military service; he fell on a bottle fragment and was seriously wounded on his right hand, cutting the flexor tendon of the thumb; but he has been cared for to perfection in the Lausanne hospital and is beginning to get back a little the use of his hand. One hopes that eventually the thumb will return to normal.

I have been receiving for some months the *Hibbert Journal*—which we had not yet had in Geneva—and I have read in it your article on Pluralism, and will be very glad to read the following ones. I think poor Abauzit, who went through here 10 days ago, and who seemed to me much better, has about decided to translate your *Pragmatism*.—Have a good trip, my dear James. All our affectionate good wishes to Mrs. James and kindest regards to your children. Drop me a card from time to time in order to give me news of yourself. I wish you a happy ending to your stay in England, and a good crossing. I am glad for you that you are returning home.

As ever yours,
Th. Flournoy

JAMES TO FLOURNOY

Charing Cross Hotel [London]

Oct. 4, 1908

Dear Flournoy—I got your delightful letter duly 2 weeks ago, or more. I always have a bad conscience on receiving a letter from you, because I feel as if I *forced* you to write it, and I know too well by your own confessions (as well as by my own far less extreme experience of reluctance to write) what a nuisance and an effort letters are apt to be. But no matter! this letter of yours was a good one indeed. First of all I take note of your willingness to try my lymph-extract, which I will have sent to you immediately on my return, and which you promise to inject twice a day for 4 weeks, before getting discouraged. With me, effects begin already at the end of the first week. I am afraid that your *agraphia* (or whatever you may call it) may prove hard to change, for it seems to be a congenital idiosyncracy of character rather than a neurasthenic symptom. But your discouragement and feeling of impossibility, especially social impossibility, ought to yield. Mine yield, most beautifully. But enough of pathology—let me give some account of ourselves. We sail from Liverpool the day after tomorrow, and tomorrow will be a busy day winding up our affairs and making some last purchases of small things. Alice has an insatiable desire (as Mme. Flournoy may have noticed at Geneva) to increase her possessions, whilst I, like an American Tolstoy, wish to diminish them. The most convenient arrangement for a Tolstoy is to have an anti-Tolstoyan wife to "run the house" for him. We have been for 3 days in Devonshire, and for 4 days at Oxford previous to that. Extraordinary warm summer weather, with exquisite atmospheric effects. I am extremely glad to leave England with my last optical images so beautiful. In any case the harmony and softness of the landscape of rural England probably excels everything in the world in that line. At Oxford I saw McDou-

gall & Schiller quite intimately, also Schiller's friend, Capt.
Knox, who retired from the army, lives at Grindelwald, and
is an extremely acute mind, and fine character, I should think.
He is a militant "pragmatist." Before that I spent 3 days at
Cambridge, where again I saw James Ward intimately. I
prophesy that if he gets his health again (after a prostatic
operation, alas!) he will become also a militant pluralist of
some sort. I think he has worked out his original monistic-
theistic vein and is steering straight towards a "critical point"
where the umbrella will turn inside out, and not go back.
I hope so! I made the acquaintance of Boutroux here last
week. He came to the "Moral education Congress" where he
made a very fine address. I find him very *simpatico*. But the
best of all these meetings has been one of three hours this
very morning with Bergson, who is here visiting his relatives.
So modest and unpretending a man, but such a genius intellectually! We talked very easily together, or rather *he* talked
easily, for he talked much more than I did, and altho I can't
say that I follow the folds of his system much more clearly
than I did before, he has made some points much plainer.
I have the strongest suspicions that the tendency which he
has brought to a focus will end by prevailing, and that the
present epoch will be a sort of turning point in the history
of philosophy. So many things converge towards an anti-
rationalistic crystallization. Qui vivra verra!

I am very glad indeed to go on board ship. For two months
I have been more than ready to get back to my own habits,
my own library & writing table and bed, but Alice who seems
to grow younger and more frivolous, and Peggy, who wanted
to see more "sights" were inexorable, so I stayed to keep them
company. But waiting & dangling, and dawdling are poor
occupations for a man with work of his own to do, and very
few years left to do it in.

Sur ce, dear Flournoy, I wish you, and all of you, a pros-

perous and healthy, and resultful winter, and am with old
time affection,

> your ever faithful friend,
> Wm James

If the duty of writing weights so heavily on you, why obey
it? Why, for example, write any more book reviews? I absolutely refuse to, and find that one great alleviation.

JAMES TO FLOURNOY

> 95 Irving St., Cambridge.
> Nov. 18, 08

Dear Flournoy,

I caused to be sent to you a week ago, a supply of the
Roberts-Hawley lymph Compound. Possibly a few hints from
my own experience as to the routine of injection may save
you trouble.

I have never had *any tendency whatever* to the production
of callosities or abscesses after the *piqure,* and I fancy that
the material is not liable to produce such accidents.

The directions advise keeping the bottle aseptic by a rubber
cap. This doesn't seem very safe, for it has to be handled so.
I simply keep it on a saucer, with a cup or glass turned over
it, in a dark place not exposed to dust, and I find this sufficient.

I boil the syringe only once a day, leaving it under water,
in the little covered saucepan which I use for the purpose.

I find an anatomical forceps very convenient for handling
the syringe, cotton, etc.

I keep the alcohol used for disinfecting purposes in a wide-
mouthed bottle, and pour it into a cup, for washing fingers,
skin etc.

You will yourself find the most convenient places for injecting. The syringe should be plunged in, perpendicularly
to the surface. The directions recommend the glutaei and the
muscles beside the spine, both of which require an assistant.

I, making the injections myself, have found the best places to be the biceps; certain chosen places on the thighs; the soft parts behind and below the great trochanter; and, when one knee is crossed over the other, the soft part (tensor vaginae femoris, etc?) that forms itself in front of the trochanter and the crest of the ilium. You will perhaps find other places—I have never tried the abdominal walls!!

As I told you, I always begin to get effects within 10 days—increase of courage, loss of fatigue, activity of bowels, better sleep. It reaches its maximum in about 4 weeks, but quickly goes back unless I keep on a couple of weeks longer, when it holds good for many weeks succeeding.

Ecco! Your salvation now depends no longer on me, but on yourself!! Of course the lymph often fails, not finding the patient of the proper idiosyncrasy—I most earnestly hope and pray that you may be one of the right quality! If so, you will thank me eternally.

I saw last night the patient of Morton Prince's [14] whose very interesting autobiography is now appearing in the J. of Abn. Psych. She is a very intelligent woman, regards herself now as quite well. Prince bro't back the B phase by hypnotizing C, and calling "B" to come. It is a very complex case. The ordinary objection is that these distinct "personalities" have been organized & solidified by the operators suggestions. Suppose they have—what then? The point that is psychologically interesting is not how they arose, but the fact that a human being can continue to exist in that strangely divided shape.

We were greatly amused the other day by a post-card from Lutoslawski saying that you had refused to see him because you didn't wish to be interrupted in some Yoga exercises which you were practising. L. has degenerated very much,

14. Morton Prince (1854–1929) was Professor of Neurology in the Medical School of Tufts College; he became editor of the *Journal of Abnormal Psychology* in 1906.

morally, I think. His conceit and egotism are boundless. Good bye, dear Flournoy, and may good fortune attend you. If you write to me write a post-card only!

Your affectionate
W. J.

FLOURNOY TO JAMES

Florissant, Geneva
Nov. 30, 1908

My dear James:

This letter has two purposes.—first to thank you for all the trouble you have taken on my behalf,—the very detailed explanations enclosed in your letter of yesterday on the way of using the lymph—and for having sent me this precious liquid. Some days ago I received a letter from Dr. Hawley informing me that two bottles had been sent—then some brochures on the subject—but the bottles themselves have not yet arrived, having been put on a different ship from the letters. As soon as they come I shall let you know, and I shall follow your prescriptions like a good, obedient child, *for the love of you;* and you will not be offended if I attribute the good results which will surely follow to the autosuggestion springing from this feeling of gratitude to you and of confidence in your wisdom,—rather than to the lymph itself!

My second reason for writing to you today is to recommend to you the Abbé Baudin, the translator of your *Textbook,* who would like to write to you asking for some information and clarification, and who, it seems, feels some embarrassment about disturbing you for that. My friend [Lucien] Cellérier— in whose judgment and good sense I have great confidence— values greatly this Monsieur Baudin, whom he has seen several times during recent months in Paris, and he has often told me that the translation of your *Textbook,* after so many unhappy vicissitudes, has finally fallen into good hands and at last has a good chance of succeeding. Now, he has come back from Paris, where he saw Monsieur Baudin again; but, after all, it is much simpler to send you Cellérier's letter, itself. I have already replied by telephone that Baudin only has to write to you, and that I was certain that you would reply to him with your usual kindness. Still, to clear my conscience, I recommend him to you warmly. I actually received a card from Lutoslawski, dated from *Lugano,* informing me that if I was in Geneva he would gladly pay me a visit. I replied that I was taking a rest and isolation cure, that I was not receiving visitors, and requested him, at this time, not to make a detour through Geneva in order to see me. It seems that, even so, he did come to Geneva, and rang my doorbell in order to leave a brochure on Poland, with some lines of dedication; but he did not ask to see me, nor did he give his name or address. If I had known where to locate him, I certainly should have seen him since he was in Geneva. On the other hand, I am glad, both for my wife and myself, to have escaped him this time!

I have begun my courses again, which give me little trouble;— but as for writing, that goes no better, and I have decided to try no more. The dull, stupid book which I hoped would be finished 6 months ago will drag on indefinitely. It interests me very much to know that you have verified the existence of the case of Morton *Prince*—whose incredible autobiography I read a few days ago in the issue which had just arrived. It is only in America that one sees such things or takes note of them!—As you tell me nothing of your health or of your family, I conclude that "no news is good news" and I wish you all a good winter, as do we all. I read with admiration your article on the *Method of Hegel* in the last issue of the Hibbert Journal. Enjoy in peace your freedom and your endless holidays, and believe me, my dear James,

> Your semper idem
>
> Th. Flournoy

JAMES TO FLOURNOY

95 Irving St., Cambridge.

March 22. 09

Dear Flournoy,

I am being bombarded by notices of the great things to be done at Geneva next Summer, and with invitations to take part. A superb invitation from the rector, for the anniversary fête, with my name caligraphed upon it as never before in the history of the world; an appeal from the Committee of former students to collect signatures to an address, & subscriptions to a Jubilee foundation (I seem myself to be the only American student before my son William who ever sat on the sacred benches of the Geneva lecture rooms—at least I know of no other names); an enthusiastic invitation to a Zofingian celebration, and *anderes mehr*. On general principles I should like to come, but crowds do me no good, and if I did come it would only be as a pretext for seeing *you*. I admire very much the careful consideration which you and your colleagues have given to the program of the Congress of psychologists, and the absence of pedantry which you have shown. I hope that the results will justify your pains. It seems very difficult to make the "communication" element satisfactory at any of these large gatherings, yet communications and discussions there must be, for the social meeting, which seems to be really the serious part of the affair, to take place at all. You can have no truth without some fiction to support it!

I heard through Mrs. Flournoy some weeks ago, that you were heroically injecting the "lymph-compound," but with no results *so far*. Not hearing from you, I imagine, my dear friend, that the experiment has failed. If so I am very sorry to have been the cause of inflicting on you so troublesome a procedure. The good done to me by it has been so *sovereign*—there is no other word—that I had similar hopes for you, and thought it my duty to persecute you. But no persecution is as bad as the kind of medical persecution with remedies. I can only

beg you for absolution, in view of my good intention. I know
you must often have cursed my name, but I ask you now to
take the Curses back. I am myself undergoing an interminable
cure for my pre-cordial anguish, which forbids the slightest
exertion, but so far with no positive results! Nevertheless,
having no lecturing to do, I manage to keep up a little
trickle of work, of which I hope in a few days to send you
some examples.—I must stop here, for I am called away,

Yours affectionately

Wm James

FLOURNOY TO JAMES

Geneva, April 1, 1909

My dear James:

Your good letter comes as I return from Paris, where I spent
several days in order to give two request lectures, one on
Religious Psychology and the other on *Spirits and Mediums.*
Several times I wanted to write you from the capital, but each
time something came up to prevent it, in that feverish and
mixed-up life one leads, particularly when one is in Paris
for only a short time. The, to me, terrifying perspective of
this expedition to Paris and of the lectures has obsessed, depressed, paralyzed, inhibited, and crushed me all through
this wretched winter and this is what prevented me from
writing you sooner, in spite of my wish to do so; my courses
suffered from it, my correspondence *überhaupt* so puny
stopped entirely, my disposition turned sour over it, my wife
and children suffered the consequences of it and certainly
this unfavorable psychic disposition has also prevented me
from feeling all the good effects which Dr. Hawley's lymph
would have been able to bring about in me under other circumstances. But evidently my temperament is not particularly sensitive to this medication. I have earnestly followed
your prescriptions, and used up your two bottles to the last

drop; the two injections per day, for more than four weeks, have not caused me any inconvenience or produced any abscess or inflammation;—but neither have I felt any great effect; after about twelve days I did have a period when it seemed to me—and to my family as well—that I was more lively, a bit excited, sleeping less (for I always sleep too much, as much as ten or twelve hours out of 24 in the winter), taking things more cheerfully; but this phase of improvement, actually not very distinct, only lasted eight or ten days, and I fell back to my usual level before I had even finished the series of injections, which had no further noticeable effect. During this transitory period of improvement, I did not, moreover, have less trouble writing and working than the rest of the time. The lymph doesn't seem to have the miraculous power of changing the normal temperament of the individual. It is capable only of putting him up on his highest level and when that is by nature very low the result is hardly appreciable. If the lion and the ox, equally ill, take a drug which renders them equally healthy, the lion becomes a lion again, but the ox remains an ox! It is inevitable, and thus I explain to myself that the most marvelous of lymphs apparently has very different effects on different individuals. I am no less infinitely grateful to you, my dear James, for the attempt which your friendship and goodness gave me the occasion to make. My wife is witness that "I never *cursed* your name"; [15] even in admitting the lack of results. I remain profoundly touched by your affection and by what you tried to do to lift me above my naturally poor condition. If I regret the trouble and expense that this gesture cost you, I do not regret this experience, which greatly interested me and which definitely showed me that I must live with my nature and my defects, trying to make the best of things, without soothing myself with the illusion that I could ever change my skin or

15. In English in the original letter.

my mentality in this base world! Nothing prevents me, however, from attributing to the remote effect of this lymph the
fact that I have been very well for 48 hours since I returned
from Paris and am delivered from the burden of those lectures!
And as I shall be still much better, psychically and physically,
by the middle of August when I shall have *behind* me the
terrible drudgery of the *Jubilee* of the University and the
Congress of Psychology, instead of having them still ahead
of me, I shall be able to write to Dr. Hawley at that time
that this lymph was for me a sovereign remedy with delayed
effects, which restored me at the end of eight months. He
asked me to send him news about my health. I haven't done
so yet, having nothing very precise to tell him, and I shall
wait until August!

Once more, dear friend, the little success evident from the
lymph on my temperament does not diminish at all my gratitude for your kindness and sympathy, and I shall never be
able to thank you enough.

I do not need to tell you how happy we should be if the
program of the *Jubilee* [16] and the *Congress* should make you
decide to come to Geneva this summer. But I shall not be
indiscreet enough to insist, for I understand perfectly that
these festivities have little attraction for you, and in your
place I would look on them as you do. If I weren't bound
by a professional secret, I would whisper in your ear that
our Faculty of Théology, it seems, intends to present you with
the degree of "Docteur en Théologie honoris causa";—but I
fear that even the attraction of this title will not be very
tempting to you!!!!

I should like to tell you about Paris where I saw Ribot,
Richet, Janet, Boutroux, and twenty others; but I saw them

16. Jubilee was held in celebration of the 350th anniversary of
the University, which was founded by John Calvin in 1559 as the
Academy of Geneva.

only for a few minutes, and through the pessimistic spectacles that are part of me and which hinder me from judging sanely and impartially. The youngsters, Dumas, Revault, d'Allones, etc., give me the impression of being career men and humbug; the older ones seem to me to have shut themselves little by little into their small, limited circles, knowing nothing of any others. I was not successful in seeing Bergson. I always feel ill at ease, physically and mentally, in the atmosphere of Paris. I am not up to it, and I feel too strongly my unworthiness in front of so many great ones. The postal and telegraph strike, of which I saw part, gave me the impression of administrative, political, and social decay which promises us a pretty outcome before long!—It is Richet whom I find the most truly and completely *human* in all the milieux which I observed. And the most *astonishing* thing I saw was a new medium of Ochorowicz, a young Polish woman of 20, who moves objects without contact; I saw her depress a letter-scale, make a ball roll, etc., in conditions excluding all imaginable fraud and every known process. I believe that little by little, trained and brought out scientifically by Ochorowicz, she will succeed in producing phenomena which will convince the most refractory scientists. The very infantile, hypnoid personality which produces these feats has nothing, moreover, of the true spiritist, but seems to be only a state of childish retrogression in the medium herself.

My wife received a long letter from Mrs. James about twelve days ago, for which she thanks her very much, and to which she will reply soon. I send you all good wishes possible for your health and for the healing of your heart trouble. Please give our kindest regards to Mrs. James and remember us to your children.

Always your devoted,
Th. Flournoy

P.S.   Thank you for the clipping from the paper about the tragicomic accident of poor Strong. I hope that he has completely recovered. So, even the son-in-law of Rockefeller is not immune to such adventures!

FLOURNOY TO JAMES

April 30, 1909

My dear James,

I have just received your fine volume, *A Pluralistic Universe,* and I hasten to express to you all my thanks. I am very happy to read in it the new chapters which I did not see in the *Hibbert Journal.* Apropos Bergson, it always amuses me to see your admiration of his writings. It is not that I do not appreciate them and the magic of their style; but you make me think of a rich proprietor who does not even surmise all that he possesses and who falls into a swoon before jewels which a clever goldsmith has stolen from him and has simply disguised by means of a new and glittering setting. (This is between ourselves.)

Are you not coming to the Congress from the 3rd to the 7th of August? Should I urge you? Or should I tell you that we shall have among others Lutoslawski, Baldwin, Leuba, and a release of pigeons?

Théodore Flournoy

P.S. I cannot take this Congress seriously. Is it the effect of Hawley's lymph? My wife has written to Mrs. James to thank her apropos Mrs. Piper.

JAMES TO FLOURNOY

Chocorua (N.H.), June 18. '09

My dear Flournoy—You must have been wondering during all these weeks what has been the explanation of my silence. It has had two simple causes: 1st. laziness; & 2nd. uncertainty, until within a couple of days, about whether or not I was myself going to Geneva for the University jubilee. I have been strongly tempted, not only by the "doctorate of theology" which you confidently told me of (and which would have been a fertile subject of triumph over my dear friend Royce on my part, and of sarcasm on his part about academic distinctions, as well as a diverting episode generally among my friends,—I being so essentially profane a character), but by the hope of seeing you, and by the prospect of a few weeks in dear old Switzerland again. But the economical, hygienic and domestic reasons were all against the journey; so a few days ago I ceased coquetting with the idea of it, and have finally given it up. This postpones any possible meeting with you till next summer, when I think it pretty certain that Alice & I & Peggy will go to Europe again, and probably stay there for two years.

I got duly your good long letter about the failure of the "Roberts-Hawley Lymph Compound," also a later one acknowledging my "pluralistic Universe." I feel a sort of inward *Zerknirschung* at having, out of pure good will and "sense of duty," subjected one whom I love to the interminable annoyance of giving himself two of those injections daily for six weeks. I feel as if I owed you some kind of heavy reparation which some day I may perhaps be able to make. Meanwhile I know that you will harbor no malice or resentment, for human ignorance is so vast that the purest intentions lead to disaster and make victims, and you know that mine were pure. *I* have taken no injections for a year, and I think that I need some soon, having been lately in a bad condition of fatigue, so within a month I shall begin again. I trust I may be able to report to you the usual improvement of symptoms.

I have done very little work during this past winter, in spite of the complete academic leisure which I now enjoy. The reason is my cardio-arterial condition, structurally not bad, to all appearance, but functionally such as to produce violent pre-cordial pain whenever I exert myself strongly or rapidly, or whenever I get into any mental hesitation, trepidation, or flurry. Apparently it is predominantly a neurosis, but it makes me pusillanimous, and greatly abridges all my activities. When I get into the country (where I now am, visiting my brother in law Salter [17]) and life gets simplified, and I can walk as *slowly* as I like, in the midst of the verdure, I can do a good deal and even go considerable distances up hill. I don't think I'm any worse than I was last summer, and I hope still that the whole condition may improve. Alice will come up by the first of July, and we shall open our own house. The rest of the family, including Peggy, are very well.

What with the Jubilee & the Congress, dear Flournoy, I fear that your own Summer will not yield much healing repose. "Go through it like an automaton" is the best advice I can give you. I find that it is possible, on occasions of great strain, to get relief by ceasing all voluntary control. *Do* nothing, and I find that something will do itself! and not so stupidly in the eyes of outsiders as in one's own. Claparède will, I suppose, be the Chief executive officer at the Congress. It is a pleasure to see how he is rising to the top among psychologists, how large a field he covers, and with both originality and "humanity" (in the sense of the omission of the superfluous & technical, and preference for the probable[ )]. When will the Germans learn that art? I have just been reading Driesch's Gifford Lectures, vol. ii.[18] Very exact & careful, and the work of a most powerful intellect. But why lug in, as he does, all that Kantian apparatus, when the questions he treats of are real enough and important enough to be handled directly and not smothered in that opaque and artificial veil? I find the book extremely suggestive, and should like to be-

17. W. M. Salter was the husband of Mrs. James's sister. Their summer home, "The Salters' Hill-Top," was situated near Chocorua, N. H.

18. Hans Adolf Edward Driesch (1867–1941), German biologist and philosopher of the University of Heidelberg, was an advocate of "vitalism." He believed that the functions of protoplasm cannot be explained mechanically, that instincts and actions are inexplicable mechanically. His Gifford Lectures appeared as *Science and Philosophy of the Organism*, 2 vols., 1907–8.

lieve in its thesis; but I can't help suspecting that Driesch is unjust to the possibilities of purely mechanical action. Candle flames, waterfalls, eddies in streams, to say nothing of "vortex atoms," seem to perpetuate themselves & repair their injuries. You ought to receive very soon my report on Mrs. Piper's Hodgson control.[19] Some theoretic remarks I make at the end may interest you. I rejoice in the triumph of Eusapia all along the line—also in Ochorowicz's young polish medium, whom you have seen. It looks at last as if something definitive & positive were in sight.

I am correcting the proofs of a collection of what I have written on the subject of "truth"—it will appear in September under the title of "The Meaning of Truth, A Sequel to Pragmatism." It is already evident from the letters I am getting about the "Pluralistic Universe" that the book will 1), be *read;* 2), be *rejected* almost unanimously at first, and for very diverse reasons; but 3), will continue to be bought and referred to, and will end by strongly influencing english philosophy.

And now, dear Flournoy, good bye! and believe me with sincere affection for Mrs. Flournoy and the young people as well as for yourself,

yours faithfully,
Wm James

JAMES TO FLOURNOY

Chocorua, August 25. 1909

Dear Flournoy,

A notice from the Genevese Government announcing academic vote, and corroboration, of me as Docteur ès Sciences

19. The concluding pages of this report published in the *Proceeding of the Society for Psychical Research*, XXIII (1909), 1–121, contain the fullest, most analystical statement which James made on this subject. See also *Collected Essays and Reviews.*

Naturelles has just surprised me. So at your Jubilee you gave degrees *in absentia* and judged me worthy of that one! Thanks! thanks! and primarily to you. For it is a Flournoy degree, I know, and I trust that I shall not disgrace you. Not being a Doctor in Theology, I shan't be able to crow over Royce as I otherwise might; so there will be one joke less in the world! I had given up all thought of the possibility of a degree when I decided not to go in person.

I also have a card from Lutoslawski, after the Congress. He says: "Flournoy presided splendidly." I feel sure that you did so, but the accumulated strain must have been great, and you must now be greatly fatigued. Have you ever thought of an oceanic voyage and the *Kur?* Why not take passage in one of the *big* slower steamers, Red Star Line from Antwerp, Holland-America Line from Rotterdam (or any other line!) and come to New York or Boston (alone or with Mme. Flournoy) and stay with us here or at Cambridge—here if you come soon enough!—as long as you can stand it, and take the voyage home, with westerly winds, in October. It would be more of a change than you otherwise could get, and would enlarge your geographical consciousness—which is one great part of education! Think seriously of this, which my wife and I have long talked of as good for you, and *optimal* for us, and cable me "Prof. James, Cambridge, Mass." giving simply the name of steamer and date of sailing, if it be too soon for exchange of letters.

I hope that you will come—both of you, if possible, but it often is more curative to go away entirely alone. You will arrive here in cooler weather than if you came earlier, and I hope there may be rains, for the country has been going through a terrible period of drought. Love to you all!

Your affectionate,
W. J.

P. S.   Alice, to whom I have just read this, thinks it infamous in me to have suggested the possibility of your coming alone, and says that I judge you after my own likeness, being, she says, a man whose supreme happiness consists in absence from his proper wife! Be this as it may, of course *our* preference would be to see you both arrive together—you need no assurance of this.

W. J.[20]

FLOURNOY TO JAMES

Florissant, Geneva
September 4, 1909

My dear James:

I have not had the courage to write you until now; however, I must do it in sending you the funeral announcement, in order to give you some details. The companion of my life for thirty years of happiness, my beloved Marie, was taken from us two weeks ago. After the Congress of Psychology, in which she took part with much vigor and pleasure, I left by myself to take the cure at Ragaz, while she went to Gryon for a short visit at the home of her sister-in-law (the widow of Dr. Henri Burnier who was murdered in Leysin in 1896) who owns a chalet there. My wife caught cold while going up to Gryon in a terrible storm; at first she suffered from rheumatism with a high fever, then pulmonary congestion set in, to which she succumbed (due to heart failure). I was able to come from Ragaz the day before, and all our children came from Geneva. She did not suffer, except for some depression, and was not at all aware of her condition and that she was going; and we are very grateful for this, because it would have been a terrible wrench for her to leave us all. The weakness of her heart increased little by little in spite of all the help of medicine, and she gradually became drowsy, without

20. On the bottom of the original copy of this letter, Théodore Flournoy wrote that Madame Flournoy had died on August 22, 1909, three days before the letter was written. James died the following year, 1910, on August 26th.

pain. We brought her back to Florissant in her coffin, and the funeral service was held there on August 25 by our intimate friend Pastor Berguer. We were to have gone to Florence in September with our two older daughters, while Henri had military service and Ariane stayed with the Werners, and my poor wife would have enjoyed this period of vacation and rest so much after the busy and tiring summer. One must not count on anything in this tragic universe! Instead of going to Florence as a family, I will take my daughters, the day after tomorrow, to spend a few days at Sierre, to get them away from here. You can imagine our desolation, the frightful emptiness which my beloved leaves in this house which is so full of her ... The Werners have just moved into the house which they had built for themselves. Alice is expecting a second baby toward the end of the year; her little boy (who is 18 months old) was a great joy to my wife ... The dark mystery of this world envelopes us, and I need all the "Will to Believe" [21] I am capable of to resist this crushing blow and to see *beyond* this impenetrable mist. Enjoy your happiness, my dear James, while *you* are together, and may you long be spared the sorrow of earthly separation.—I know that I have your sympathy and that of Mrs. James. My wife loved you so much, both of you, and your children.

Your grieving

Théodore Flournoy

P. S. My son-in-law Werner, armed with his title of substitute for the Procurer General, has taken charge of the business of the corsets: Mme. Culey excused herself for all sorts of bad reasons (they must have been sent to St. Petersburg by mistake, with other corsets!! etc.), and finally offered to return the money which Mrs. James had paid in advance; on Werner's insistence, she has at last undertaken to make the corsets again, and to send them to you, paying half the customs charges herself, as damages for this year of delay. She

21. In English in the original letter.

must show Werner the shipping receipt when she has sent
them; she is obviously dragging it out, but Werner has her in
hand, and the hussy will finally have to do it.

FLOURNOY TO JAMES

Geneva, Sept. 6, 1909

My dear James:

I was profoundly touched by your invitation, from Mrs.
James and you, to my wife and myself to go and visit you
this autumn. Alas!! Your letter crossed with mine which I wrote
you last week... Thank you even so. I am very touched by
your precious friendship. I leave today for Sierre with Marguerite, Hélène and Ariane, for a fortnight, during which
Henri is on military service. I must do my utmost not to
burden the young people too much with my grief.

My deepest regards to you, and thanks to Mrs. James for
the letter addressed to the one for whom I mourn.

Th. Flournoy

P.S. I had nothing to do personally with your "Doctorat
honoris causa;" I merely voted, as I should for my colleagues,
on a proposition presented spontaneously by the "Bureau du
Sénat" of the University. There was no need to draw your
name to the attention of our university authorities!

JAMES TO FLOURNOY

Chocorua, Sept. 28. 09

Dear Flournoy,

We had fondly hoped that before now you might both,
accepting my half-invitation, half-suggestion, be with us in
this uncared-for nature, so different from Switzerland, and
you getting strengthened & refreshed by the change. *Dieu
dispose*, indeed! The fact that *is* never entered into our imagination! I give up all hope of you this year, unless it be for
Cambridge, where, however, the conditions of repose will be

less favorable for you. I am naturally most anxious to hear how the shock and strain have affected your condition, but I adjure you not to write until the moment of spontaneous impulse occurs, and then as briefly as you please. I am myself going down to Cambridge on the fifth of October for two days of "inauguration" ceremonies of our new president, Lawrence Lowell. Our former president Chas. W. Eliot resigned after 38 years of authority, and Lowell is a man of more varied intellectual interests, from whose administration a very good influence may be expected. There are so many rival universities in our country that advantage has to be taken of such changes to make the newspapers talk, and keep the name of Harvard in the public ear, so the occasion is to be almost as elaborate as a "Jubilee", but I shall keep as much out of it as is officially possible, and come back to Chocorua on the 8th to stay as late into October as we can, tho' probably not later than the 20th., after which the Cambridge winter will begin. It hasn't gone well with my health this summer, and beyond a little reading, I have done no work at all. I have however, succeeded during the past year in preparing a volume on the "Meaning of Truth"—already printed papers for the most part—which you will receive in a few days after getting this letter, and which I think may help to set the "pragmatic" account of knowledge in a clearer light. I will also send you a magazine article on the mediums which has just appeared, and which may divert you.[22] Eusapia P., I understand, has just signed a contract to come to New York to be at the disposition of Hereward Carrington,[23] an expert

22. "The Confidences of a 'Psychical Researcher,'" *American Magazine*, October, 1909; reprinted in *Memories and Studies*, 1911, under the title "Final Impressions of a Psychical Researcher."

23. Hereward Carrington, 1880——, was the most active of the group investigating the Italian medium. In 1909 he published *Eusapia Palladino and Her Phenomena;* he was a translator of Flournoy's *Esprits et médiums*, 1911, which appeared the same year under the title *Spiritism and Psychology*.

in mediums' tricks, and author of a book on the same, who, together with Feilding & Bagally, also experts, formed the Committee of the London S. P. R., who saw her at Naples and were absolutely converted to belief in her genuineness. She seems to be the pivot now of a revolution in public opinion from which great effects will probably flow. But she is nothing compared with Ochorowicz's young polish lady, and I should greatly like to know whether you have any positive belief about her. I shall see Eusapia, probably, but only once. After Courtier's report on Eusapia, I don't think any "investigation" here will be worth much "scientifically"—the only advantage of her coming may possibly be to get some scientific men to believe that there is really a problem. Two other cases have been reported to me lately which are worth looking up, and I shall hope to do so.

How much your interests and mine keep step with each other, dear Flournoy. "Functional psychology", and the twilight region that surrounds the clearly lighted centre of experience! Speaking of "functional" psychology, Clark University, of which Stanley Hall is president, had a little international congress the other day in honor of the 20th. year of its existence. I went there for one day in order to see what Freud was like, and met also [Carl Gustav] Yung of Zürich, who professed great esteem for you, and made a very pleasant impression. I hope that Freud and his pupils will push their ideas to their utmost limits, so that we may learn what they are. They can't fail to throw light on human nature, but I confess that he made on me personally the impression of a man obsessed by fixed ideas. I can make nothing in my own case with his dream theories, and obviously "symbolism" is a most dangerous method. A newspaper report of the Congress said that Freud had condemned the American religious therapy (which has such extensive results) as very "dangerous" because so "unscientific." Bah!

Well, it is pouring rain, and so dark that I must close.

Alice joins me, dear Flournoy, in sending you our united love, in which all your children have a share.

Ever yours,
W. J.

FLOURNOY TO JAMES

Dec. 31, 1909

My dear James:

The awful dejection in which I drag myself about and which makes every effort so difficult has made me neglect my correspondence more than ever. Nevertheless, I cannot finish the year without at least having said *thank you* for your letters which I have left unanswered, particularly for that of September 28th, so full of interesting things. Since I wrote to Mrs. James, nothing particular has happened to affect the bleak and sorrowful course of existence. Alice and her twins are well, thank God; but each time I see these babies, it makes me feel more cruelly the absence of my dearly-beloved wife, who would have found such joy in them and who would have been so helpful with them. Alas!—Alice and her husband and we all have been deeply touched by the superb gift which Mrs. James and you sent several days ago for this young family.—Thank you! We owed you so much already, and we shall never know how to show you all our gratitude! Claparède is probably going to have the medium [Francesco] Carancini come here (they say he is still better than Eusapia). I read with interest your fine article on mediums, and your book, *The Meaning of Truth;* but I have so much trouble in fixing my attention.—

All our good wishes for the health and happiness of you and all your family.

Always yours,
Th. Flournoy

95 Irving St., Cambridge.

Jan. 26. 1910

Dearest Flournoy,

Your sad little card of new year's greeting came the other day and made me feel the atmosphere of your changed life. Simultaneously came a most kind letter from your son-in-law to Alice, telling a good many details about your interior as well as about his own, so that I now feel as if I knew the facts. What a comfort Doctor Henri, now so responsible a man, must be to you in these days. Time brings everything in to *some* kind of a new equilibrium, but we feel as if the equilibrium *ought* not to be restored, in a case like yours. That is a false feeling, if yielded to. The daily life has its own rights, sovereign above the rights of the grave. I hardly know why I write this—it seems, dear Flournoy, as if I were trying to teach *you,* which of course I'm not. It is only a general reflection prompted by the general situation in which you are. I sent you the other day a characteristically impudent and shallow article on Eusapia P. (by Münsterberg), thinking it might amuse you. There is no limit to his genius for self-advertisement and superficiality. Mendacity too! He would have the readers think that Morselli, Bottazzi, Ochorowicz, Richet et al are "spiritualists," and by lugging in pragmatism (!) he tries to insinuate that I also am one.*

The winter is passing very easily here—beautiful weather on the whole. Isn't Switzerland suffering from the floods which are now ravaging France? I am feeling better than for more than a year past—the result of having given my heart a big *rest.* I know now what the indications are, and it is a great comfort. I must lead an *extremely* sedentary life, and fortunately I am becoming 'adapted' thereto. Boutroux is coming to give some lectures on the Hyde foundation in the month of March. He seems, in spite of his somewhat invalid appearance, to be a man of extraordinary ability to turn off work, and of extraordinary Schlagfertigkeit with tongue and pen.

Likewise very gleichgesinnt with myself—I expect great pleasure from their visit. Shall you ever come? I shall without
doubt go to Europe next summer, and shall of course hope to
see you.

Ever affectionately yours,
W. J.

* You will doubtless have seen Bagally's exposure of Carancini in the last S. P. R. Journal.

FLOURNOY TO JAMES

Geneva, March 15, 1910

My dear James,

I finished my University courses three days ago. There is
not the joy, alas, any more, of other years when *she* was here
to rejoice with me over being free at the end of the semester
and about the vacation. The distress of her absence flattens
all incidents, agreeable or disagreeable, under a uniform layer
of indifference and sadness. I must be thankful, however, for
having been able to face—although very badly—the exigencies
of the winter and my courses. I am taking advantage of this
moment of freedom and leisure to thank you for your affectionate letter of the end of January, as well as for the magazine
(*The Metropolitan*) containing Münsterberg's article [on Eusapia Palladino] and your fine lecture on the "Equivalent of
War." I hope that there will be someday an account of Eusapia's séances in America by Carrington or some other man
more serious than this joker Münsterberg.

It is a known fact that Eusapia cheats by every means at
her disposal when she is allowed to do so. In the seances
which I attended a dozen years ago, with Myers, at Richet's,
one of us was constantly under the table to hold her ankles;
I recall the contractions I observed all along her legs, her
calves, while the spectators indicated the production of phenomena. Fraud with the feet, which Münsterberg allowed to
take place (if indeed he didn't intentionally encourage it in

order to support his preconceived ideas) does not explain the innumerable happenings which occur when she is controlled in all 4 limbs, and the séances take place in sufficient light.—What, in retrospect, goes far to convince me of the authenticity of the phenomena which I saw produced by Eusapia (at Richet's and at Schrenck-Notzing's) are the séances which we have just had with Carancini, and which are only a vulgar imitation of Eusapia's phenomena. I attended only three séances because of my lack of spirit and my fatigue which scarcely permit me to go out evenings; but that was enough for me, and all my colleagues, Claparède, Battelli [physiologist], Yung, Guye etc., are equally unanimous in considering Carancini an out-and-out humbug; even his trance, from many indications, is counterfeited and *badly* so at that. He takes advantage of the darkness to free one of his hands, following the classic procedure, moving with the feet also, and all these phenomena can be explained easily—each one in concrete detail—by some fraudulent process. Two séances, in which he had unwillingly to agree to allow a little red light and to have his legs tied together, remained absolutely without result—to the great despair of Baron Ehrhardt, a German painter living in Rome who is a convinced admirer of Garancini and who doesn't leave him alone a moment: a fine type of sincere and enthusiastic spiritist, a victim of his own naïveté and duped by Carancini. If this Carancini does produce *real* phenomena, one must believe that the climate of Geneva paralyzes them absolutely, and he is going to set off again for Rome to renew his strength; after leaving Geneva, he was to go to Belgium and Paris to give some séances, but his failure with us seems to have taken away for the moment his desire to continue. Baron Ehrhardt, who has devoted a good portion of his fortune and his life to Spiritism, and who seems to begin to feel his blind faith in Carancini shaken, makes us really pity him: it was tragically and comically moving, at the same time, to listen to him, the other evening, beseeching and imploring "Intelligence" please to allow us one small convincing phenomenon; but nothing happened—in conditions of supervision adequate to exclude fraud. With Eusapia, in the same conditions, I had seen a number of phenomena. The two mediums are completely different.

To change the subject, a few days ago I received from the president of the *Association of Swiss Christian Students* in Lausanne (which has a reunion each autumn at St. Croix sur Yverdon) a letter saying: "Please tell us if it is true that Monsieur W. James may be coming to Switzerland; if so, tell us whether you would consent to invite him to our conference (from the 8th to the 11th of October, 1910): he might speak to us on an educational subject, for example, or on anything he wishes. It would be magnificent! provided it isn't a castle in Spain!" You enjoy a reputation without equal among our students (and all the Protestant public) in French-speaking Switzerland, and I understand the desire which these young men have to see you and hear you. I have told them that I would transmit the message to you, but they will write to you directly. I do wish so much that your health and travel plans may allow you to grant them this favor!—All my children and grandchildren are well, thank Heavens! I hope that you and yours are well also. My kindest regards to Mrs. James.

> Always devotedly yours,
> Th. Flournoy

JAMES TO FLOURNOY

> Lamb House, Rye, Sussex
> April 9. 1910

My dear Flournoy,

You will doubtless be much surprised at the above address. Alice and I arrived here the day before yesterday, learning that my brother, who has been quite ill, was very lonely and craved our society rather urgently. I was intending anyhow to go to Europe not much later than this, to get my circulatory organs patched up again at Nauheim. For a year past they have been developing in the wrong direction and it is important to do something to check the process, if possible. I got your letter (about Munsterberg, Eusapia, etc.) about a fortnight before leaving home, and I am very desirous of seeing you again. Of course from Nauheim I shall repair to Geneva, but if you could yourself come to Nauheim before that, it would be still more pleasant. The fair Marguerite might accompany you—I think she would enjoy a German Kurort for a short time.

Eusapia's visit to America has not been a success from the point of view of investigation. Poor Carrington had to promise her enormous pay, and to raise the money he had to give sittings to every idle rich person who asked for them, hoping to invite some serious experts gratis with the surplus. But the experts became suspicious of him, and 6 or 8 of them raised money elsewhere and had some sittings by themselves, which in the end ceased without producing any unanimous results. They disagreed as to methods, and made Eusapia angry, and the whole thing "fell through." Eusapia's trip to the U.S. will simply have spoiled her, and discredited everyone else. I wish that Ochorowicz's little Polish lady might be authenticated— it will be a scandal, after what he has published, if the case ends there. Eusapia's type of performance is *detestable*—if it be not fraud simulating reality, it is reality simulating fraud! Of course Münsterberg's article about her is simply infamous. The gentleman who seized her foot was a stranger to M——g, and none of the company knew what had happened till after the sitting was over, when he informed M——g and one or two others. M——g tells everybody (or gives them to believe) that this man was his employe, acting by his direction! In point of fact he was one of the guests whose payment made it possible for Carrington to invite M——g *gratis*. M——g is indeed a "fumiste," as you say.—But *basta!* enough of this painful subject! Much more pleasant is the subject of Boutroux's visit—the gentlest and most modest of philosophers, without an enemy in the world. They stayed with us for 2½ weeks and we were able to protect him from too much fatigue. *She* needed no protection, excellent wife that she is. His lectures, of which he gave 12, were exquisite for clearness, breadth, and sincerity, and I think that the book which will follow— "Contingence et Liberté"—will inevitably have success, the times being now fully ready for that way of thinking, as they were not when he pub'd his first book. I found him very easy to talk with, our ideas being so fundamentally alike.—We shall stay with my brother most of this month. We go then to Paris for a week or so, to try some high frequency electricity in the hands of one Dr. Moutier, to reduce my arterial tension if possible. Thence to Nauheim early in May. Believe me dear Flournoy with love from us both to you and all of yours,

W. J.

FLOURNOY TO JAMES

Florissant, April 18, 1910

My dear James,

I was very happy indeed to learn from your affectionate and interesting letter that you and Mrs. James are in Europe; but I was very sorry to hear of your brother's poor state of health, and of your circulation trouble which is going to make you take a new cure at Nauheim; all my good wishes that even before the cure the climate of Europe will do you good!—Your article in "The Nation" on Boutroux interested me greatly; and yesterday I read in the Débats the one by Boutroux on Harvard, and his very attractive picture of your home. That reminded me of the many times—even last autumn—

you so kindly invited us too to enjoy your delightful hospitality, which circumstances or the deficiencies of my nature
never permitted us to enjoy. My dear wife would have been
so happy to go to America once to see you!—I am very touched
by the way you urge me to go make you a visit at Nauheim,
but I dare not promise it: merely going to Lausanne costs me
such an effort! As soon as I step outside the routine of daily
occupations, I am assailed by memories, the past obsesses me.
It is now just thirty years since we were married (April 15,
1880), and six years since we lost Blanche upon returning
from Rome; there is for bereaved hearts such an irony and
such a cruel contrast in the return of spring and the shining
of the sun! For weak natures and half-failures like me, even
when they are spared material worries, it is a difficult thing
to face life; and it is in particular a practical problem, infinitely
delicate and agonizing, to blend the worship of the past which
one *cannot* and does not *want* to forget with the demands
of the present, the pressing duties of each instant; I think
that this blending is possible only by faith in the future, which
renders to the soul the serenity and the inner strength to live;
but when one is not a mystic by temperament, this faith in
the suprasensible realities of the Beyond calls for ceaseless
effort, a perpetual renewal of inner decisions which are tremendously exacting—but it is not the author of *The Will to
Believe* who needs to have these elementary banalities pointed
out!

I am now reading *The Riddles of the Sphynx* by Schiller,
which I had never read before and which interests me doubly,
for itself and as a shadow coming before the substance, or
rather as the first outline of his humanism. I learned yesterday
that the French translation of your *Pluralistic Universe* has
just been published, under another title, but I have not yet
seen the book; I shall run through it one of these days and
I hope that it is well done in good, clear French—which, alas,

is so rare! The translation of your *Psychologie* by Baudin is really as well done as possible.—All my good wishes for your health and that of Mrs. James and your brother. I shall be so happy to see you. Have a good time and a good electric cure in Paris!

> Always your devoted,
> Th. Flournoy

JAMES TO FLOURNOY

> Sufficient address:—
> Bad-Nauheim
> May 29, '10

My dear Flournoy—I have been here now for 12 days, and shall probably remain for 4 weeks more at least, after which a fortnight on your shores, and then as straight home as possible. I have a perfectly definite diagnosis (aortic enlargement as well as some mitral insufficiency) wh. perfectly explains all my symptoms—hitherto explained by "nervousness"!—and the progress of which these baths will probably check for a time. At any rate, I can now with a good conscience *vivere convenienter naturae* and not *aufreiben* myself with vain social futilities, as has to a great extent been the case hitherto. No more dinner or lunch parties for W.J! Only gleichgesinnte Menschen, or persons with whom I have some serious interests in common. And even, of *those,* no Abauzits or Lutoslawskis! I wish that I might see *you* just now; for my brother, so far, declines to come hither, and *Klammert sich an* my wife, who stays with him, and I am quite alone. I don't suppose, however, that you can easily get so far, or get away at all from the university at this time of the year. If not, the meeting is only postponed & not for long.

The baths here reduce one's strength so that my brain is unfit for writing, and I only send you this short note, *which needs no reply*, to tell you where I am. I spent 10 days in Paris (partly with Strong & partly with the Boutrouxs). I consulted Dr. Moutier there, who told me that his d'Arsonval currents could do nothing for me, for my general arterial tension was normal—just what they find here. Paris was splendid, but fatiguing. Among other things I was introduced to the Acad. d. Sc. Morales, of which you very likely have heard that I am now an associé étranger (!!) Boutroux says that Renan when he took his seat after being received at the Académie française, said: Qu'on est bien dans çe fauteuil (it is nothing but a cushioned bench with no back)! Peut-être n'y a-t-il que cela de vrai! Delicious renanesque remark! Believe me, dearest Flournoy, with the hope that you are feeling more like your ancient self than when you wrote to me last,

> yours ever affectionately,
> W. J.

FLOURNOY TO JAMES

Florissant, June 6, 1910

My dear James,

Your letter moves and grieves me greatly by informing me that your heart troubles were not merely a neurasthenic symptom but are due to an incurable *organic* lesion. Experience proves, happily, that one can reach the most advanced age with heart trouble, provided that one takes good care of oneself; and I like to think that there is perhaps something providential in this illness: it is going to oblige you, as you tell me, to renounce all tiring social affairs—and by the same means you are going, I hope, to recover the leisure and strength which will allow you a long and fruitful career as a thinker and writer. The retreat and tranquility which are thus imposed upon your body—while they are a terrible trial for an active and energetic nature like yours to endure and in this you have my profoundest sympathy!—will result in *longevity,* and a guarantee of intellectual production by you for the good of all those about you, near and far! It is thus that evil will be turned into good, in your own case—as we must believe will happen also in the cosmic processes generally!—But, alas, how many renunciations, precautions, privations are going to be exacted of you! I pity you with all my heart. May the cure at Nauheim be at least a powerful palliative for your ills!

Although I am by temperament and by actual circumstances the extreme opposite of Abauzit and Lutoslawski, my visit to Nauheim would not bring you the element of optimism and of comfort which I should wish; therefore it is fortunate that external things are preventing me from going to see you, in spite of all my longings to do so. Alice's little twins have the whooping cough. We have taken the little boy to Florissant so he will escape the contagion, and as Henri is in military service (in Geneva, fortunately) for 7 weeks, I cannot dream of leaving the house, where, without being able to replace my dear wife, I am nevertheless a support for the children. If the whooping cough is over in time, I shall take a cure at Ragatz, with Marguerite, from the 10th to the 21st of July, then return to take care of my grandchildren in August while Alice will go to the mountains for a rest. But I hope very much that in the first week of July I shall be able to see you, according to your present plans for coming to Switzerland; wherever you may be, I shall, in any case come to you, before my cure at Ragatz and your departure from Europe.—I hope that you have good news from Mrs. James, and from your brother. Two days ago, I sent you a little book of *Souvenirs* of my poor wife, in which I have taken the liberty of citing a passage from one of Mrs. James's letters. All my good wishes for your cure, my dear James,

Affectionately yours,
Th. Flournoy

Florissant, July 4, 1910

My dear James,

I was extremely touched, as were my children, by your very affectionate and sympathetic letter (including that of Mrs. James!), and I wanted to thank you sooner; but I didn't manage it! I was much troubled by the discouraging news of your health; and by your uncertainty and lack of confidence over the results of your cure at Nauheim. Since then, I have not heard anything of you; yet this is the time when, according to your plans, you counted on spending some days in our country. I hope to hear soon that your cure was completed with better results than you dared to hope,—that your organic lesions have been checked—that you are at last enjoying all the benefits of Nauheim, and that you feel as well as possible despite the state of your aorta and of your heart. I have just noticed that your intellectual activity has not slackened in recent months, since the *Hibbert Journal* of the day before yesterday, contains a study from your pen on the mysticism of [Benjamin Paul] Blood. I began to read it at once, but unfortunately my powers are so diminished and limited at the moment that I shall have to make several attempts at it. A week from today (Monday, July 11th), we plan to go, Marguerite and I, for a cure at Ragaz. But I am not giving up the prospect of meeting you somewhere, here or elsewhere; as soon as I know what you are doing, I shall arrange to see you; I can visit you at Nauheim if you are still there, or return from Ragaz to see you wherever you are, here in Geneva or elsewhere; (my cure at Ragaz is quite flexible so that without inconvenience I can interrupt it as I wish.) The whooping cough that Alice's children had is coming to an end, fortunately. In August we shall bring the three children to Florissant, while Alice goes for a rest in the Engadine with Ariane, and in September, I hope to take Henri, Hélène and Marguerite to Florence; we have been thinking of doing that for so many years; for me it will be painful every moment to be there without Marie—but one must make the effort to rise above self for the sake of the children!—I think very often of you and Mrs. James, with the ardent hope that the cure does you all the good it possibly can. Believe me, my dear James, with profound affection, always your devoted,

Th. Flournoy

JAMES TO FLOURNOY (postcard)

Hotel Beau Rivage [Geneva]
July 4th. [1910] 8 p.m.

We arrived here a couple of hours ago, and I should be paying you a visit this very night, only I feel fatigued. I propose to take a cab and be at Florissant tomorrow morning at *about* ½ past 10. Don't come here, till I have seen you alone. I have to consult you about certain things apart from my brother.

Your faithful
Wm James

JAMES TO FLOURNOY (postcard)

Hotel Beau-Rivage
July 7th. [1910]

Dear F.—I am very sorry, but I can't see you tomorrow. My dyspnoea has increased so that conversation of an interesting sort is too *lästig*. Quite done up by a visit from [Dickinson S.] Miller this morning! Tomorrow our Cousin comes from Lausanne.

The brother is having a good day, and I don't feel tragic in spite of my discomfort.

W. J.

Friday, Florissant, July 8, 1910

My dear James,

I am distressed to learn from your card that you are not well. It fills me with remorse to have contributed to your fatigue. The day before yesterday, you seemed to me less well than on your first visit, the day before that, and I fear there was too much activity and excitement for you in Geneva. I earnestly beg you to rest as much as possible. Alice Werner told me that she expects you tomorrow afternoon with Mrs. James and your brother; but, it seems to me that you will do better not to come yourself: all these outings (and especially conversation, even reduced to a minimum) don't help you. I would be desolate if you were to leave Geneva less well than when you came; do us the kindness of not bothering about us and of not thinking that you must make or receive any calls. I shall know from Mrs. James if I can see you for a moment on Sunday. (I depart Monday morning for Ragaz with Marguerite); but if there is the least chance that a visit, even brief, would risk upsetting you, I shall give it up, thinking myself already privileged to have been able to spend some moments with you this week. I can't tell you how grieved I am that Nauheim has agreed with you so little—at least up to the present, because I always hope that the benefits may be felt later on. In the meantime, you must be restricted to the most absolute quiet.

I hope your brother will escape the attack of gout which seemed to threaten him.—I should not have insisted upon having you to lunch the day before yesterday, if I had known how the least effort increases your dyspnoea. Now, I insist you give up every effort. I should like to stand guard at the door of your hotel in order to prevent all calls (commencing with my own).

With heartiest good wishes,
Th. Flournoy

JAMES TO FLOURNOY

Hotel Beaurivage [Geneva]

Saturday [July 9, 1910]

Dear Flournoy,

Your two letters, of yesterday & of July 4th. sent to Nauheim, came this morning. I am sorry that the Nauheim one
was not written earlier, since you had the trouble of writing
it at all. I thank you for all the considerateness you show—
you understand entirely my situation. My dyspnoea gets
worse at an accelerated rate, and all I care for now is to get
home—doing *nothing* on the way. It is partly a spasmodic
phenomenon I am sure, for the aeration of my tissues, judging
by the colour of my lips, seems to be sufficient. I will leave
Geneva now without seeing you again—better not come, unless just to shake hands with my wife! Through all these years
I have wished I might live nearer to you and see more of
you and exchange more ideas, for we seem two men particularly well *faits pour nous comprendre.* Particularly now, as
my own intellectual housekeeping has seemed on the point
of working out some good results, would it have been good
to work out the less unworthy parts of it in your company.
But that is impossible!—I doubt if I ever do any more writing
of a serious sort; and as I am able to look upon my life rather
lightly, I can truly say that "I don't care"—don't care in the
least pathetically or tragically, at any rate.—I hope that Ragaz
will be a success, or at any rate a wholesome way of passing
the month, and that little by little you will reach your new
equilibrium. Those dear daughters, at any rate, are something
to live for—to show them Italy should be rejuvenating. I can
write no more, my very dear old friend, but only ask you to
think of me as ever lovingly yours,

W. J.

Grand Hotel Hof Ragaz
Ragaz (Switzerland)
July 20, 1910

My dear James,

Since I left Geneva, I have not ceased to think of you, of your health, and your journey. I did not reply to your last letter, so affectionate and so touching, in order not to risk fatiguing you and disturbing you on your arrival in England. But we are very anxious to have news of you and of your brother; and if Mrs. James, in the midst of her preoccupations and duties as nurse, could send us, one day, two words on a postcard, I should be profoundly grateful to her. We are longing to know how your trip went off, and how the London doctors found your heart. I am dreadfully sorry that this sojourn in Geneva went so badly for you and will leave you such unhappy memories! I hope that by the sea or at least at a lower altitude, you will feel much better and that the beneficial effects of the Nauheim cure are beginning to show— and for your brother also. I regret very much having missed his call when he had the kindness to come to Florissant with Mrs. James a fortnight ago.

Since we have been here, Marguerite and I, the weather has been very bad: always cold and rainy, with the exception of one single day which gave us hope for good weather, but the next day the cataracts began to fall again. Everywhere there are traces of the ravages of floods and the threat of new disasters. A sad summer! Although I never came here with my wife, the hours of atrocious anguish that I passed here a year ago before my departure to see her again one last time have left their imprint everywhere in this place; and not having the compulsory distraction of my occupations at Geneva, I am a prey to memories. Thirty years of happiness gone by become a hard test, when they are no more! I have to control my feelings and listen to the concerts of the Kursaal, in order not to sadden unduly poor Marguerite, who is charming and for whom it is a pity not to have society other than mine, during this cure! In ten days we shall return to Geneva. I cordially shake your hand, my dear James, and I cannot tell you how much I ardently desire to have better news of your health. My respectful good wishes to Mrs. James and to your brother.

> With warmest regards,
> Th. Flournoy

JAMES TO FLOURNOY (postcard)

> London, Aug. 12, 1910

En route for Liverpool where the journals report smooth sea. Your card after Ragaz reached my wife yesterday—you say naught of benefit received, but I hope there has been some, in spite of the deplorable weather. I am still in pretty miserable shape with *athemnoth* & weakness, but near home now, & not afraid of the voyage. My brother seems much better. All loving wishes!

> W. J.

Note on Sources
and Previous Publication
of Letters

The sources of this correspondence are chiefly at Harvard University in the Houghton Library collection of James papers and Flournoy family papers. The originals of the correspondence printed here are there except for the items listed below. I indicate as among the papers of the late Madame Werner-Flournoy those letters which I transcribed in Geneva directly from her papers. Her son, Professor A. R. Werner, informs me that he believes the James letters were deposited at Houghton before her death in 1965. Originals not found at Houghton may be in the possession of Dr. Olivier Flournoy of Geneva, grandson of Théodore Flournoy.

JAMES-TO-FLOURNOY LETTERS AMONG
FLOURNOY FAMILY PAPERS

July 4, 1892	(copy in Houghton)
December 31, 1893	(copy in Houghton)
August 13, 1895	(copy in Houghton)
January 1, 1900	
June 25, 1902	
January 1, 1904	(copy in Houghton)
May 23, 1905	(copy in Houghton)
Feb. 9, 1906	(copy in Houghton)

June 15, 1906   (copy in Houghton)
August 25, 1909

FLOURNOY-TO-JAMES LETTERS, LOCATION
OF ORIGINALS UNKNOWN

April 21, 1908   (copy in Houghton)
September 20, 1908   (copy in Houghton)
November 30, 1908   (copy in Houghton)
April 1, 1909   (copy in Houghton)
September 4, 1909   (copy in Houghton)
September 6, 1909   (copy in Houghton)
September 31, 1909   (copy in Houghton)

PREVIOUS PUBLICATIONS OF JAMES-FLOURNOY LETTERS

September 19, 1892   LWJ (I) and TCWJ (II)
December 31, 1893   NEQ
August 13, 1895   LWJ (II) and NEQ
August 30, 1896   LWJ (II) and SLWJ
December 7, 1896   LWJ (II)
June 17, 1898   TCWJ (II)
January 1, 1900   NEQ
April 30, 1903   LWJ (II)
January 1, 1904   NEQ
May 23, 1905   NEQ
February 9, 1906   LWJ (II) and SLWJ
June 15, 1906   NEQ
July 1, 1906   NEQ
January 2, 1907   TCWJ (II)
March 26, 1907   LWJ (II) and TCWJ (II)
January 3, 1908   LWJ (II)
August 9, 1908   LWJ (II)

October 4, 1908	LWJ	(II)
June 18, 1909	LWJ	(II)
August 25, 1909	NEQ	
September 28, 1909	LWJ	(II) and SLWJ
May 29, 1910	LWJ	(II)
July 4, 1910	LWJ	(II) and SLWJ

PREVIOUS PUBLICATIONS OF FLOURNEY-JAMES LETTERS

| October 9, 1904 | TCWJ | (II) |
| March 16, 1907 | TCWJ | (II) |

ABBREVIATIONS

LWJ = Henry James, *The Letters of William James*, Vol. I and II

TCWJ = Ralph Barton Perry, *The Thought and Character of William James*, Vols. I and II

SLWJ = Elizabeth Hardwick, *The Selected Letters of William James*

NEQ = Robert C. Le Clair, *New England Quarterly*, December, 1953

Index

Abauzit, Frank: translation of *The Varieties of Religious Experience*, 107, 139, 142, 150, 157, 159, 184, 192; as a person, 147, 166, 235; family problems, 153, 169, 178; criticism of his translation of *Varieties*, 185, 189; translation of *Pragmatism*, 197, 203; mentioned, 111, 132, 154, 160, 196–97

Agassiz, Louis, 65

Angell, Frank, 176

Archives de Psychologie: founded by T. F. and E. Claparède, 4; W. J.'s admiration of, 151, 156; mentioned, 113n, 127, 139, 142, 145, 147, 181

——articles in: on "Hélène Smith," 114; on F. W. H. Myers, 142; on F. C. S. Schiller's *Humanism,* 160; on C. R. Richet, 176; W. J.'s "La Notion de la Conscience," 187; by Binet, 188

Baldwin, James Mark, 26, 58, 84, 91n, 159, 215

Bashkirtseff, Marie, 111

Baudin, Abbé: translates *Principles of Psychology,* 208–9, 232

Bergson, Henri: W. J.'s opinion of, 138, 164, 190; T. F.'s opinion of, 169, 189, 190, 215; and pragmatism, 184; W. J.'s discussion of his theory, 190; W. J.'s meeting with, 205; mentioned, xix, 138n, 163–64, 189, 190, 194.

Biélèr, Monsieur, 11

Billia, Lorenzo, 202

Binet, Alfred: W. J.'s estimate of, 181, 188; T. F.'s estimate of, 184; mentioned, 39, 102

Blood, Benjamin Paul, 236

Boutroux, Emile E. M.: relation to W. J., 184n, 205; W. J.'s estimate of, 213–14, 231; mentioned, 107, 184, 226, 234

Bradley, Francis Herbert, 36, 166